Flying High
On Wings of Memories

Book III of
The Eagle Must Fly
An Autobiographical Trilogy

Gisela Scofield

COVER PICTURE

The cover art for this book is based on my favorite vintage Pan Am travel poster shown below.

Also by Gisela Scofield

Parts I and II of "The Eagle Must Fly" trilogy:

"My Childhood in Hitler's Germany"

"Growing Up British"

Available on amazon.com

TO

BOB

September 1929 – August 2003

Sometimes we have to wait until we are 60 to find our soul-mate.

CONTENTS

ACKNOWLEDGEMENTS

With grateful thanks to my dear friend Janet Crane who is an amazing artist, poet, and writer in her own right, and who's patience, hard work, and faith in me over the last five years has enabled me to get my story written and the "Eagle to FLY."

PREFACE

Time is once again suspended.

I look back on my childhood and ponder – how many times have I been blessed with love and opportunities I could never have imagined. In my childhood in Hitler's Germany, had my Father lived and raised me, what would my life have been like? Would I have enjoyed any of the opportunities thrown my way the way they were as a result of me growing up British? I think not.

I am who I am and all the things I have accomplished because my Father gave his life to the Third Reich, and Hitler, to be cannon fodder in the hell of a Russian winter. This, all because he was unfortunate enough to have tuberculosis. The same Hitler and Third Reich that failed its people and forever trashed them in the eyes of the world. This failure would bless me by being found and rescued by a British soldier who fell in love with my Mother in the shell and rubble of what was left of a bombed out city. Hamburg, Germany was a Phoenix that would eventually arise and become reborn in the tender hands of the Allies and The British Control Commission.

British Army Captain Arthur Edwin William Wheeler spoke fluent German, and as a result was commissioned and sent to Germany to help the city of Hamburg and its people rebuild. He did an amazing job for two years, helping to rebuild that war torn city, devastated and completely burned to the ground. Subsequently he rescued my Mother and six year old me, by taking us to live in a new country and giving us a new beginning - and me a rebirth.

As a result I grew up British, and thanks to Arthur Wheeler and the life and education he provided for me, I was now able to follow my dream. To Fly.

The Eagle will fly. The Eagle must fly. Oh Yes and The Eagle will fly high - on wings of memories through these pages.

I am that Eagle, and will intermittently express my feelings and emotions through that mighty bird – the symbol of all three countries of my life.

.

Flying High

My life has been long
Said the bird to the sky.
I've sailed in your wind
And on clouds up so high.

I've traveled so far
On wings that are strong.
They've taken me round
This world for so long.

I've made a few nests
But the trees seemed to sigh
"You know you are best
When you just go and Fly!"

-   Janet Crane

CHAPTER 1 –

NEW BEGINNINGS

The heady smell of jet fuel and airport bustle came to a sudden end as the forward door of the big Pan Am jet slammed shut and the handle slipped into the "Locked" position. I was sitting in the first row of the First Class cabin directly behind the cute little lounge area decorated with a large Hawaiian flower arrangement that I had passed upon boarding. Seated next to me was a new friend I had been introduced to upon check in. Her name was Chloe and she and I had both been accepted to start class in New York to train as stewardesses for Pan American World Airways. It was January 31st, 1964.

We had boarded the Pan American Round The World Clipper flight together in great excitement, with four other new classmates from Sweden. The six of us stowed our luggage and snuggled gratefully into the comfortable softness of the spacious seats while carefully removing the small sparkling white pillows and light blue Pan Am blankets awaiting us in every seat. Chloe and I sat together in the first row behind the bulkhead decorated with a large metal antique Clipper Ship hanging from it. All Pan American aircraft were known as 'Clippers' and a metal Clipper Ship adorned the forward bulkhead on every airplane.

Chloe looked at me, grinned, and grabbing my hand said, "Can you believe we are really doing this and are on our way to America?" It was a surreal moment for both of us.

The reality of this giant step in our lives hit home with gusto. We were committed now with that slamming door. The giant steps were pulled away and the big Boeing 707 jet pushed laboriously forward and turned onto the taxi way from its gate at London Airport, England en route to New York 5000 miles away across a cold, stormy winter Atlantic Ocean. Our eyes filled with tears as we held hands and left our loved ones and Homeland behind. With just the required $300 in our pockets and hearts full of hope and anticipation, we gave in to trust for what lay ahead.

We all met at Gate 25 in Terminal 3 when we checked in at the Pan Am counter. Chloe had come from Devon on the beautiful, rocky south coast of England, with her parents to see her off. I had arrived with my Mother and Clifford Duits, a man I had known for years and dearly loved. To my delight they had recently married and had driven me from our home in Wimbledon to the airport to see me off. The four Swedish young ladies had arrived from Stockholm earlier in the day and joined us at the gate. We had been given special "Crew Pass" tickets, and the agent in the smart, soft light blue Pan Am uniform, smiled and introduced us as 'class mates.' She grinned and had a bright twinkle in her eye as she handed us those First Class boarding passes. "The back of the airplane was over booked and is completely full - but I have to get you all to New York today, so I have no alternative but to put you in First Class. Welcome to Pan Am."

We introduced ourselves to each other and to our excited but somewhat overwhelmed and slightly emotional parents. As my hand shook Chloe's and our eyes locked, I knew we would become close friends. That certain, gut feeling does not happen often in one's lifetime, but when it does – you just know it is good and will last.

With the door now closed, the stewardess assigned to our cabin came around with glasses of Champagne or mimosas, while the Purser welcomed us on board and went through the departure announcements. She made them first in English and then in German because the flight had come from India via Frankfurt. All this as the aircraft slowly made its way, in line, to the long departure runway, newly extended at the far side of the airport perimeter for transatlantic jet flights.

Chloe and I locked arms in excited awe as the stewardesses secured the cabin for takeoff. We continued happily sipping our mimosas out of tall stemmed glasses with the Pan Am logo on the side. Ten minutes later the Captain came over the aircraft PA system, welcomed us on board and explained our route and how high we would be flying. He said the flight would be eight hours and twenty minutes in duration – a little longer than usual due to a strong head wind across the Atlantic. However, in spite of that, he anticipated a smooth crossing until we approached the Canadian coastline, at which time we could expect a slight "chop" of turbulent air. With that he wished us a pleasant flight, again welcomed us on board and directed the stewardesses to take their seats as we were next in line for takeoff.

Our glasses were collected, hastily stowed and the galley

secured. We took in every move as the stewardesses took their seats next to the exit doors and strapped themselves in. Minutes later the engines roared to life and when the Captain released the breaks the aircraft lurched eagerly forward like a proud race horse out of the starting gate. I felt Chloe tense a little as we rolled with increasing momentum down that long runway. Finally the nose slowly rose off the tarmac and we sailed effortlessly, in spite of a very heavy load of passengers, freight and fuel into a cold, wide and open winter sky - heading towards the north and west.

I watched the London skyline gradually slip from view as the big airplane banked slightly to the left. We had taken off towards the east, into the wind and our flight path took us over my Wimbledon home in south east London, and on over the shining silver ribbon that was the River Thames. I eased myself back into my seat. The mimosa together with the pain medication I had taken earlier for my broken left wrist and badly bruised and painful left knee, was gradually rendering me into a state of drowsy euphoria. I had acquired the injuries a week earlier when I had run my Messerschmitt off the road on my way home from a farewell party that my friends had thrown for me. Now, all the excitement of the last hour had taken its final toll, along with the medication and the mimosa. As a result, while the monotonous drone of the four big engines labored on and continued our lengthy climb into the heavens – I slipped gently into a deep sleep.

I did not hear the chime from the flight deck alerting the crew that we were passing smoothly through 10,000 feet on our way to the promised cruising altitude of 30,000 feet. It was now safe for the stewardesses to get up and move around the cabin and start our elaborate lunch service.

I was once again embarking on a monumental change in my life, and as I drifted deeper into the abyss of sleep, time seemed to spin backwards. I was back in another place and another time, when I was seven years old and on board the life altering flight I had taken seventeen years before. That amazing flight gave me an opportunity and opened a door that would enable me to embrace this one – and many more to come.

For a moment in my dreams, time was suspended and I found myself back there, as the small chartered British airplane took off from my still bruised and battered German homeland in 1948 and flew me to the stars......................................

****

Our dramatic arrival into the beautiful city of New York was anything but beautiful. The airplane dropped out of the sky and slammed into the runway with an enormous THUMP. It slid and bounced and groaned until it finally came to rest at the insistence of the cockpit crew, and not of the incredible downpour of water and wind engulfing it. Our approach to the city had been decidedly crab like, as we fought the heavy crosswind from the Atlantic Ocean.

The long, time consuming taxi into the gate, felt as though we were rolling all the way back to London at zero feet. Our eyes were glued to the window. We were so very much on edge as we tried in vain, to get a glimpse of our new home, but the weather obliterated every chance. The north eastern sea board of the United States is not the most desirable location in the throes of winter in late January. The weather was mean, cold, wet and unwelcoming – but we had arrived.

NEW YORK. NEW YORK. USA.

We were met after our release from customs and passport control by a member of the training team from the New York crew base who politely piled us into a crew van, and without further fanfare, drove us through blinding rain to our new home in Kew Gardens, Queens. The building housing the Pan Am trainees was just one of a gazillion in that concrete jungle. We were in awe of our surroundings as we literally blew out of the crew bus and strained against wind and rain to retrieve our bags.

Once inside the warm, welcoming lobby of 'The Forrest Park Towne House,' we were assigned our rooms. Chloe and I were to share a two bedroom apartment with two other trainees already there. The other four trainees from Sweden were given a two bedroom apartment on the floor above ours. Then, with instructions to be down in the lobby at seven o'clock sharp in the morning, for pick up to the training school, our happy Pan Am greeter left us with a cheery wave to find our way to our assigned apartments.

The apartment in The Forrest Park Towne House was quite luxurious to our naive European eyes. It accommodated four trainees and was fully furnished, including linens, dishes and cooking utensils. It was very comfortable and also had a resident supervisor from the training school living on the premises, in case we needed help or assistance with anything. The facility was specially selected by Pan American to house its trainees for the six week training period because it was very convenient to the airport and Hanger 14. We had been informed in our 'acceptance letter' that we would be required to reside there for the duration of training – even if the trainee was local and from the New York city area.

We arrived at our designated apartment to find the door ajar and music playing. Chloe pushed the door open with her suitcase and I poked my head inside and called out "Hello – anyone home?" A young Asian girl came running from somewhere inside, grabbed the door and flung it wide.

"Yes, yes. Hello – are you our new roommates? Oh welcome, welcome. Come in please – we have been expecting you, but the weather has been so bad we were afraid you could not land today. Micky, Micky our new roommates are here," she called excitedly over her shoulder at a half open door where we could hear water running. "Micky is in the shower," she explained excitedly helping me in with my bag. "My name is Akita – I am from Tokyo and Micky is from Manila. Come in and let me show you your room." With that she grabbed a bag and pulled it behind her into an open door.

Our bedroom consisted of two twin beds, two bedside tables with a chair beside each and a large oak dresser. A door opened into a walk in closet, the likes of which Chloe and I had never seen. A window looked out onto the street and the labyrinth of tall concrete buildings that made up Kew Gardens, Queens, New York. The apartment was clean and our room mates were welcoming.

We were home.

****

The next morning, at 6:45 a.m., thirty-five young ladies from all over the world descended into the spacious lobby of The Forrest Park Towne House. The excitement was intense. Everyone introducing themselves to everyone close by, and exchanging information about past, present and future hopes and plans. All the trainees had passed mandatory checks and qualifications two pages long, before the interview process in their homelands had even begun. This included our height, our weight and of course, languages spoken. This group of young ladies was without a doubt – the crème de la crème of the world.

A large bus was parked and ready out front, to transport this treasure to the Pan American Training School at Hanger 14, Idlewild International Airport – the world was at our feet and waiting. It was February 1st, 1964.

When the door of the elevator opened onto the lobby and Micky, Akita, Chloe and I spilled out into the mayhem, we were overcome and unprepared to see so many strikingly attractive, glamorous young women in beautiful clothes looking like they had just stepped out of a magazine. Even more amazing was the multitude of languages being spoken casually and with ease. French, German, Italian, Portuguese, Russian, Polish, Arabic and Hindi – even Japanese and some I could not identify. It was very exciting and exhilarating to join and find ourselves part of this diverse group.

On the dot of seven a gentleman entered the lobby and the noise level closed down slowly, as though someone was turning off a tap of running water.

"Good Morning Ladies. My name is Bill Viola and I am delighted to be your instructor for the next six weeks. Please be good enough to board the bus and we will be on our way to the training center, and welcome on board. We are delighted to see you and cannot wait to begin."

Sitting on the bus on our way to training, Chloe and I were able to look around and check out our fellow classmates. The thing that struck us immediately was – we all looked alike! In spite of the fact that we came from amazingly different back-grounds and parts of the world – we all looked alike! It was as if we had been cloned – that was the Pan Am way.

The training center was very close to our residence and would only be a short bus ride away, which was the idea. On this first morning we were all picked up to make sure we all got to the center at the same time and acquired all the necessary information regarding training. Sitting there and listening to all the happy chatter I was overwhelmed by the amount of talent on this bus. Not only were the languages from all over the world, but many of these ladies were nurses also. It was exhilarating to know that the passengers on our long around the world flights would be so very well cared for, no matter what the situation. A child's ears hurting, a heart attack, a baby born, or even – heaven forbid – an emergency evacuation.

We were on our way to Flying High!

New Beginnings

CHAPTER 2 -

TRAINING
"THE GIRLS IN BLUE"

W e poured out of the bus upon our arrival at Hanger 14 in great spirits and full of anticipation. Bill Viola directed us to an open door and led us inside to a spacious classroom on the left side of the entrance. He took his place beside a large desk at the front of the room and bid us find one of our own. Chloe and I slid into a desk on each side of the aisle in row two.

When we were all seated Bill welcomed us again to the training center and let us know how important we were to the Inflight Service Department. Pan Am was in a growth spurt, acquiring not only new airplanes but also new routes. We should all be very proud, because we had beaten out hundreds of other candidates and been specially selected to join Pan Am at this exciting time. Our languages and different cultures were a very necessary addition to that program.

The morning continued with the filling out of many official looking forms which was quite time consuming. We were given our Pan Am IDs and our training schedule and the layout of the buildings and offices that would be important to us during training and beyond. We were told that our classes would start every day at 3 p.m. and end around 11 p.m. This unusual starting time caused some lifted eyebrows around the room, but was probably done on purpose to get us ready for unaccustomed flight departure times we would be scheduled for on our bid lines in days to come.

Uniforms were next, and we were all trotted around the corner to the Uniform Fittings Center, where we were each met with persons wheeling a tape measure after we stepped off the dreaded scales. The uniform was designed by famous Beverley Hills designer Don Loper and was well known around the world as being Pan Am 'Tunis Blue.' It consisted of a fitted jacket and pencil thin over the knee sheath skirt, a fitted short sleeved white blouse that was worn outside the skirt, and a long rap around winter coat that tied at the waist and went almost down to our ankles. We also got a pale blue fitted smock which we donned on board for the food service and a very perky little hat with a small wing on the side to which was pinned the round Pan Am logo. We would be required to pay for our first uniform – approximately $288 which would be gradually deducted from our pay checks – then Pan Am would supply any further uniform items going forward.

After our fittings and before leaving the uniform department we were reminded of what was expected of us during training by the female staff. We were required to dress very conservatively every day in 'business attire' consisting of blouses, jackets or sweaters and skirts with medium to high heeled shoes. Absolutely no slacks of any kind or flat heeled shoes. We would also be required to buy an elastic girdle because we were not allowed to wear garter belts to hold up our stockings. Our uniform skirt was tight fitting and we could not show any panty or garter belt lines through the material. It was to be a smooth sleek fit.

This information caused quite a commotion and alarm amongst most of us European girls. We had never even seen such a thing as an elastic girdle down to our thighs – let alone wear such a thing as that. Little did we know that we would be subjected to daily 'girdle checks' after arriving in class, to ensure our compliance and also to get us used to shoehorning ourselves into such a contraption on a daily basis. It was like wearing armor plating and very uncomfortable in flight, because your body would swell due to airplane pressurization. The higher the airplane flew, the tighter we were squeezed.

After graduating and having now experienced one of our normal 10 hour flights encased in one of these gismos, I did a little shopping in a shop I had found by accident just around the corner. It was an Emporium where the local "Ladies of the Night" did their shopping, and lo and behold, there I acquired stockings with an elastic thigh top. Praise the Lord - I did not need a girdle of any kind to keep my stockings up!

Lunch at the cafeteria was next, and then onto the medical department for the first in a long series of shots – starting out with tetanus and typhoid. Afterwards, with our arms burning and throbbing we were unceremoniously released to the bus and the short ride home.

Next day we started off with a Grooming class where we were shown how to apply make up by a beauty expert from Macy's Department Store. We arrived to find a myriad of little bottles and jars on our desks. These were creams, foundation, rouge etc., all things that most of us had never worn and were not too delighted to be expected to wear from now on. ONE ONLY lipstick color was allowed – Revlon's Persian Melon!

This was definitely our 'day of discontent.' Many of us had never worn make up before – maybe a little lipstick – or not. America was way beyond Europe or other parts of the world regarding make up. It was normal and expected for American ladies to wear make up on a daily basis when out in public or going to work. This was really alien territory to most of us. We all had good healthy young skin – but if we wanted this wonderful job, we had to do it Pan Am's way, much to the amusement of the three American girls in the class. They really helped us a lot and gave us much encouragement. Next we learned how to apply eyebrow pencil and mascara. We all complied during this class and got a kick out of seeing how different we all looked with make up on, often causing great merriment and much embarrassed laughter.

This done we were informed of what we could and could not do with our hair. It had to be well maintained and short – one inch above the collar at all times and the top of the ear may never show. No artificial color and definitely no wigs were permitted. Jewelry was also a no-no. No necklaces or bracelets – if you had pierced ears you may wear a single pearl or small gold ball on the ear. Furthermore, no eye glasses or contact lenses could be worn.

We absorbed all this information in serious silence. Some of us were still nursing very sore arms from our shots from the day before. It was a lot to take in and get used to, and we were all relieved when we were released and it was time to go to supper in the cafeteria.

That afternoon we resumed training in the hanger with Bill Viola and were introduced to a Pan Am bar service. This was the first time he had seen us today and he made us feel good by telling us how bright and professional we all looked with our new made up faces. It was very kind of him because we all felt very uncomfortable and self-conscious. His praise made us relax, forget our faces and how we looked, thus enabling us to focus on our bar service training, and what he needed us to know.

The Pan Am First Class bar service in flight also proved to be a big challenge. Most of us did not drink anything other than a glass of wine or beer now and then. Some trainees for religious reasons were not even permitted to drink alcohol at all and had not ever been around any. Now we were required to learn how to memorize and mix drinks we had never heard of before. Manhattan, Bloody Mary, Martini, Screwdriver, Whiskey Sour and Mai Tai - all had to become second nature to us.

We learned how to stock the bar and take drink orders, but we also had to become familiar with the full range of fine wines, Champagne, cognacs and cordials, and when and how they would accompany our meal service. It was all 'hands on' and so very much to learn that had our heads spinning.

Suddenly Bill called on me to take a turn at mixing and delivering a drink to him and Jenny. Jenny was a Purser on Special Assignment to the training school to assist with the training of new hires. I was the first trainee to start. I was very tickled to be called upon first, and I had a jovial skip in my step as I took their drink orders and went over to the mock-up bar to fix them. Bill was to have Whiskey on the rocks and Jenny ordered a Bloody Mary.

When I got there I realized I did not know what KIND of whiskey – ooops – I forgot to ask. European men usually want Scotch whiskey and will just ask for 'whiskey' but Americans will ask for Bourbon, Scotch or Rei or even Irish whiskey. Sheepishly, back I went to ask.

Bill would like Scotch. No problem.

I thought I did a really good job of mixing the drinks and was quite pleased with myself when I delivered them very professionally on a small tray placing a small Pan Am napkin down first and then setting the drink on top. The room was quiet – everyone holding their breath, waiting for the scene to play out. Bill looked at his drink while in deep thought. Then, smiling up at me said.

"Gisela, I asked for Whiskey ON THE ROCKS. You gave me ONE small ice cube in here, and what about Jenny's Bloody Mary. I don't see ANY ice in her drink at all!!" NO - I did not want to dilute her Bloody Mary with water – ice is water and she did not say she WANTED ice!!

With that he jumped up and with much good humor started pushing me back to the bar. "Now, gather round everyone, let me show you all how we mix a drink on Pan Am." With that he took a glass out of the rack and filled it to the very top with ice. Then he poured the liquor over it and set it down. "That is how you mix a drink Ladies. We do not COUNT the ice cubes on Pan Am – all drinks, mixed or otherwise, are made this way. The glass is filled to the TOP with ice – THEN you add the liquor."

We all stared in disbelief. We had never seen anything like that before.

We were dumfounded all the way home on the bus and that night, many of us were mixing drinks all night long in our dreams, panicked in this alien world while swimming in an ocean of ice.

CHAPTER 3 -

LEARNING A NEW NORMAL

The next day, the four of us roommates decided we should go early and check out the commissary shop before class. It was like a commissary shop on a military base – selling everything you might need for house and home and of course, travel - at very good prices. We checked out the array of Samsonite luggage. We all would need to buy a large Samsonite suitcase after graduation, because the ones we had arrived with from home were either old and very heavy, or very pathetic looking and too small. This Samsonite luggage was also especially made for crew and had very hard shells which could withstand a great deal of knocking about while traveling around the world.

Next we went and examined the make up on display and played with some of the samples and demos – cracking up when witnessing some of the results. Then, still laughing we made our way to the cafeteria for a bite to eat. Some of the offerings on the menu left us shaking our heads. Breakfast was served all day, but some of the dishes were a puzzlement. What in the world were grits? Hash browns? Eggs over easy???

We decided to play it safe and ordered hamburgers. They were the biggest we had ever seen and looked juicy and delicious, served on a plate with a napkin. We sat very quietly and politely – waiting for our knives and forks to arrive. We waited, and waited. Then realizing that they were not coming Mickey got up and went to the counter to ask for them. The staff looked at us as though we had three heads, and then laughingly explained that in America burgers are eaten with your fingers.

REALLY – no kidding – well OK then! Chloe and I had been fascinated by the American table etiquette since our arrival here. In England you ate with your fork in your left hand and your knife in your right. You cut up your food one piece at a time and slid it up the back side of your fork - including peas. NEVER may your fork be turned over and used like a 'shovel.' In America we notice that you cut everything up into pieces - then put your knife down and eat everything you have just cut up with your fork in your right hand. It was all very different and this eating your hamburger with your hands was just another new twist.

It was a fun way to start the day but it made us all very much aware that we were in a foreign land and had much to learn - beyond our training.

The day before, our group of trainees had been divided into two groups. Seventeen young ladies were in one class with a Purser/Instructor on assignment to the training school, and eighteen in our class with Bill Viola. At three o'clock on the dot we were all seated at our little desks when Bill Viola arrived with his usual happy smile and cheery greeting. After checking to make sure we all had our ID's on us he unlocked a closet behind his desk that was full of supplies including our Pan Am In Flight Manuals. We each got one and were told in no uncertain terms that these were sacred and must NEVER leave our side! They MUST be taken with us on every flight. A supervisor would check that before every assignment and take us off the line if we did not have it in our possession. The manuals were fat and heavy but contained every single thing we would ever need to know about being a stewardess. They must therefore be readily available to reference at any given time around the world while working. Our in-flight bible!

This done, Bill asked us to pick them up and to follow him down the hall to a 707 aircraft first class cabin mock up. The mock up was complete with seating, six abreast – three on each side of an aisle and a fully equipped galley with working ovens. Quite intimidating.

Pan Am's meals were all prepared by Maxims of Paris and the First Class 'President Special' service was considered the ultimate in-flight dining experience. All meals were offered off an elegant menu and cooked to order.

We were here to be introduced to the finest china, silverware, linens and French crystal stemware that we would be using to deliver our fine dining experience to our passengers. Now we had to learn how to set up the carts and tray tables in First Class to start the elegant service.

There would ultimately be six carts in the aisle. We had to learn how to set them all up for each course plus the appropriate wine or Champagne.

The first cart, specially set up for this purpose would start the ball rolling. The cart was a small compact, collapsible two shelf contraption that we set up with crisp linens. The shelves snapped into place and were very sturdy - unless - of course, you were not diligent and careful when assembling it, and the class was quite often interrupted by howls of horror and frustration when a beautifully set up cart collapsed when rolled into the cabin and the contents shed far and wide.

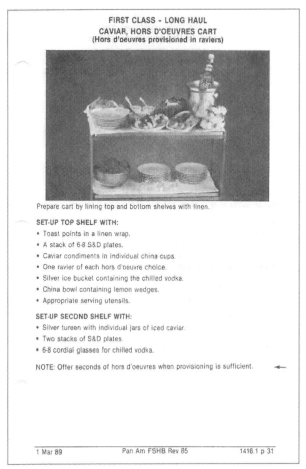

FIRST CLASS - LONG HAUL
CAVIAR, HORS D'OEUVRES CART
(Hors d'oeuvres provisioned in raviers)

Prepare cart by lining top and bottom shelves with linen.

SET-UP TOP SHELF WITH:
- Toast points in a linen wrap.
- A stack of 6-8 S&D plates.
- Caviar condiments in individual china cups.
- One ravier of each hors d'oeuvre choice.
- Silver ice bucket containing the chilled vodka.
- China bowl containing lemon wedges.
- Appropriate serving utensils.

SET-UP SECOND SHELF WITH:
- Silver tureen with individual jars of iced caviar.
- Two stacks of S&D plates.
- 6-8 cordial glasses for chilled vodka.

NOTE: Offer seconds of hors d'oeuvres when provisioning is sufficient.

| 1 Mar 89 | Pan Am FSHB Rev 85 | 1416.1 p 31 |

Page from THE MANUAL on setting up the Hors D'Oeuves Cart

The cart would stop beside each passenger and we would place a large, snow white linen napkin on the tray table. Then place silverware wrapped in a large folded linen napkin with a button hole in one corner that could be fastened over a shirt button, on the table to the passenger's right. The crystal wine glass with the Pan Am logo was to be placed above the silverware roll-up and a water glass was placed to the right of that. A small bread and butter plate is placed at the top left of the passenger, with a butter dish with butter, next to it. Tiny crystal salt and pepper shakers were placed in the middle - the salt to the right and pepper to the left. The display was finished with a small china vase containing a flower placed in the center above the salt and pepper.

It was all quite exquisite and very chic.

The class was now seated in the rows of airplane seats pretending to be passengers, and we could follow each step in the In Flight Service Manual with photographs or diagrams on every page. We could not believe all the details involved that we would be required to learn by heart.

Cart Two. Dinner began with a cart containing a large showpiece tray presentation of various hors d'oeuvre choices. It included Russian Caviar set on ice in a large silver ice bucket with all the condiments in little china cups and not forgetting the iced bottle of Vodka with glasses. The large selection included smoked salmon, shrimp, and little toast points in a linen boat as well as a china bowl of lemon wedges.

Then followed four more carts in easy succession.

Cart Three. Salad and/or soup, in a large silver soup tureen with a large, heavy silver ladle. China bowls, pepper mill and breadbasket.

Cart Four. Roast Prime Rib of Beef or Rack of Lamb with large silver carving knife and fork and heated dinner plates. A silver Bain Marie, the bottom of which was filled with hot water to keep the vegetable and starch choice nice and hot in their separated compartments.

Cart Five. A large fruit basket along with a multitude of different cheeses on a carving board. Small plates, crackers and biscuits in a linen boat. Port wine and Red wine, glasses.

Cart Six. Desert - Ice Cream, Sherbet or Berry Tart. Silver coffee and tea pots, cream and sugar and a stainless pitcher of milk for the tea. Bottom shelf has Cordials – Cognac and Liqueurs of every kind and glasses.

We learned how and where all this food, liquor and equipment were stowed, and we learned how to operate the ovens without burning ourselves or the food. Different foods cooked at certain temperatures and we had to know all this. Also for the First Class breakfast service the passengers had their choice of eggs. We learned how to boil, scramble and fry eggs at 30,000 feet. Quite a trick!

Now we had to learn HOW to serve all these delicacies from an open rolling cart with class and panache - using a fork and spoon in one hand. As you can imagine, my dear reader, this all was a gigantic learning curve, resulting in a multitude of disasters with many a tear shed and a foot stamped in frustration.

One by one over the next days, we all took our turns at doing this over and over again till practice made perfect, and we could all serve our mock passengers the caviar, pâté de foie gras or smoked salmon without a fumble. We learned by doing and eating EVERYTHING over a period of several days, to the detriment of our expanding waistlines. Woe betide - the ever lurking scale and that tight fitting, made to order uniform skirt!

The soup also was quite a challenge. Guiding the hot liquid into the soup bowls using the heavy silver ladle without spilling it all over the cart or the passenger – especially in turbulence – was no easy feat.

Thereafter came the carving of the giant beef rib roast or rack of lamb while wielding a large silver carving knife and fork. Not for the faint of heart! The cooking of that rib roast was enough to give us all giant heart palpitations. NEVER may it be overcooked – dear Lord thank heaven for the trusty thermometer which kept an eye on it while in the oven and let us know when it registered 'rare' and the beef was done. The vegetables were also served from the cart with a fork and spoon - potato croquettes, buttered green beans, snow peas or whatever was on the menu.

While this cart was in the aisle the galley girl was dishing up the other entree dishes the passengers had selected that were not eating prime rib or lamb. The entrees had to all come out at the same time as the cart. They could have chosen a variety of different dishes such as lobster thermidor, veal with tarragon sauce or Cornish game hen. She had to remember to always place the meat or fish at two o'clock on the plate – the vegetable at six and the potato or rice at ten – and NEVER, EVER forget the parsley garnish!

After four full days of this we were in overload with our hair on fire. So much information to learn, and it all had to be perfect before we could move on. We each had to take turns working the galley and cooking the food, while others worked the cabin service. The weekend arrived not one minute too soon. Many of us said that it had to ease, we could not possibly keep up a pace like this. One trainee quit – she was from Italy and could not handle the stress while also having trouble keeping up, having to learn everything in English.

Little did we know what was to come!

CHAPTER 4 -

AN INTERESTING BREAK

The weekend was a welcome and very needed relief. The four of us roommates slept until almost noon on Saturday. It was the honest sleep of sheer exhaustion – otherwise known as 'Fried Brain Syndrome.' We had no idea how we were going to absorb it all to the high standard required.

Chloe and I woke up – slowly, reluctantly and with great effort – to the smell of coffee. Akita had dragged herself out of bed and managed to plug in the coffee pot a little while earlier, but that was as far as she got, because when Chloe and I entered the kitchen Akita was fast asleep lying with head on arms across the kitchen table. We did not disturb her as we filled the kettle with water to make tea. Coffee could not fix what ailed us – yet – that transition would come with time, but now we needed - TEA!

We padded silently around the kitchen in stockinged feet fixing toast and trying not to wake Akita, when Mickey swayed in, rubbing her eyes - hair standing on end. It took a while for us all to settle down – the tea and coffee were a tremendous help and a little toast and jam did not hurt on an empty still churning, stress filled stomach. We were trying to get used to the texture of the bread – it was very alien to us – so soft and smoochy – we were used to harder, more heavy bodied bread, but this did the trick today. We had the day off but we were required to start the new week on Sunday afternoon. It was the beginning of Emergency training.

We sat quietly talking about our first week and what all was expected of us. We were totally in awe as we realized that we were indeed now working for "The Worlds Most Experienced Airline." We had had no idea what that meant, but we were starting to find out – a little more each day and with every test.

The Pan Am flight-line, In-Flight Services, had set the standard for the rest of the industry. Its creator Juan Terry Trippe had insisted on nothing but excellence since its beginning, and as a result Pan Am had become a cultural icon of the 20th century and was the unofficial flag carrier of the United States. Its logo was well known around the world second only to Coca-Cola.

Juan Trippe would lead Pan Am from 1927 to 1968 and would swell the company into a global network. It would fly to every continent except Antarctica. It could take you to 86 countries and pretty much to anywhere in the world you needed to go. Should trouble arise, be it armed conflict or natural disasters of any kind – it would be there to help with desperately needed supplies flown in, and passengers dead or wounded flown out.

The transportation of our armed services was felt to be a great honor and taken very seriously by the company. I would enjoy flying many a Military Charter flight to and from Vietnam – feeding these incredibly wonderful troops EVERY FOUR HOURS as required. We would have food and supplies bursting out of every available nook and cranny on that 707 jet airplane! By the time we landed 14 hours later – we all were FAMILY – we knew everything there was to know about those wonderful young guys going to war. They introduced us to all their loved ones. They shared their lives, their hopes and dreams, through stories and photographs on this long flight to who knew what.

Very emotional, sad, quiet and somber going to Vietnam – but very joyous coming home with jubilant, if damaged and sometimes broken young men! The airplane would become airborne on the wings of loud cheers and the singing of the Star Spangled Banner. There was not a dry eye in the crew.

****

We would find out, over time, what it meant to wear the Pan Am uniform around the world. We would learn that in that uniform you automatically became an unofficial ambassador representing the United States of America. That carried a lot of weight but was also a tremendous responsibility. We would be treated like Rock Stars at our layover stations and in the five star hotels around the world where we would stay. Pan Am crews were invited to visit or dine at any Officer's club on US Bases around the world. We also had the privilege of being invited to visit many elite private clubs in places like Beirut, Teheran, Hong Kong, Rio, Bangkok and New Delhi while in those cities, to enjoy their facilities at any time. We were offered Pan Am discounts everywhere for many things which was wonderful, and I would very often take advantage of one offered by Vidal Sassoon to get my hair done in Knightsbridge, when in London after visiting my Mother.

When wearing that light blue Pan Am uniform crowds would part to let you pass. Gentlemen would smile and ladies eyes would follow us with envy. We were living their dream. Children would run up to us and excitingly state that they wanted to be a stewardess just like us when they grew up. It was truly unnerving at first but you soon got used to it and acknowledged it with a smile, a greeting or a wave.

For now however, we had to concentrate and apply ourselves like never before to the rigors of this airline's training program and all that that entailed. So very much was at stake. Our passenger's very lives and well-being while in our care. We had no idea what awaited us or how intense our training would become. For now our weight was checked once every week and we were informed from the first day of training that many of us would not graduate. The standard was incredibly high and some would not be able to survive. We would be tested every other day on what we had learned, and you were required to pass with an 85% plus grade on every test, in order to stay in training. It was indeed daunting, especially because we had already lost a trainee, before the end of the first week.

Now, feeling somewhat revived after eating, we got dressed and thought it might be fun to take a break from our studies and make our first trip into Manhattan and get introduced to New York. We also decided that we really needed to watch our money, so elected to explore the New York subway system instead of taking a taxi into the city.

We were not impressed.

It was freezing cold and the carriages rattled into the litter strewn unkempt looking station covered in graffiti. We huddled together nervously, all the while watching intently for our stop at Grand Central Station. Finally, our destination reached, we happily joined the powerful flow of humanity bursting out of the train. We looked around thoroughly traumatized by the size, height and business of it all. It was indeed a 'Grand Station.' The crowd was intense in this location and we had to be careful not to get trampled by overzealous New Yorkers running every which way in great abandon.

We made our way to the exit having decided our first point of interest would be Rockefeller Center. We joined the thickest crowd and like the front wave of a tsunami we were exploded out of the terminal, spilling into canyons of solid granite thousands of feet high - that was Manhattan at every turn. It took our breath away it was so overwhelming and intimidating. The momentum of the crush of people exiting the station bore us slightly to the right and there facing us was the most unbelievable sight.

We were right in front of the Pan Am Building at 200 Park Avenue.

It was startling because it was so unexpected. We had all heard about it – but to now suddenly find ourselves standing in its shadow was quite intimidating. When I finally wrenched my eyes back to the pandemonium of the street, my searching eyes landed on a wonderful sight. I grabbed Chloe's hand and started to pull her along behind me while calling over my shoulder to the other two girls,

"Over here – praise the Lord - I see a policeman." So with help and salvation in our grasp we pushed our way through the avalanche of people, and landed at the officer's feet. We burst out of the crowd, smiling and so happy to be liberated.

"Good afternoon sir. We would very much like to go to the Rockefeller Center," I stated cheerfully.

The officer turned, looked at us as though we were something the cat had dragged in – threw his hands onto his hips and said in the most obnoxious, flippant way I had ever heard.

"OK - SO GO AHEAD!"

WELCOME TO NEW YORK!

We finally were directed and found our way to the ice rink full of wonderful, happy, energized, swirling skaters. We were awed by the large, beautiful bronze statue of Prometheus gazing proudly and overlooking this amazing scene – to music. We stayed a goodly while, happily taking it all in. Finally the cold and biting wind started to gnaw on our stomachs and we realized we were hungry, so decide to look for somewhere to eat. No problem – eateries are everywhere in Manhattan. We found a small drugstore/cafe and were ushered into a cozy room filled with little round tables with cheerful checkered table cloths. The waitress handed us an enormous menu which was a real puzzlement to decipher, but we all found something familiar and ate heartily.

Once again refreshed we wondered down to Central Park and back up to Macy's to check out this department store we had heard so much about. Time seemed to fly by and when we came out of Macy's it was getting dark and lights were twinkling on the street in the cold, stark air.

We made our way home the same way as we had come – by graffiti decorated, rattling subway cars – worn out and cold, but in awe at all we had seen and done. It had been exciting and perfect stress relief from the rigors of the introduction to our new world, including getting used to American money. So very baffling. Every denomination was the same size and color - this required some serious attention and was very alien to us.

That night, we went to bed and dreamed of skaters floating around a rink to beautiful music and soft lights.

CHAPTER 5 -

HELL WEEK

N ext morning we got up and hit the books. It was Sunday, but we had class, so after eating a light lunch, dressed "down" for what we knew would be emergency training. We were allowed to wear casual clothes and sneakers but needed to be sure to pack that 'super' manual that may NEVER leave our side. It was as fat and heavy as any old family bible - but pack it we did in our new Pan Am tote bags issued at the Uniform Center.

The class day started with us learning world geography and flight routes, then a mammoth amount of three letter codes for airports around the world that we had to memorize. SFO, MIA, LAX and on and on and on...............! We learned what kept the airplane in the air and what to do if it fell out of the sky.

We had three aircraft types – the 707, the 727 and the DC8 and we were required to learn EVERYTHING about all three types. The seating configurations, where the life rafts were located, the first aid kits, the fire extinguishers (different kinds) and the portable oxygen bottles. We had to know where they were all stowed – each aircraft was different – and how to use them.

Besides the different aircraft types that we would be flying, now it was the fire extinguishers turn to stretch our overloaded brains to the limit. We learned that there were foam extinguishers and dry chemical extinguishers and water extinguishers and CO_2 extinguishers – all used for different fires AND OF COURSE we had to know which was which and doing what!! This was 'hands on' and we each took turns at operating every single piece of equipment.

As though this was not enough information to absorb on the first day of "Hell Week" the last thing on the schedule for that day was "THE FILM!" We all fell into our desk seats worn out after the exertion of the day, and sleepily gazed at the screen in the darkened classroom.

"The Film" was about an emergency that occurred eight years before in 1956 to one of Pan Am's Boeing Stratocruisers flying from Honolulu to San Francisco. The Pan Am Clipper 'Sovereign of the Skies' was on the last leg of a round-the-world-flight when it had just passed 'The Point of No Return.' This is the moment in time when you can no longer turn around and go back to the departure airport, for many reasons – lack of fuel, winds and weather aloft et cetera, et cetera, et cetera. You HAVE to go on to your destination.

The movie and the plight of this aircraft, passengers and crew was so dire that it scared us poor girls watching this film half to death. It certainly brought our tired bodies and overloaded brains back to reality and we sat watching what was unfolding on screen with now rapped attention.

The Pan Am Clipper was over nothing but miles and miles of Pacific Ocean and unable to reach San Francisco or return back to Honolulu. Flying at 21,000 feet they were losing altitude after two of the four engines failed – a ditching was unavoidable. Fortunately they had managed to contact a Coast Guard cutter gunboat, the "Pontchartrain" that happened to be on assignment as a weather ship and patrolling in that remote area of the Pacific. They were there so they could assist ships in storms or an emergency should they be needed. Their assignment so far had been uneventful and boring on this mighty ocean that could turn violent in a heartbeat – but not today. Today all was peaceful and the ocean just had a slight swell with light winds - so the crew of the Pontchartrain was relaxed and at ease. Little did they know this peace would soon be shattered and the emergency needing their attention would be the most unlikely they could have imagined.

Their help was going to be needed by AN AIRPLANE!

The Captain of the Pan Am Clipper made contact with the Pontchartrain and the two Captains brainstormed and created a plan between them they thought would work. The Clipper would ditch in the ocean alongside the ship, but they had too much fuel on board to make a safe attempt. There could be an explosion and fire resulting in much loss of life, or the airplane fuel tanks being still so full, would cause the fuselage to sink much more quickly and thus hamper escape from the cabin. It was therefore decided that the Clipper would circle in place through the night, if possible, till it had reached 2000 feet above the waves. The crew prayed that the two healthy engines would hold and not fail and also that the sea – which was running with 5 foot waves – would flatten out a little more.

I could relate, and relived the stress and fear along with those on board. I was sent plummeting back in memory to a situation that I had lived through a little more than a year before as a stewardess with British European Airways.

By now we are all sitting huddled and hunched, white knuckled – some in tears – watching the movie and terrified in our seats. The Pontchartrain was filming every second of the Clipper's plight. Perfect for a training session later!

As the soft first gentle streaks of the new dawn lit the sky across the vast Pacific to the east, the Captain circled the weather ship one last time and positioned The Sovereign of the Skies into position. The ship had created a "foam" runway on the surface of the water to help the approach. It was a sickening few minutes of wait until the Stratocruiser leveled out eased downward and kissed the surface of the water. When it did - bits and pieces of the giant propellers bit into the ocean and broke off. Now at the mercy of the sea it hit a large swell, the left wing dug into the rolling water, the craft lurched violently and broke apart. The tail section of the airplane snapped off and sank immediately.

During the night the Captain had, of course, been in radio contact with San Francisco. They had suggested moving all the passengers as far forward as possible, over the wings, because of the likelihood that the tail would break off on impact with the ocean. This had been learned from a previous accident not involving Pan Am, but with this aircraft type. The Purser – who was female - and the two Stewardesses had miraculously got that accomplished after getting everyone into life vests. Then, after the tail sank, the entire crew had performed brilliantly. The giant aircraft was floating by its wings, with the jagged hole in the fuselage where the tail had broken off, gaping eerily at the sky and open ocean.

In two minutes the crew had all the passengers in life rafts or in the arriving boats from the Pontchartrain. The Purser and the Captain were the last to leave. The Sovereign of the Skies sank, being sucked into the depths of the great Pacific Ocean, less than fifteen minutes later.

We sat in our seats in the training school in Hanger 14 in stunned silence. Not a single life had been lost. The Clipper had 31 souls on board including three small children. Thanks to their brutal training the crew had been able to perform a miracle. Now it was our turn to learn how to perform that same miracle!

I think what hit home most amongst us girls on the ride home that night was the enormity of the responsibility we carried when boarding our flights. Unexpectedly, the beautiful, very elaborate inflight service we provided our passengers was just 'lagniappe' – an added bonus. The SAFETY of every soul on board our aircraft was in our hands and THAT was our FIRST responsibility.

Having had the unenviable experience of a serious in-flight emergency while flying with BEA - I always had a moment of silent prayer before takeoff on any flight with Pan Am, especially once I upgraded to the Purser position. Then once again the world was spinning on MY shoulders. It was a heavy burden to bear and I took it very seriously all my flying career.

From this time on in the late 1950's till now, every time the world experienced an in-flight emergency or tragedy, so very much was learned, revised and implemented and as a result that knowledge makes today's in-flight experience without a doubt the safest way to travel. The glitz and glamor and luxury are gone – but safety has replaced it.

Before leaving class yesterday we had been instructed to bring bathing suits and swim caps for water training today, and right on schedule a Pan Am shuttle bus arrived to take us to a large local indoor swimming pool. After donning our colorful array of swimwear and tight fitting swim caps to protect our hair, we filed out to the biggest pool I had ever seen. There waiting for us was a very fit, athletic gentleman in swim trunks and a Pan Am tee shirt who greeted us with great gusto and informed us his name was James and he would be doing water training with us today. So without further ado he told us to line up along the length of the pool.

Suddenly, out of seemingly nowhere, a female instructor arrived in great haste and with frantically waving arms called a stop to the proceedings. James looked up startled – silenced in mid-sentence.

"One minute, please James," she called out, coming to a breathless halt at his side. "I see that seven of these ladies are inappropriately attired." Then, without further ado and great fanfare, she proceeded to pull seven of us out of the group and bade us follow her to the changing rooms.

What had we done? NOTHING – we were wearing bikinis!

Minutes later we returned to the astonished class wearing the most hideous and unbecoming black bathing suites this world had ever seen.

This accomplished, James resumed control, and said cheerfully as though the interruption had not happened,

"OK ladies let's get started – I need you all to dive into the water and swim to the other side of the pool."

Eeeeeeer WHAT?!!!!!!!

Five out of our group did as told and the rest of us stood staring hesitantly either at the water or at James, or both – dumfounded, and some with real panic starting to show. Most of us could not dive, some had fear of putting faces in the water – two in the group could not swim. The two American girls and three others were able to do the assigned task and struck out smoothly across the pool. The rest of us were sheepishly 'stuck.' I was luckier than most in as much as I could swim quite well and had done some 'life saving drills' before with BEA. Also I had spent a great deal of time at the beach or by some exotic swimming pool, so I was not afraid of the water – but I had never learned to dive.

After some hesitation it was reluctantly agreed that we could jump in and the two that could not swim, terrified of looking bad and being sent home, grabbed the hand of their nearest neighbor and jumped squealing into the pool. The original five were the only ones who swam with an over arm crawl, the rest of us had only ever mastered very awkward looking breast stroke. We arrived at the other side gasping and spluttering for precious air and very embarrassed indeed. This was not a good way to start learning lifesaving techniques - with us being the lifesavers!

Next came the Ditching Drill. James informed us that this class was usually taught in the bay or somewhere in the ocean, but since this was February we had to do it in this Olympic swimming pool.

We eyed the large packed life rafts sitting at one end with some trepidation. They looked like they would weigh a ton.

Sure enough, without further ado, James called upon two of our number to go and collect a life raft and bring it to the side of the pool. As we had feared, this was no easy feat as they were

VERY heavy. Never mind. We all had to do it in turn, so that we knew what to expect should we ever need to use them. Now we all lined up along the side of the pool and another assistant called Beth came around and handed us each a life vest. We were told to put them on, tie them tightly - but DO NOT INFLATE!

At this moment I had a vivid flashback to another moment in time when I had given the exact same instruction to a cabin loaded with passengers - and been totally ignored!!

Now we were instructed to all line up along the side of the pool while two of us were told to lift the raft up and F-L-I-N-G it into the water. ARE YOU KIDDING!!! Most of us were about five foot three or four and weighed only about 100 pounds soaking wet – about the same weight as the raft!

It took mammoth effort to accomplish this, but the raft did 'its thing' and inflated immediately upon hitting the water with an enormous WHOOOOOSH! This having been accomplished James instructed us to inflate our vests, jump into the water, swim to the raft and climb in.

Finally and with great effort we all managed to do this only to discover that these life vests, once inflated, were a terrible bulk and drag around our bodies and made swimming almost impossible. James barked orders and did his best to settle us down and calm our fears while running up and down the side of the pool. We struggled with enormous effort to do his bidding. We had to swim, and then climb into that giant floating elusive rubber raft, that now took up most of the Olympic pool and loomed menacingly over us.

It took all our strength – and often the help of fellow trainees, who pushed, tugged and pulled – to help us clamber up and over the bulging lip on that raft. When in, we all fell into a heap gasping for air, traumatized and often crying and hugging our bruised flailing bodies. Thoroughly exhausted we sat shivering and dripping water, like drowned rats on the wet floor of the raft. This was all happening in the calm, warm waters of an Olympic swimming pool. How could this possibly be accomplished in a wide open ocean, with freezing cold five foot waves, at the dead of night and in full uniform with hungry sharks circling the crash site!

We were scared, dejected lost souls shivering and dripping water - when James jumped in like a Jack in the Box. He was cheerful and very animated.

"Congratulations Ladies – good job. Now that you have all done it, it will not be a problem to repeat it when you come back tomorrow. Tomorrow WE WILL DO IT WITH ALL OUR CLOTHES ON!"

Having delivered this bombshell with a happy smiling demeanor he announced, "Now, let me show you where all the goodies are stowed that you will need to survive with your passengers. Gillian, why don't you reach over the side and retrieve the large bag of emergency supplies next to you on that side of the raft?"

Gillian - a sweet, slight girl from Thailand jumped to her feet in shock when called upon like this by James. As a result her feet shot out from under her on the rolling, wet and uneven floor of the raft, her inflated life vest pushing her head back at an uncomfortable angle causing her to disappear over the side with an enormous splash. Naturally – as luck would have it, she was one of the two non-swimmers in the group trying desperately to not draw attention to herself. Fortunately Beth, James's assistant, was right there in the water beside the bobbing raft, to help her back to the surface of the pool and stabilize her gasping, shaking body. She burst into tears of embarrassment and frustration.

James was not in the least bit put out and after Gillian had been unceremoniously retrieved from the water and once again settled in the raft, he reached over the side and hauled aboard a large bag of life saving equipment. Beth now joined him in the raft and proceeded to hand out a medical kit, hand flares, some fishing gear and many kinds of food rations. A kit to turn salt water into drinking water came next, and we all desperately tried to concentrate on all the information pouring out of James like a flood.

Even though we all felt like drowned rats and totally overwhelmed by all this very important information, we tried hard to concentrate on everything we were being shown and told to learn the art of survival. James showed us how to use the drinking water kit to remove the salt from the sea water, how to protect your eyes from glare from the sun. How to treat sea sickness and to stave off hunger by rationing out candy and gum and vitamins. How to protect and treat sunburn by wearing your outer garments. How to deal with emotional disturbances - phenobarbital tablets could be used as a sedative should they be needed.

Our brains were fried while our bodies shook still dripping water. Finally, it was over. James perused our sad and dejected disposition and took pity.

"Ladies you all did well today – you have all survived a ditching. Please take off your life vests and leave them here in the raft. You may go, and Beth and I will see you tomorrow. Please be sure to bring an entire extra change of clothing with you when you come."

The subsequent hot shower so badly needed to return us back to the real world followed, and we climbed gratefully into our clothes still in a complete daze. As the crew bus delivered its battered and exhausted cargo back to the Towne House, we were silent and in fear.

****

The next day James and Beth greeted us cheerfully upon our arrival at the pool and took us gently but positively through all we had learned the day before. They were both wonderful instructors and obviously dealt constantly with the panic and fear of new hires being introduced to this reality for the first time. Going through that training in our street clothes the next day was very humbling and traumatic however, and the learning curve was enormous. Our silent fear returned in earnest upon our ride home that night, our brains in a lather. We were learning what it meant to be a stewardess for Pan Am.

Till now we had had no idea of that reality.

How in this world could we possibly do what the crew of Pan Am Flight 6, on board the Sovereign of the Skies had achieved half way between San Francisco and Hawaii in that wide open Pacific Ocean? The magnitude of such a thing was overwhelming.

Could we - would we - be capable of doing that if called upon - and succeed as they had?

Yes – we now can – and we would succeed just as they had.

****

The agony continued the following day. The only good thing about going to school the next day was the fact that we could 'dress down' in casual clothes and tennis shoes. That did not mean pants or jeans. Dear reader, these were not yet acceptable attire for the fairer sex – of quality.

Today, James would lead us through a crash on land in Alaska.

This is very intensive survival training, introducing us to exposure to the elements in maybe deep snow and very low temperatures. James managed to put us all into deep shock with the first words out of his mouth that day.

"Ladies, I need you to know that the very best way to combat exposure to extreme cold is to strip off all your clothes and huddle tightly together."

EEEXXXCUSE ME?

Was James suggesting we take all our clothes off and huddle with the pilots?

YES HE WAS – AND ANYONE ELSE YOU COULD GET CLOSE TO.

Other than that, warm dry clothing is the best protection. Also, it is very important to try and keep your socks and shoes dry. He went on to warn us of frost bite, and never place a victim near an open fire.

Once again we were on full alert and absorbing every detail.

These very important facts stressed and understood, James now regaled us with grim stories of hunger and how to avoid it to the best of our ability. Depending on what food source if any, you have access to, try to eat four ounces of solid food every two hours. This will really increase your resistance to severe cold and help to negate the effect.   R-I-G-H-T

Next we went around the corner and down to the Boeing 707 mock-up. Here we were shown where the life rafts were stowed in the cabin ceiling, and had to go through the mammoth task of opening the compartments and getting the heavy rafts down and dragging them to the Emergency Exits. The first tears of the day were shed here, as the heavy rafts were freed and sometimes tumbled down on outstretched hands and upturned heads unable to cope with their instant release. Then the difficulty of dragging them down the aisle to the wing exits. In a REAL emergency however, the adrenalin would be in full swing and this problem would not exist as adrenalin and trauma produce incredible strength and ability.

This task learned and completed successfully, we went on to be introduced to the emergency slide in the aircraft doors. Here we all had to take turns and one by one open a door and successfully inflate the slide. We were timed and tested on how fast it was that we managed to open the door, insert the bar to the chute into its anchors on the aircraft floor, then pull the tab and inflate it. Now we had to jump into the slide evacuating the aircraft, remembering to remove shoes beforehand.

All was done in a very timely manner and James was pleased with how well we had accomplished this.

"Don't forget, you have to be able to do that in a ditching too. Those chutes will become life rafts when you come down over water." R-I-G-H-T

We were released to the cafeteria for sustenance which we sorely needed. Our heads spinning, our hair on fire.

Upon return to class we once again addressed the fire extinguishers. The different types, where they were located on all three airplane types – and how to use them. Everyone had to work each one in turn.

Then, mercifully, we were dismissed for the day with heavy homework assignments.

The next day we had First Aid instruction with a Miss Ingles, an elderly nurse from the local Red Cross Office, who proceeded to teach us how to handle a heart attack in flight and later how to deliver a baby. She then proceeded to very patiently inform us how to treat and handle every ailment known to man at 30,000 feet. An hour later we had to sit through a long session on health hints for the tropics, and how to deal with water deprivation, bugs, disease and fungal infections.

Our dinner break came as a blessed relief after which we spent the rest of the night with Miss Ingles learning and getting certified on CPR for adults and babies.

We were now completely worn out and frazzled, but before we could be released for the day Miss Ingles gave us an exam on all we had learned from her in First Aid and CPR. We had to pass this in order for us to receive a certificate of completion from the Red Cross. This all was separate and apart from the stringent, heavy duty exams we had to take and pass for our Emergency Equipment Training in order to graduate.

Those dreaded exams came all too soon. We were so worn out physically, but emotionally too, from all the long hours of homework and study we had all done during this time. There had been no 'time out' for fun or play. All that we had gone through was deadly serious and we had to apply ourselves 100% to go on.

None of us had any happy memories of that week and we lost another trainee due to the workload and stress. We were beaten up and emotionally fragile, but we needed to be able to recall every minute and every second of all the information we had been given in "Hell Week" for time immemorial. Our lives and the lives of our passengers would depend on it.

Some of us – at a later time – would thank the good Lord for the agony and intensity of this training.

****

Now that this mind blowing intense period of trauma and brain overload was done with, you could expect, dear reader, that we would be left to relax and absorb. However, you would be utterly wrong, because what followed now was our introduction to crash/cabin emergency procedures on dry land.

Upon arrival at Hanger 14 the next day, we were herded into a cabin mock-up further around the airport perimeter. Once there, we all took our seats in the mock cabin and then each one of us in turn was selected to act as "stewardess" and sit in the bulkhead jump seat facing aft. We, and this trainee, went over everything in great detail that we would need to do to prepare the cabin and passengers for an emergency landing.

Suddenly a male voice (the Captain) came booming over the intercom. "BRACE FOR IMPACT - BRACE FOR IMPACT." We all did and proceeded to experience a very real simulated crash with appropriate crashing noise. Then rattling and shaking and pumped in smoke filling the cabin, as the lights flickered and slowly petered out.

The "stewardess" was now required to jump up – access the outside for signs of fire – if none observed, open the door inflate the slide and repeatedly yell at the top of her lungs "LEAVE EVERYTHING, COME THIS WAY" and evacuate the aircraft in less than 90 seconds.

Now the rest of the class (passengers) would jump up and attempt to exit the airplane as directed. The only problem was, by now you could see nothing in the dark and the very realistic, simulated smoke. It was a very traumatic lesson, but one we will never forget. We had to get down very low in the aisle in order to count the rows and follow the emergency lighting to the exit door. The designated stewardess was timed as to how long it took her to empty and then check the cabin.

A very intense day of learning indeed.

Then we were given one day off to recoup and get ready for the dreaded Emergency Equipment Exam. The final outcome of everything learned during that intense Hell Week. Eight of our group did not/could not pass those necessary compulsory exams, and sadly were forced to depart back to their home country that same day. They were called out of class one by one and when we returned back to our apartments that night – they were gone – as though they had never existed.

C-R-E-E-P-Y to say the least.

We all – in quieter personal moments, questioned what we had gotten ourselves into – always waiting for the dreaded "other shoe to drop" when we would be asked/required to leave. Friendships however, made during this stressful time, would last a lifetime. Also, unknown to us at the time – this experience had made us stronger, wiser, more confident in ourselves and we held our heads higher and our backs and shoulders straighter than ever before We were on our way to becoming 'real stewardesses' for the world's best and most experienced airline.

Even though a tad premature – it was a feeling of pride never experienced before by me, or for that matter, any of us. It felt good. Suddenly we were a tightly bonded group, feeling confident and ready to face any adversity we might be confronted with hereafter.

The Eagle flexed her wings – gently – feeling the 'lift' and growing confidence and strength.

CHAPTER 6 -

A FLY IN THE OINTMENT

Acold winter sunshine dawned and engulfed the training program. The temperature was warmer in than out, but sunshine we had. We had been beaten and tested under fire. Those of us remaining to continue after "Hell Week" were a strong, united group. We went on to learn how to make announcements in every language known to man. How to make our passengers happy, comfortable and safe in our tender loving care. We lived every day in the aircraft mock up and fine-tuned everything from meals to service, and as a result the remaining weeks flew by. We worked hard, studied hard and nailed all the remaining daily tests of what we had learned in days gone by.

And so the days dwindled down to THE FINAL EXAM – that would make or break us as a Pan American Stewardess.

The exam was long and intense.

As we finished, we got up and one at a time handed Bill Viola our papers. Then, silently stole out, leaving the room to seek space and fresh air outside the hanger. We all met and commiserated in the Cafeteria – thankful that it was over, but too afraid to eat anything – our stomachs still stressfully churning.

Later we made our way around to the Uniform Fitting Center for a final fitting or to pick up our uniforms most of which we had been told were ready. One final fitting and we could take them home – graduation was three days away.

As it turned out, there was one fairly large 'fly in the ointment' however. During our six weeks of training – we had eaten everything that we had cooked, on a daily basis in the cabin mock up galley. Very rich and exotic foods we were not used to eating. Without fail – the scales BONGED as we stood on them one at a time before our fittings. We had all gained excessive pounds and were required to go on instant diets in order to graduate and fit properly into our blue uniforms. We all sucked it in to fit into those pencil thin body hugging skirts that day – but we were definitely in trouble.

We would have to be perfect on the day of graduation – starvation was in order – and we were each given a time to be at the Uniform Center to be weighed and measured bright and early every day between now and that big day. We were going to be on probation for six months after graduation and most of us were not in compliance, weight wise, so would start that time having to go on a strict diet to melt off the extra pounds gained in training. Those dreadful elastic girdles all the way to our knees that we were forced to wear – saved the day after all and were a great help to shoehorn us into our skirts on graduation day – but it would not be enough.

That evening found us at our desks talking quietly while waiting on the results of that dreaded exam. Right on time Bill Viola came into the room with a thick bunch of papers and said cheerfully.

"OK young ladies – I have the results of your efforts and I will announce them in alphabetical order."

SSHHEEZZZZAAMMM!

Chloe was given the wonderful news before me because her last name preceded mine in the alphabet. Her excitement was tamed a touch, as she spent the next few minutes squirming in agony of anticipation in her seat, until my name was called and I was told I had 'nailed it' also. We had all passed except for two of our classmates – one from Russia and the other from Poland – both we suddenly realized, were missing. Sadly, their failure was probably the result of a language barrier. How hard must it have been to do all we had been required to do in a language not their own? English. Or maybe not. Neither one could swim and we literally had carried them through the ditching process. Either way it was heartbreaking – but they were no longer in class. Upon our jubilant return home to the Towne House, we found that they really were gone, along with all their possessions and their beds made up with fresh linens. We never saw them again. Had they been a figment of our imagination? It was a tad sobering.

No, C-R-E-E-P-Y.

Now Bill Viola was discussing where we would be based, and he announced in a very cheery tone that this entire class would be based in New York.

NEW YORK - I felt the breath leave my body and I shot a look of helplessness at Chloe. She jumped in horror and mouthed at me "OH NO!" We had survived six weeks of intense training in this city, but she and I and the four Swedish girls we had come over with, had agreed after a long conversation over time, that we did not think we could live here in New York. The culture shock and the density of buildings in this giant maze of concrete jungle of a city, was too great, plus the biting negativity and attitude of the people that lived there. NO - we hated New York and had been praying this would not be our fate. What could we do?

Our ride home that night was so very bitter sweet. We had passed and been accepted into the fold of the most prestigious and famous airline of the world, yet we sat together in silence as we listened to the excited chatter of the rest of our classmates. Akita and Mickie were happy and excitedly making plans. They had expected to be based in San Francisco and flying to countries closer to their homeland due to their language skills – they were ecstatic to be flying European routes instead. Suzanne and Mona, two of the Swedish girls we had come over from London with were waiting for us in the lobby with long faces. Suzanne had been crying. We were a pathetic looking bunch.

"I cannot do zis!" Suzanne stated quietly. "I 'ave ze job of my dreams and I cannot do it." Mona too, shook her head in heartbroken misery – but said nothing.

"Do you think we could talk to Bill Viola in the morning and explain how we feel? I'm sure he would be as unhappy as we are that we are thinking of resigning. After all, Pan Am has spent a lot of time and money on our training." Chloe stated with her practical down to earth British thinking mind and attitude. All three of us stared at her silently – a slight glimmer of hope creeping into our tired downcast hearts and bodies. Could that be a possibility? Maybe they had another base we could go to. None of us cared which one – it just could not be New York. That city and its culture had beaten us to our knees. So it was agreed, that we would go a little early to class in the hopes of being able to talk with Bill before the start of the day.

We all had a restless, sleepless night and agreed over breakfast that we were united. We could not graduate if we had to stay in New York. It was just Suzanne, Mona, Chloe and I – the other two Swedish girls had decided to 'suck it up' and stay because they would get to fly home to Sweden frequently. They were not happy, but decided to give it a try.

It was the saddest, motliest crew of four that knocked on Bill Viola's office door the next day, one hour before the start of class. Hanger 14 was quiet and empty yet – trainees and staff would not arrive till later, but we knew that Bill would be there – he liked to come in way ahead of the class to get set up for the day.

"Come in," his cheery voice called, and we opened the door. He sat behind his desk and looked up startled when he saw who had come to disturb his quiet morning. We stood there in the shadow of the open door like four statues, unable to move. He jumped to his feet and said "Ladies, this is an unexpected pleasure. What brings four of my star pupils to my office at this hour – come in – come in," while holding out his hand in greeting.

We all moved forward in unison but with dragging feet. I found myself, suddenly, somehow, having been maneuvered into the point position to shake his hand and look into his surprised face, ahead of the other three.

"Good – gggood – good morning Bill," I stuttered as I shook his hand. "I hope we are not disturbing you, but could we please speak with you for a minute before class?"

"Of course you can Gisela – come in ladies, have a seat and

tell me what is on your minds." He was surprised but warm and friendly and seemed genuinely happy to see us. He was very proud of the fact that so many of his class had passed the Final exam with such high marks.

We all sat. Suzanne had tears running down her cheeks which she hastily wiped away in embarrassment when she saw Bill looking at her with a very puzzled expression on his face.

"Ladies, do I sense that something is very wrong? I would have expected that you would all be dancing in the aisles with excitement after what you have accomplished. We are so very happy to have you in the Pan Am Family and the four of you are the stars of my class. What could possibly be amiss?"

"Yes, yes Bill – we are very ecstatic indeed and proud of our achievement – but we do have a mammoth problem." I hung my head and looked at the floor – I could not go on.

Finally, between the four of us we were able to explain to Bill Viola, our teacher, mentor and surrogate father figure for these last traumatic six weeks – what in the world ailed us. He sat back in his chair and studied us in turn. The silence was deafening. It was as if he was penetrating deep into our soul with those soft, dark brown eyes. After a while he said, "Well ladies, you have really thrown me a curve – as they say in New York. Of all things – I did not expect this." We were all silent – he in deep thought and the four of us in utter misery.

"Let me think this through – talk to a few people including crew scheduling. The only other base I could send you to has just received the last full class and it is New York that now really needs you with your languages. Let me see what I can come up with – I could not bear to have to accept the resignation of my four star graduates."

We left his office and somehow managed to suffer through a whole day of class. As if our traumatic emotional status was not enough, we got three more shots in the arm from the Medical Department. Then with our arms on fire, we went to get weighed in the Uniform Center after skipping lunch at the Cafeteria. It was fortunate that we were in no mood to eat. This helped when we stood on the scales.

The day dragged on and we found it impossible to concentrate. Finally, Bill Viola came in for the last two hours of the day to go over our announcement technique and to distribute our Announcement Handbooks. The announcements on all Pan Am flights had to be read verbatim from the book. It was done by the Purser working the front of the airplane, and then by the language qualified stewardess on board, depending where the flight was going or where it had come from in-bound to the United States.

Finally the day was over and the class was dismissed. Bill indicated that the four of us should remain behind as he left the classroom. After everyone was gone he returned with a manila folder in his hand and sat down at his desk. You could have heard a pin drop.

"Ladies, PLEASE don't look so grief stricken - the world will not end today, I promise. I have talked the situation over with 'the powers that be' and also with scheduling. The last class went to San Francisco which is very senior and hard to get into, but lately we have had some people retiring or transferring out to other bases – Miami, Seattle and London. Soooo, even with the new class transferring in – they still have some openings and I can offer you San Francisco if you would be open to that idea?"

We were speechless. Could this be possible? Not one of us believed in our heart of hearts that we had a China man's chance to have this amazing airline want us enough to accommodate us like this. Four pairs of eyes lifted off the floor to find and rest on Bill's face.

Was he – no, surely not – WAS HE OFFERING US SAN FRANCISCO?

YYYYEEEEESSSSSSS!

The Eagle will fly the world after all...

Bill Viola 1964

CHAPTER 7 -

GRADUATION AND GOLDEN WINGS

Graduation day dawned bright, crisp and clear. A watery sun slid in and out of tiny wispy clouds and danced off some early signs of spring in the form of bright yellow Forsythia, scattered around the tall gray buildings that made up Kew Gardens in February. Class II of 1964 was gathered in the lobby of the Towne House – coiffed with make up on and perfectly outfitted in their Pan Am uniforms.

It was on the dot of 12:00 noon, and we were ready to start the first day of the rest of our lives by getting on the waiting bus that was to take us over to the airline terminal for our graduation ceremony and pictures. So, when the bus driver opened the lobby door we swept out of the Towne House and onto the bus in a great tidal wave of bright, Tunis Blue.

We were proud. We were excited. We looked amazing - and oh so very Pan Am beautiful!

Upon arrival we were met and paraded through the airline terminal with all eyes upon us. We were walking on air as we were escorted to a steep staircase in the center, which curved to one side. Here we were instructed to go to the top and line up by height, working down the side with our arm on the banister, one stair at a time – the tallest at the top and so on down to the bottom. Chloe and I were about the same height and landed pretty much in the middle, while Mikey and Akita were two of the shortest in the group and ended up on the bottom two steps.

Graduation Class

After the class pictures were taken we were ushered into a large side room, to be the guests of honor at our graduation ceremony. Once again we were lined up and then, with a band playing the Pan American Airlines signature tune – the same music that welcomed every Clipper passenger on board Pan American aircraft world wide - we came forward, one by one, to be 'pinned' with our 'golden wings' and receive our well-deserved diplomas from a proud and smiling Bill Viola.

Now, with gold wings on our uniforms we were each handed a glass of champagne and Bill welcomed us officially into the Pan Am Family, stating that this would be the ONLY time in our careers with Pan Am, that we would be permitted to drink in uniform! He once again emphasized how proud we should be, to not only be wearing the Pan Am uniform, but stating once again the fact that for each one of us that graduated, one hundred applicants had not made the grade to be accepted. Not only that, but we had lost twelve in this class alone since the start of training. On that note Bill raised his glass in a toast to Class II and wished us safe and happy flying. After we had toasted ourselves, Bill told us to relax, have fun and enjoy our graduation party – which we did, happily mingling with our guests - as the band played on.

This was an amazing moment for me and I took myself quietly away to the ladies room. I stood and looked at myself in the mirror for the longest time, trying to get used to the amazing, brilliant Tunis Blue and all that it meant. I was used to seeing myself in dark navy uniforms, and this seemed strange.

I stared on – transfixed, as though in a dream – at the strange image in the mirror.

One of the things I had learned quite early on in my training with this amazing airline – was how little I knew. It was very humbling. I had come to them as quite a seasoned stewardess from a very reputable European airline – but I knew NOTHING compared to what I needed to know, to fly with Pan Am.

I had earned my wings as a "Seven Day Wonder" with BEA. We had been taught how to done a life vest, where the first aid kit was, and how to use the portable oxygen and fire extinguishers.

How to make "Welcome Aboard" announcements, and how to handle different currency – what more did you need to know? Nothing - and they NEEDED me and my languages on line, desperately - and so I graduated after only seven days! Some – sadly, did not. It was all too much, too sudden and too fast for people from outside the airline industry. However, thanks to the amazing lessons learned with Lufthansa – I had no problem with what was expected of me with BEA. I am happy with the job I did for them. I worked hard, was responsible and reliable and I believe I did a really good job.

BUT - Knowing all that I know now – I KNEW NOTHING!

I HAD SLAMMED A DOOR SHUT IN ENGLAND – BUT A WINDOW BLEW OPEN IN AMERICA.   GO TO IT - AND FLY.

The die was cast. I took one more look at my image in the mirror, turned and quietly left the empty restroom and rejoined my friends and the party.

****

Two days later the four of us found ourselves on an airplane to London. This was the way we would get to San Francisco. We had no domestic connection in those days, Pan Am flew to the 'Gateway Cities' of America only. So we had to fly to London from New York in order to get to San Francisco. No problem.

Chloe and I both briefly connected with our families in England. It was bitter sweet. We had to tell them that we would not be able to come to London often – we would be flying to the 'other' side of the world from Europe. Our flights would take us to Asia, the Pacific Islands and Australia instead.

I did not connect with Ollie. He apparently knew of my graduation and transfer to San Francisco through a buddy of his in Air Canada. I missed him terribly, but was not yet strong enough to see him, so did not dare to connect.

He in turn honored me by staying away, although he knew I was there. Our love, our bond to each other – though denied, would last a lifetime.

The flight to San Francisco was so long and we thought it would never end. We flew over the North Pole and had to land in Winnipeg, Canada to refuel. It was sixteen hours since we left London, and it was the longest I had ever been airborne. Another learning curve.

Upon arrival in San Francisco we were met by a supervisor from that base, who showed us around to all the crew facilities and made sure we would be able to find our way around the system. He then drove us to a small hotel across from the terminal and gave us some maps of the city and some leads as to where to look for apartments, while also giving us an insight as to where other crew members lived.

We had five days to get settled at Pan Am expense, before our first assignment.

When we were in crew scheduling we had been told that for our first month we would be "flying in the pool." This meant we would be on reserve and would not have a 'hard line' of flying. Next month we could 'bid' to be awarded a 'hard line', but this was a very senior base and we had a whole new class ahead of us, so our chances of getting a line would be slim to none. We should be prepared to remain 'flying in the pool' for a good while!

By now it was late afternoon and we were stressed and worn

out and had jet lag – big time. We decided to drop our bags in our rooms and then come down to the small restaurant, grab a bite to eat and turn in for the night. Chloe and I were sharing a room and Mona and Suzanne were sharing, so that is what we did – tomorrow was a new day and we could start fresh to house hunt.

Jet Lag.

They do not train you or give you the slightest idea what a CURSE THAT IS! We all went so happily to bed upon our arrival in San Francisco, desperately tired, and fell asleep immediately that our heads touched the pillows.

Two hours later we were up and ready to start the day – the only problem was it was only 12:45 a.m. Now we are wide awake and cannot shut it down again. We get up to pee. The four of us rolled and turned – rolled and turned – got up to pee – 2:50, 3:25, 4:33 - all night long. We were all awake as the sun kissed the horizon in a soft saffron haze. We remained laying traumatized in our disheveled sheets, staring at the soft morning light hitting the ceiling.

Did I imagine it – or was that a knock on the door. I lay still, my brain in some form of paralysis. It was 6:35 a.m. It was indeed a knock. I got gratefully out of my trashed bed and was in total shock upon catching sight of the wild looking personage that looked back at me in the mirror as I passed it, on my way to the door.

"Who is it?" I said addressing the locked door while trying to engage my brain.

"It is Suzanne – ve cannot sleep any longer and ve vere vondering if you guys had di same problem."

I threw the bolt, flung the door wide and dragged the poor girl bodily and in silence over our threshold. In spite of myself and the condition I was in, I smiled, and giving her a big hug said, "Welcome to the exotic world of travel. Come on in, we are up too."

Over time we would all learn to deal with that phenomena so that it would not take its toll on us. For now – we were babes in arms and learning to cope. Jet lag was only the first of many such problems.

Pan American World Airways – 1964 Graduation

CHAPTER 8 -

SAN FRANCISCO -
A CITY ON A HILL

Eight o'clock found us in the hotel cafeteria eating breakfast and pouring over our notes and maps that Pan Am had provided us with upon arrival. During one of my sleepless 'walk abouts' during the night I had gone down to the front desk and chatted with the night manager who was having coffee with a local policeman.

They were very friendly and found great mirth in my sleepless predicament, even though neither one of them had ever done any overseas flying and could not relate to my problem in the least. I asked them if they could recommend an area near the airport where we could start our apartment hunt in the morning. They told me that many stewardesses lived about 12 miles south in San Mateo –

a nice little town - we could catch the local Greyhound bus around the corner, and check it out. Then after a little more good natured teasing and banter, I thanked them and left to resume my tossing and turning in my wreck of a bed.

Now, over my bacon and eggs, I told the girls of my night time adventure to the front desk.

"San Mateo – I've heard it is really nice there," Mona said, looking at me with somewhat bloodshot eyes while sipping her hot tea.

"But I had kind of hoped we could find something in the city," Chloe said looking up from her spread out map. "It is not much further away than San Mateo and the transportation is really good too. We could use the buses from the downtown Air Terminal going right into the airport. It would be so much fun living in The City by the Bay."

"But can ve afford it?" Suzanne chimed in wistfully.

Obviously much had to be considered but nothing could be gained by sitting here, so we returned to our rooms and got ready to start our adventure.

We spent the next two days exploring every lead and idea in all directions. We were fascinated and totally captivated by the weather, the trees, the flowering shrubs – the bright sunny, happy color of it all. Such a far cry from the overpowering walls of grimy, gray granite that had harbored us for all those weeks of winter on the other side of the continent.

Those difficult weeks had truly been a baptism of fire – but we had survived to land in Eden!

On the afternoon of our third day we got on the bus to San

Francisco. We enjoyed the morning wondering around our new hometown. China Town, the shops, the sunshine, the feel and happiness, the entire atmosphere of this city by the Bay. We had lunch sitting on the Wharf watching the seals playing and sunning themselves on the rocks below. We took pictures with new little cameras that our families had given us before leaving home with instructions to record everything – so we could share it with them.

It was hard to tear ourselves away from all this fun but we had to get back to the reason we were here. We left the Wharf reluctantly and started to wonder up Main Street to van Ness Avenue checking out the shops as we went. At Jackson Street we turned the corner and started walking up the hill towards Pacific Heights. It was a very pleasant street with local type shops and restaurants with little tables out front.

On the corner of the second block was a large house that had a sign outside stating "Vacancy." We entered the lobby and knocked on a door marked "Office." A lady in a business suite got up from behind her desk to greet us as we filed in the door one by one. We explained who we were and what we were looking for and she was very helpful and assured us that she was bound to have something available that would suit.

She picked up a bunch of keys off her desk and bid us follow her. We took the elevator to the second floor where she opened a door and we walked into the largest apartment we had ever seen. We were in an older part of the city, and this great old house had tall open ceilings and wide corridors leading to large bright rooms. The apartment had two bedrooms, a kitchen, enormous living room and spacious bathroom. It was fully furnished and had windows from floor to ceiling facing Gough Street which went for many blocks down the hill from Pacific Heights and ended up in the Bay. We were in awe – speechless with delight.

"Oh this is brilliant." I said, walking to the window. "But sadly – I'm afraid we probably could not afford it – how much is the rent?"

"It is $200 a month plus utilities," our guide informed us cheerfully.

I was thunderstruck and swung around to face her almost knocking a lamp over in my excitement. "Excuse – excuse me. Did you say TWO HUNDRED DOLLARS?" I asked totally dumfounded – my eyes the size of saucers.

"Yes, I did indeed," she said smiling at our reaction. "Plus utilities of course."

We all four gasped in unison – in happy, total disbelief.

WE WERE HOME!

We could not believe our luck. It was all we could have hoped for – but to be able to afford such a place and in the city, was indeed mind boggling. We had seen so many apartments of all shapes and sizes in our quest. Some we could afford and some not – but we did not see anything that took our breath away like this one had. We signed the paperwork and before leaving made arrangements to have a telephone hooked up. This was a requirement so that Crew Scheduling could connect with us at any time, day or night.

We were told we could move in right away so we were all set as we left grasping four brand new keys in our excited clammy hands. Our bus ride back to the airport hotel was quiet and uneventful. Each of us deep in thought and a little scared at the giant step we had taken. We had flashbacks of what all had happened to us since leaving the safety of our families and homeland. It was daunting and sleep eluded each of us that night.

The next day dawned with the rising sun fighting to erase the morning fog which draped, caressing the City by the Bay with a gentle blanket in the early hours of every day. We decided to 'splurge' on a taxi to carry us, our bags and uniforms safely to our new home in one trip. We got up early and with much laughter, difficulty and confusion, managed to shoe horn ourselves and our belongings into the taxi to start this new and exciting chapter of our lives.

The Eagle had her wings – and now poised on the edge of the abyss - it was time to fly.

CHAPTER 9 -

HOME SWEET HOME

We moved into the building on the corner of Jackson and Gough in the city of San Francisco, California, on March 24, 1964 with great fanfare and glee. It was fun settling into our respective bedrooms and unpacking our things for the last time. It felt really good and calming to know that this was now permanent – this was home. We had been on the edge of temporary, impromptu time for so long, always waiting for the other shoe to drop. It was unnerving and stressful – but now we had landed. It felt really good.

We spent the afternoon exploring our immediate surrounding neighborhood. The little shops and restaurants on Jackson Street that led to Van Ness Avenue and the bus stop. Then we climbed the hill that was Gough Street all the way to the top and the little park there at Pacific Heights. From here we had an amazing view down the steep hill and all the way to the Bay. We sat for a while on a little bench under the lush foliage of a large Southern Magnolia tree overlooking the city – just taking it all in. Soon however we needed to head back down – we needed to buy groceries, set up our kitchen and finish unpacking. Reluctantly we started walking back down Gough Street. When we came back to our building I realized that although our apartment was on the second floor, if we opened our living room window we could step right down onto the street, the incline on Gough Street was that steep on this side of the building.

We soon ended up back on Jackson and Van Ness to do our shopping. We bought groceries including a bottle of wine and returned home in great spirits to put our purchases into the biggest refrigerator any of us had ever seen. It even had a separate compartment at the top that was a freezer and we could make ice cubes – should we ever have need for such things - or freeze meat and vegetables while we were gone.

We decided Mona and Suzanne should buy the groceries that they liked to eat and Chloe and I would do the same. It would be easier to keep track of our money that way too. The two Swedes liked Muesli and cold cuts on rolls for breakfast but Chloe and I liked to have eggs with bacon. We had the hardest time making a decision about the bacon. It was so streaky and fatty – hardly any lean meat on any brand we picked up to compare. Now we had to make a decision on what bread to buy – all so very soft and mushy – no substance. Then we found San Francisco sour dough bread. We had no idea what that meant, but it felt right to the touch so in the bag it went.

We were in the middle of unpacking our groceries when there was a knock on the door. It was the guy from the telephone company - to hook us up. Now we really were all set and as soon as we were alone again Chloe called Crew Scheduling to let them know we had an address and a telephone.

"Excellent," said Joe the scheduler for that shift. "Could I please speak to Suzanne."

With an amazed, questioning look on her face, Chloe turned on her heel and handed Suzanne the phone. Suzanne took the phone gingerly from Chloe in startled panic.

"For me?" she said meekly, her eyes as big as saucers. She stared at the receiver in her hand in disbelief and quietly said, " 'ello - zis is Suzanne"

"Ah Suzanne good girl. Do you have a pen and paper? I have a trip for you for tomorrow – I need you to write it down," said Joe happily. Suzanne - in surprised shock, started flailing about looking for something to write on and gesturing that she needed a pen. Chloe handed her the pen, note pad and the Bid Lines we had already placed next to the phone for just such an occasion – never thinking it would be needed immediately on our first call.

We all watched in great excitement as Suzanne wrote down all the information for her first trip. It was a double Bangkok. Pattern 96 on Line 35. She would be gone for almost 2 weeks. Please pack accordingly Joe instructed. "You are on Reserve and could be reassigned while down line – so be prepared for any eventuality." He hung up.

Suzanne sank deep down into the nearest easy chair and looked at us in panic – the dead phone still in her limp hand. We all stood as if frozen in time.

I was the first to gather my wits as I replaced the receiver in its bracket and grabbed the Crew Bid Lines that had fallen to the floor. "Suzanne, how exciting." I exclaimed turning the pages to find line 35 and check out her flight pattern. "Look your first stop is to Honolulu then you go to Guam and Manilla and on to Bangkok."

I could hardly control my excitement when the phone began to ring again and we all spun in unison to look at the loudly jingling instrument. We looked at it as though it was hot to the touch. No one moved. I was the nearest one to it and found myself reaching out with shaking hand to pick up the receiver. "Hello."

"Hi, this is Joe in crew scheduling again, could I please speak to Gisela."

"This is Gisela, Joe, can I - can I - can I help you?" I stammered weakly.

"Oh, hi Gisela. Yes I see I have a trip for you for tomorrow also. You can ride the same bus from town to the airport as Suzanne. Your trip checks in a half hour later than hers. You will do Tokyo outward bound through Anchorage, Alaska and returning via Honolulu – you will be gone 11 days please pack according to the climate at your lay-over stations or also for any eventuality, should you get rerouted off your pattern, down line. You will fly Pattern 23 on Line 105. Have a good trip – your roommates can expect to be airborne also shortly after you leave – I am working on that now – I was waiting for you guys to call in to let us know you are settled"

The phone went dead. The room reverberated with the sound of stunned silence.

"Great Heavens Ladies," exclaimed Chloe unable to stifle her excitement. "That calls for a cup of tea to calm our nerves - I'll put the kettle on." With that she swept dramatically out of the room in the direction of the kitchen. In England when an unexpected situation arrives – good news – bad news – panic – trauma – stress – it can always be fixed or endured by having a cup of tea.

So we did. The wine temporarily forgotten.

Suzanne and I had spent the rest of the evening agonizing over what to pack in our new Samsonite suite cases for our trip. I was going to Alaska for a two day layover – in freezing cold March weather - before heading for Tokyo. I packed a spare uniform skirt and two uniform blouses. I would wear my black uniform boots and heavy overcoat, but I would need sweaters and rain gear for Tokyo – and my bikini for Honolulu and three days in the island sun on the way back.

Suzanne was having trouble closing her suitcase so we all had to sit on it to make the lock click shut. None of us slept very well that night. Too much excited anticipation of what awaited us – what was to come.

****

The morning dawned cool and misty with fog shrouding the City by the Bay, in a thick vale of smoky white. By nine o'clock the pale morning sun was already working hard to burn it off however and the city spires had already cleared the mist. The day promised it would turn bright with sunshine, a blue sky with a slight westerly wind off the ocean.

Suzanne and I donned our uniforms and after one more hesitant glance at the long mirror in the hall way – hugged our roommates and left the apartment for the airport. Her check in time was eleven o'clock and mine was eleven thirty – we would be there in plenty of time.

The crew room was alive with hustle and bustle and noise. Crews were coming and going in every direction. Some incoming Pursers were sitting at little round tables filling out paperwork and trip reports. Other crew were sitting in the lounge area sleeping or working on their bid lines which were due to be turned in by midnight. At the far end the pilots were working on their flight plans with the dispatchers, getting weather, fuel and any other pertinent information needed for their trips.

Suzanne and I stood in the doorway, panic gripping at our hearts, trying to decide where we fit in. A young pilot came up behind us and picking up Suzanne's heavy suitcase which had not yet cleared the busy entryway said. "Good Morning Ladies – you look lost can I help?"

At that moment I saw a stewardess get up from behind one of the large desks on the far side of the room and wave at us.

"Over here ladies – you must be the latest new members of the Pan Am family that I was expecting to join us this morning. Come on over here and I will check you in – please leave your bags in the racks by the door, they will need to get Crew Tags on them which I can give you now." We gratefully approached the check-in desk after thanking the young pilot for his assistance and gentle persuasion in getting us through the door. The stewardess introduced herself as Linda Kelley, the In Flight Supervisor for that day. She gave us a warm smile while settling herself back behind the desk and handing us a crew tag to fill out and put on our suitcase. We looked at them with a puzzled expression and she laughed at our confusion and said.

"Here let me show you what you have to do with them. You go ahead and write your name at the top and then each line down gets the flight number, the date and destination throughout your pattern. This ensures that your suitcase stays with you for each flight. When you leave here today you will not see it again until you arrive and go through customs at your destination. Now, please tell me which of you is Suzanne?" Suzanne eagerly raised her hand and stepped forward.

"Hello Suzanne allow me to be the first to welcome you on board your first flight. You are checking in for Pattern 96 to Honolulu. This is your crew list and your Purser is already here in briefing room 2 over there by the door. Now please step on the scale and then you may go ahead and join her there. Please adjust your hat – it is slightly askew." Then with a smile she marked down Suzanne's weight on a sheet with her name and Pattern number on it, and turned to me.

"You must be Gisela – welcome on board Pan Am also. Did you all find somewhere nice to live and are you settled in? Let us know if you need help with anything. I will be the Supervisor for the four of you in-coming girls. This is my phone number, feel free to call if you need help or advice." I thanked her and told her we were all in good shape, had found a great apartment and were happy and excited to start flying. I assured her I would pass her name and phone number along to the other three in my group.

"Good, good I'm happy to hear that. It will take one or two trips to get comfortable with the routine." I felt her eyes peruse and sweep over my body - taking in every minute detail of my appearance. "You look very nice Gisela – please step on the scale. You are on Pattern 23 to Anchorage – your Captain is here but not yet your Purser. This is your Crew List and you will meet and brief in room 4 at 11:30. You still have 45 minutes so help yourself to some coffee if you'd like – it is over there on the counter," she said pointing to a small kitchen area.

I thanked her and walked over to a counter to fill out my Crew Tag for my suitcase. It felt good to be back in a crew room. The atmosphere was familiar, businesslike but warm and friendly – full of motion, coming and going and anticipation. It would also serve as a warm haven to come back to at the end of a long trip where you kick your shoes off and detox. I looked at my crew list. Longer than I was used to seeing. It consisted of three flight deck crew and six stewardesses which included two Pursers – one for each cabin. The airplane was a Boeing 707.

I filled out the crew tag and attached it to my suitcase and lifted it onto the rack under our flight number. Then I made my way to briefing room 4 and sat down at the long table. Two other stewardesses followed me in and we introduced ourselves. They were Japanese and roommates and flew together often. They told me they would go to visit their families upon arrival in Tokyo and not stay with the rest of the crew at the hotel on the Ginza. They were very friendly and excited to know that this was my first flight. At this point our two Pursers and another stewardess came in, pouring over a sheet of paper they had been given at check-in, and discussing its contents excitedly. Behind them came our three pilots.

We all sat down around the big table and introduced ourselves. I was welcomed warmly by all and found myself relaxing in the comfort of familiarity and crew camaraderie.

It felt really good – I was where I belonged.

CHAPTER 10 -

SPREADING MY WINGS

T he Captain's briefing the morning of my first flight with Pan Am, turned out to be longer than usual because of the information that he had and we needed to know.

On Friday March 27, 1964 at 5:36 p.m. – three days ago – the earth had moved in Alaska caused by a ginormous earthquake and creating a violent tsunami. We were going to be the first flight back into the town of Anchorage since the quake, carrying assistance and supplies greatly needed there. It was the largest quake ever recorded – 9.2 on the Richter scale - a disaster of great magnitude. It hit Alaska in the Prince William Sound area about 70 miles south east of the town of Anchorage. The great Pacific Plate located underground in that area, lurched northward with great force and jammed itself underneath the North American

Plate. The ground shook for four l-o-n-g minutes and continued shaking with many smaller aftershocks. A tsunami followed claiming many lives as it rolled southward throughout the great Pacific basin.

I was mesmerized. No – stunned. The color draining from my cheeks. Hadn't I lived this once before - off the coast of Africa while based on the island of Malta with BEA? Could history repeat itself – surely not. I listened to the Captain's briefing as though floating through a dream.

Anchorage had sustained a great deal of structural damage – especially in the downtown area along with loss of life. Fourth avenue – where our hotel was located was now a crater, it had moved 14 feet straight down and was inaccessible so we would be staying in a small motel closer to the airport.

This terrible occurrence would be a turning point in earth science over the next fifty years. The quake and resulting tsunami would force great leaps and bounds on how to handle and predict these phenomena. It would spawn amazing research and knowledge gained, thanks to more modern instruments acquired over time, which we could not begin to imagine in 1964.

The information given, the Captain continued our briefing by telling us that the weather was quite good - we should have a smooth ride and the flight time would be a little more than 3½ hours. We all sat in stunned silence quietly absorbing what had been disclosed. Then, without further ado, the pilots left and we were now able to brief on our cabin procedure for this leg of our trip.

The senior Purser, Travis, was a seasoned steward that had been with Pan Am for about 10 years. He now broke the silence by looking at his in-flight paperwork and informing us that due to the situation in Anchorage we have a full load in both cabins. We would be serving dinner and he therefore needed experienced stewardesses in both galleys due to the short flight time. So he proceeded to allocate the tasks to the appropriate stewardesses. I – being new and the most junior - was assigned to work the economy cabin with Bob, the junior Purser, who seemed very nice, friendly and laid-back. With that, we too got up and with some trepidation, made our way to the crew bus that would carry us out to the airplane.

Our flight to Anchorage – though full – was smooth and uneventful. Bob took me under his wing and I felt right at home and fit into the team without incident.

Anchorage, however, was indeed a disaster. I will never forget the sight of the devastation with toppled buildings and streets turned into large craters, some miles long, with cars and houses tumbled into them on each side. We were indeed the first flight into there since the town was struck and they were happy to see us because we brought supplies badly needed in their plight.

The small airport motel was off the beaten track and had not sustained much damage. The staff worked hard at making us comfortable and the food was, surprisingly, quite good. The weather however, was another story. It was cold and gray with some sleet in the wind which turned out to be just as well, because it discouraged us from wanting to venture out. The motel manager had also warned us that even walking around would be very dangerous. Much of the damage was still undetected and we could easily fall into a hidden crevice or walk under standing but unstable structures.

He was right – we dare not risk that – if one of us got hurt and were unable to fly, Pan Am had no replacement crew here and our Tokyo leg would have to cancel. As a result we made ourselves comfortable – wrote letters or made use of quite a substantial library the motel had, for use by patrons staying there during the long bleak winter months.

The pilots, however, did venture out. They needed to get back to the airport to check on the airplane and supervise the maintenance and refueling for our trip, since so many of the services had been disrupted, abandoned or broken down. Many airport staff had been pulled away being needed elsewhere or even taking care of their own homes and families.

We departed the mutilated, broken city two days later with a light load. As a result Travis, the senior Purser gave me permission to sit in the last row of seats instead of my jump seat for takeoff. This gave me full view of the devastation, as we rose into the heavens heading out over the Bering Sea. It was a sad departure from this amazingly beautiful state. I would return many times more on layovers, to enjoy nature in all its special splendor set in its high mountains and crystal clear lakes.

Bob had decided that since we had such a light load - only sixty three passengers in the aft cabin - it would be good for me to "get my feet wet" and work the galley. As soon as the Captain chimed that we had passed through 10,000 feet, I jumped up, changed into my smock, turned on the ovens and set up the two coffee makers. Before take-off and while the others were welcoming and seating our passengers, I had been checking and counting all my meals and equipment to make sure I had everything on the commissary load sheets that I would need. All seemed in good order – in fact we had been catered ten more meals than we would need.

Bob and Miki, the Japanese stewardess, started doing the beverage service. They had taken drink orders during taxi and before takeoff so they were now busy mixing the drinks in beautiful glassware with the Pan Am logo on it and delivering them to our passengers in the cabin. My ovens were now getting nice and hot and I loaded the large foil pans of Chicken Veronique – made with white wine and grapes – into them, along with the pans of potato croquettes and broccoli. This done I slammed the doors shut - the main course was cooking and under control. It felt good - now I just had to remember to put the rolls in the oven to warm before the chicken was finished cooking.

I was surprised at how easily everything came to mind without me panicking and needing to check my "cheat sheet" of notes. Our intense weeks of training and those practice meal services we had repeated day after day in the aircraft galley mock-up in Hanger 14, had indeed left their mark. I was relaxed and really enjoying being the 'chief cook and bottle washer.' I finished the job by putting the large extension shelf into place across the mouth of the galley, ready for the large china plates.

I checked the chicken and found it was bubbling nicely in the middle pans on the oven shelves. I stirred it and then rotated those pans to ensure even cooking with the pans on each side of the ovens. Now I was ready to add the rolls to the mix. I gave Bob a five minute warning that I was ready to start the service and took the china plates out of the warmers and place them on the extension shelf ready for me to dish up.

Bob and Miki went through the cabin and picked up trash and empty glasses. It took a little time as they did all this with trays because, of course, the glassware had to be collected and stored back in the racks that it had come in when loaded on the airplane.

I dished up the Chicken Veronique, potato croquettes and broccoli on plates four at a time - being careful to place each item "just so" on the plate with the required piece of parsley for garnish. Bob got the trays out of their container facing the aisle, placed a plate and a hot roll on each tray and handed them two at a time to Miki to 'run,' starting at the forward bulkhead of the aft cabin. The trays looked very appetizing with a small china dish of shrimp salad, a strawberry tart and a selection of cheese and crackers. The rolls and plate with the garnished entré finished off a perfect picture.

When Miki had served half of the cabin Bob broke off, picked up the coffee pot that I had prepared and ready for him, along with cream and sugar on a small tray and started the beverage service. The trays now came out of my galley from containers underneath the ovens, so I helped Miki by handing her the completed trays. When she told me she was serving the final passengers with their tray, I filled the tea pot and handed her a small tray with lemons, milk and sugar. She could now serve anyone wanting tea instead of the coffee Bob was serving.

While they were in the cabin I took down the extension shelf and started cleaning up and storing everything I had used. This done I went into the cabin and started to collect the used trays. The passengers all seemed happy.

However, after picking up two or three rows I realized I needed to stay back in the galley. Bob and Miki had the cabin under control. I also realized that my hair and clothes smelled of food and I did not look very presentable. It was more than two hours since we started the meal service and my galley was now knee deep in trash and dirty trays which needed my instant attention. It had been hectic and I realized I was quite tired but the main thing was – I had done it and everything went quite well. Bob proved this to be true, when he proceeded to pour a coke and hand it to me with a big smile on his face.

The cabin lights were dimmed and the passengers made comfortable with their pillows and blankets. Most slept, but one of us had to be in the cabin at all times. We checked on the ones sleeping and brought drinks or magazines to anyone awake. Then we gratefully took it in turns to sit on the jump seat next to the rear door, pull the curtain shut, kick off our shoes and just relax with a coke and a cigarette.

During my rest time the Captain invited me to sit in the cockpit to eat my crew meal. He was interested in hearing about my past life as a stewardess with a British airline – his son had just gone to Spain to fly propeller airplanes for Iberia. He had heard that Europe was hiring a lot of pilots that had been furloughed due to the incoming jet services being flown in America and Canada. Europe was happy to get these pilots, as they would continue flying propeller airplanes for some time to come. The Captain did not know that I had first-hand information of this, due to the fact that the love of my life had been just such a pilot.

I must admit I had been a tad blown away by the overall age and experience of the Pan Am pilots. They were much older than I was used to. As a rule, the Captains of most European carriers would most likely have flown in WW II and been the same age as the Pan Am pilots - but the First Officer in the right hand seat, would be much younger and usually in his mid-twenties. The pilots in all three seats with Pan Am were ex WWII or that vintage.

I finished my crew meal and excused myself from the flight deck. I needed to get back to my galley to get ready for the breakfast service. It would be quite a trick to get ready for breakfast and one I was dreading. I was beyond relieved that I was not in the first class galley, where I would be expected to create 3 minute eggs – Eggs Benedict or perfect eggs of any variety known to man. These things were not easy at 30,000 feet above the Pacific. I however, being in the rear cabin, only had to scramble eggs for sixty-three passengers and serve them with hot sausages.

The eggs were loaded ready for the oven in large pans which were very wobbly and hard to control after the lid came off.

The cabin was dark. The flight as smooth as silk. Almost all our passengers were sleeping. I pulled six pans out of the cooler and placed them in the hot ovens – three on each side, along with the warming sausages. Now I had six large pans of eggs and sausages in each oven. The idea is to cook the eggs – stirring constantly – and then store them and keep them hot in the large silver tureens borrowed from first class, until all had been cooked and it was time to dish them up and serve them. This time span could not be too long. The eggs would turn green in the silver tureens if left too long. Time was of the essence.

I was deep in thought as I opened the right hand oven to place the last pan of eggs onto the very hot oven shelf. With spoon in hand to stir the eggs in the other pans, it was at this moment in time that the 'wheels came off' and we hit a ginormous bump in the road. Unseen turbulence at 30,000 feet.

N-N-N-N-O C-A-P-T-A-I-N!

You cannot do turbulence NOW!

He must have heard me because the First Officer came over the PA apologizing for the fact that we had hit a 'slight chop' but are climbing to a higher altitude and should bypass it and be back in smooth air momentarily.

"A SLIGHT CHOP?"

You have got to be kidding as the eggs blanketed my hair and ran down the back of my neck. The sausages flew out and smashed with gay abandon on the galley floor. How lucky that they had a cover on the pan and therefore did not decorate the floor of the galley individually and on mass. The eggs however were everywhere on me and that hot oven shelf.

Soon, very soon - a smelly blue haze of smoke was cascading towards the ceiling and morphing with deliberate, billowing slowness, into the cabin of sleeping passengers.

Suddenly – as I tried to stabilize the situation by gingerly swabbing the eggs out of my eyes and immediate vision, and then forcing myself to gather the sausages in their pans off the floor – I heard a voice raised in panic from the cabin.

"We are on fire – Oh no – Dear Lord - we are on fire. Help – Help - we are on fire!"

We landed in Tokyo in the early morning having calmed our panicked passengers – assuring them that we were not on fire, and serving them a delicious breakfast.

Later, when on our way to the Ginza and our hotel we stopped at a tiny little shop, tucked into the corner of a house made of bamboo. The First Officer and the Navigator got out and soon returned smiling, carrying a large box and placed it in the trunk with our bags. I turned around in the bus, my hair still plastered to my head under my uniform hat, and gave Bob an inquiring look.

He laughed at my pathetic disheveled appearance and said, "Sake - for our debriefing party tonight. Welcome to Tokyo and Pan Am. Today you have been baptized – tonight we will celebrate that and welcome you into the 'family' – after your shower, of course." He grinned and I smiled weakly, still smelling of burnt eggs and orange juice - but feeling great.

CHAPTER 11

THE LAND OF THE RISING SUN

One of the more special things about being a Pan Am stewardess was the fact that we stayed in five star luxury hotels everywhere in the world. Many of them were owned by Pan American and this was the case here in Tokyo. We arrived in the city in the middle of rush hour traffic – or so I thought. Little did I know that this chaos and confusion of people, bicycles, trucks, mopeds and cars – was normal traffic on the Ginza in central Tokyo at any time. The city was pure mayhem and noise.

Our crew bus deposited us in front of a tall beautiful hotel with two large ornate and heavily carved pillars on each side of an elegant entrance way. As the bus came to a stop, several uniformed footmen and porters seemed to appear out of nowhere, to help us out of the bus and with our luggage. The nine of us spilled sleepily out of the crew bus and entered a large, wide lobby filled with amazing, ornate antique Asian furniture and statues. As the great heavy glass doors shut behind us – the mayhem was suddenly cut off – silenced – and soft gentle Oriental music replaced it.

We congregated around the front reception desk and were greeted by three smiling ladies in the most exquisite Japanese kimonos. We seemed to be creating quite a flutter with the patrons and staff coming and going through the lobby. There was a beautiful display of Bonsai trees of all shapes and sizes arranged in a circle of meticulously raked sand and set off by a gently gurgling fountain. I stared enchanted at this peaceful scene, letting the fatigue slowly flow out of me and totally unaware of the envious looks thrown in our direction by passers by. Little did they know how tired were our bodies. We had been on our feet for more than sixteen hours by now. We were weary – but we may not show it. We were Pan American Crew, we were in uniform and had to look and act as fresh as if our day was just beginning. The smiling ladies behind the counter knew and understood our silent plight and worked swiftly and bowed gracefully as they handed us each a room key and an envelope containing our per-diem. Our rooms were ready and waiting and we turned in unison and glided gratefully to the elevators.

We had decided on the bus that we should all go to our rooms and 'crash' for now. It was late afternoon and we could shower, relax, order room service and then sleep and meet for breakfast in the Coffee Shop at eight the next morning. That way we would be in sync with their time zone and we would not have much, if any, jet lag. The two Nisei stewardesses on our crew had departed to stay with family – being sure to leave contact information with our Captain and the front desk. Bob and the other stewardess on our crew, Jaquee who was French, had been flying out of San Francisco for more than three years and knew the city of Tokyo well.   Both had some favorite spots they thought I would like to see, and as a result could not wait to introduce me to The Land of the Rising Sun.

Travis, our senior Purser would hang with the pilots – or not. They had flown together many times, but he too had some favorite places he liked to visit, this side of the Pacific. So it was arranged we would all meet for breakfast – spend the day however we wanted and meet in the lobby for dinner. Pan Am crew mostly 'hung' together when outside of the United States and a lively debate would be had over breakfast about our dinner plans for the night. Much later it was decided we would all find our way to the Navigators room – and take care of the Saki.

When checking in the Captain had asked to see the Pan Am Crew Log Book that was always kept at the front desk, and had discovered that another crew was also here that might like to join us – we certainly had enough Saki to sink the Titanic – so he had left messages inviting them. Jason, the Navigator planned to fill the bathtub with Saki and put his and several other crew member's small coffee/water heaters that we all carried on our lay-overs, into it before leaving for dinner. It would then be a perfect warm temperature for consumption upon our return.

Navigators, as I would learn over time were very special, amazing people. They could - upon demand - conjure up the most amazing ideas, tools, equipment, gadgets and friends as needed, anywhere in the world. Maybe it stemmed from the early days of flight, when they would be required to tinker, nudge, manipulate and fix airplanes and enable them to take off and fly from locations not yet familiar or equipped for such things.

We had a fun crew. We had a great plan and left the lobby weary but in good spirits to go 'crash.'

I awoke the next morning in The Land of the Rising Sun – but the sun had not yet arisen. It was only 5:30 a.m. local time, according to the clock next to my bed. Too early to go down for breakfast. A little jet lag yet, to be sure. I remained laying there amongst the warm pillows thinking about all that had happened the days before. Reliving every minute of my first trip as a stewardess with the world's most loved and experienced airline – Pan Am.

My body ached. I realized that I must have used some muscles on that last long flight that I did not know I had. The flight had been the longest and busiest of my airline career. I climbed stiffly out of bed and decided to shower again and let the piping hot water just run over me and those tight muscles. I did that and it felt wonderful. I dressed slowly enjoying the anticipation of the day ahead.

Finally, I pulled the heavy drapes aside and looked out of the window at the breaking dawn. I was on the 6th floor of the hotel and looked out over the Ginza which was already in frantic, noisy motion. Happily the glass was too thick for any noise to penetrate.

I turned and gathered my dirty uniform pieces, stuffing them into the large laundry bag provided for us. I filled out the laundry sheet, placed it in the bag and hung the bag on the outside of my room door. It would all be cleaned and returned to my room by the end of the day. I checked the time – it was just after seven o'clock. I realized that I had thoroughly enjoyed my lazy morning but now I needed a cup of tea and to join my crew. I grabbed my uniform purse, left the room and went down to find both.

I crossed the busy lobby - already filled with many ladies coming and going in colorful kimonos. The only ladies not dressed in kimonos were from elsewhere in the world and visitors to Tokyo. I made my way slowly around the beautiful Bonsai display, marveling at the amazing artistry and design and found the

Coffee Shop around the far corner. The Captain and First Officer were already there and waved for me to join them. Pretty soon other Pan Am crew members trickled in and joined us even though they were not on my crew but were recognized by my companions. That crew was scheduled to fly to Hong Kong tomorrow night – I was introduced as one by one, they sat down and tables were joined together to accommodate the growing group. Finally Bob arrived and soon after him, Jaquee also joined us. Most of them were strangers to me – but we were "family" and it showed, as we all dug into a healthy breakfast. The next hour was spent laughing and sharing airline stories, in warm familiar friendship and camaraderie, all the while shaking off the stress and fatigue of the day before.

When Bob, Jaquee and I hit the street that morning, the sun was shining brightly but it was a tad chilly and I found myself wrapping my white silk uniform scarf, tighter around my neck. We turned left on the Ginza joining the mayhem for several blocks before arriving at the nearest station, where we hopped on a train to the Oriental Bazaar. We spent an enchanting morning going through the Bazaar with its hundreds of magical displays, stands, textures, smells, music and shops. I bought several little treasures to bring home to decorate our new apartment – but I did control myself knowing that I would be returning to Tokyo many times from now on. I discovered shopping was such fun and un-complicated because we did not have to fight with the strange Yen which was the currency of that land, everyone was more than happy to take American Dollars for our purchases.

Suddenly we realized how late it was. Time was flying by and we had further plans for the day. It was almost April, and Jaquee had noted over breakfast that it must be "Cherry Blossom Time" in Japan – and we should go and find some. The opinion around the table was that we should start at the Temple and the Old Edo

Castle that was now the Imperial Palace. There we would get a nice sample of ancient Japan amid an abundance of cherry trees, atmosphere and ambiance.

We left the Bazaar and returned to the Harajuka station and took another train back to the Yasukuni Shrine area and the Palace. Here we came out of the station and back into the crowded hubbub of the inner city, crossing the busy street at great risk to life and limb – in spite of the fact that we crossed at a legitimate crossing.

I realized quite suddenly that I loved this land that was so very different from anywhere I had ever been before. I made a vow to myself - I would come back, many times - as often as I could on future trips. I was very much aware that as a very junior stewardess in a very senior crew base I would not have enough seniority to hold a bid line and would spend many a year "flying in the pool" on reserve. BUT over time, I would learn that you could be called out on wonderful, senior trips, that you would never be able to hold as a junior stewardess, unless you were "in the pool!"

With this determination in mind I would, later, when back in my room, read up and learn more of this magical country's amazing history, for I was enchanted, intrigued, mesmerized, and – in a word – hooked.

In 1869 a seventeen year old Emperor decided to move Japan's capital city from Kyoto to Tokyo. Until then it seems, Tokyo had been just a very small fishing village named Edo. However, Edo boasted of an old castle, built during the Shogun Era in 1457. So far the ruling Emperor of Japan had always resided in the capital city, which was Kyoto, since the year 794 - but in 1869, the new young Emperor decided to change that. He had been eying the old castle in Edo and its history with the Samurai – it touched his heart and his soul, and he decided to move into it and make Tokyo the capital. Thus this amazing city was born.

Sadly, the city has always been susceptible to natural disasters and both fire and earthquakes plagued the city constantly, thus needing continuous and intermittent rebuilding. Even in more recent years, the city endured two major catastrophes. In 1923 a mammoth earthquake hit the Islands of Japan, killing almost 140,000 people. Then, during World War II, in 1944 and 1945 the city suffered incessant bombing which basically destroyed Tokyo and tragically killed 200,000 civilians.

As a result, the city was completely rebuilt and was "show cased to the world" with the Olympics in October 1964. The reborn city – a Phoenix – not unlike Hamburg, Germany, the city of my birth – is rebuilt, resurrected, triumphant and reborn out of the ashes of war. All this information awaited me at a quieter time when I could close my eyes, lay back and inhale it – but now, we were moving on.

We continued down a very narrow old side street, with many fascinating little shops on each side. There was much hustle and bustle, with some very interesting characters emerging from within the depths of some of these vintage bamboo structures. Many were illuminated by swinging lanterns and decorated with colorful ribbons. This is the Orient I had read books about and dreamed of since I was a child. I was in a total euphoric dream state, and as a result unwittingly dragged behind my companions who suddenly emerged out of my happy haze, with hands on hips. They had turned and come back looking for me – only to discover my body pressed hard against a window gazing with longing into the depths of a shop filled with exquisitely carved statues and antique Oriental furniture.

"Gi, we are not going to achieve our goal today if you do not move along. You are missing precious time out at our destination." With that Bob took my hand and while smiling, unceremoniously dragged me the last few yards to the gateway of the

Imperial Palace.

Even now – 50 years later – I am totally at a loss to explain the emotion that swept over me as we burst out of that gloomy narrow street, bustling with noise, action and humanity and into an explosion of color and gentle serene motion. It was breathtaking and I gasped with pure unexpected delight.

I felt as though I was looking deep into the heart of the most magnificent Monet picture he had ever painted - and it had somehow been set into gentle motion. The explosion of the Cherry blossom trees in all their glory, swaying in the bright sunlight – was mesmerizing. However, the spectacle did not end there. Under those heavily laden, swaying blossoms, the most amazing scene was playing out. A group of Geisha, in exquisite colorful kimonos and beautifully painted faces, were gently walking under those trees, taking in the soft sunshine. They all carried colorful umbrellas to shade their long, slender, delicate necks from the rays of the sun. Their beautiful, thick blue-black hair coiffed and piled high with pins and flowers to hold it in place.

The beauty of that scene will remain with me forever. It is now 50 plus years later – and I see it still, as though I have remained standing there, holding my breath – in suspended time.

That is how the Eagle was introduced to this magical place called 'The Land of the Rising Sun.'

CHAPTER 12 -

BLUE HAWAII

My lay-over in Japan was amazing. It was such an incredible 'fluke' that my first trip took me to Imperial Japan at the most perfect and desirable moment of their year. Cherry Blossom time. That is hard to repeat. I would return many times to Japan – but rarely this special time of year.

In fact, I was not able to repeat it again for many years – with much time and much life in between. In the meantime, the Pacific Rim and all the exotic lands that that encompassed, would become familiar 'stomping grounds.'

We left Tokyo in a brisk rain storm and I wondered what that might be doing to my perfect "Monet Cherry Blossom" picture. Sadly, that was now in my rear view mirror because my crew and I were headed for Hawaii and I had no time to dwell on it.

I would be working with Travis in the first class cabin and we were scheduled to have a full load to Honolulu on the island of Oahu in the Hawaiian Island chain. Travis had taken pity on me and decided I should work the cabin with him. It would give me a lot of help and insight into what I would need to know when working the First Class galley. He was right. The long and complicated six cart aisle service came alive to me on that flight. I learned so very much from this experienced, seasoned steward and was able to handle the galley with ease on my next leg back into San Francisco.

I loved working the cabin in first class. Setting up the tables for the elaborate dinner service with the white linen table clothes and the colorful flowers placed in a tiny vase on each table setting. The ladies were very impressed and loved that, along with the piping hot towels we offered them to freshen-up before dinner. Then, later, after the caviar, lobster thermidor and the roast beef had been enjoyed and put away – it was fun serving the passengers that had elected to move and sit in the cute little lounge, all the way forward by the entry door. This was a very sought after area for socializing on these long flights. The Gentlemen would light up everyone's cigarettes with their fancy, expensive lighters and the wine and Don Pérignon would continue to flow with gay abandon.

I also prized the large beautiful flower arrangement always there on the little table in that lounge area, to greet our passengers when they arrived on board. So beautiful and usually very tropical. Perfect for our destination. In the 1960's flying was a very special event. Our passengers all arrived on board dressed in their best clothes. In those days, flying somewhere was an 'occasion' and a lot of planning and effort was put into it. The ladies would board wearing beautiful dresses, with hats, gloves, high heels and furs. The Gentlemen would be dressed in business suits or fancy sport's jackets, starched shirts and ties.

Sometimes these long flights were quite traumatic and difficult for young children and it was a trick to keep them happy and occupied. They were not allowed in First Class, so families were sometimes split up and parents would take turns sitting up front and then back with their child in coach if they did not have a nanny or companion with them to care for the child. Often, while on a break, one of the stewardesses would take the child by the hand and walk up the cabin to the flight deck and introduce him or her to the pilots. Most of them had children of their own and welcomed the intrusion. They would show and explain all the 'bells and whistles' on the flight deck and help them put on a head set so that they could listen to some airline 'chatter' between aircraft. Then they would fill out a little "In-Flight Passport" we had given the child upon arrival on board. It would track the route flown by them that day and the Captain would sign it, thus giving them a log of their travels – to be continued on their next flight with Pan Am. Then, before the cockpit called us to return the child to the cabin they would be given a set of the Pan Am pilot wings with our name and logo - all very much fun and happily received.

****

Our arrival in Hawaii was a dream come true for me. A very important moment in my life. A real milestone, due to the fact that this moment in time was a promise kept.

I had made a vow on the occasion of my sixteenth birthday, while out and sitting with a bunch of dear friends in a freezing cold movie theater. We were all frozen to the bone, in the depths of a snowy English winter. Bored and snowbound at home we had elected to make our way, on foot due to the inclement weather, to the pictures – which we did. So now we sat huddled and shivering while watching Elvis Presley cavorting around on a warm, tropical beach in Hawaii with a bunch of beautiful women. I made a vow in that theater - to move heaven and earth to go there, and forever leave behind these cold English shores with the rain and ice and snowy winters.

Now, I was finally here – in Paradise, living my dream. I had sacrificed much to do it, but - here I was.

The young Eagle with its claws deep in the lake, triumphantly hauling its prey skywards.

****

The airport building in Honolulu was still under construction when I arrived in March 1964 – but no matter – it was magical. After landing and taxiing in, Travis opened the door and I will never forget standing behind him and being struck by soft, warm, perfumed air as that heavy door swung open. A crowd of beautiful Hawaiian girls with long black hair, soft brown skin and wearing grass skirts, came swarming towards the airplane to greet us. They were waving excitedly, carrying garlands of tropical flowers, called leis. The airstair in place, Travis stepped aside, and with Hawaiian music playing I went slowly, and with reverence, down the stairs, to stand at the bottom, to help our passengers deplane.

Upon reaching the tarmac one of these smiling girls threw a lei around my neck and wished me, "Aloha!" The greeting of the Islands.

There would be a lei for everyone on that airplane – passengers and crew – it was exotic and totally charming. I was still breathless with delight when we picked up our bags and went through customs and passport control along with everyone else. We were all still wearing those beautiful leis and totally intoxicated with their perfume when we filed out of the building. Our stretch limousine was waiting at the curb to take us for the short drive to the hotel.

The five star Royal Hawaiian Hotel on the beach at Waikiki awaited us in tropical splendor. It was the first hotel to be built on Waikiki. The crème de la crème of hotels was PAINTED PINK. As a result it would hereafter be lovingly nicknamed by my fellow crew members as "The Pink Palace."

The building glowed in the soft afternoon Hawaiian sunlight set in the midst of lush gardens filled with amazing exotic flowers and mango trees. I stepped out of the limo and in the confusion of unloading crew and bags – I just stood transfixed in awe. All I needed now was for Elvis to come strolling around the corner and the scene would have been complete. I however, would have fainted dead away.

A nudge from someone passing returned me to reality and the here and now.

We entered the most exquisite wide open, breezy wood-paneled reception area with high ceilings and ceiling fans turning lazily above us. There were flowers and lush palms everywhere. At the desk we were handed a glass of pineapple juice, a room key and an envelope with our per-diem in it. Our per-diem was always given to us at every destination in local currency. We received $20 a day for meals and incidentals. This was wonderful because I could not possibly eat $20 worth of food in a day and so I was able to save most of it and never even touch my salary.

We were required to fly seventy hours every month at a starting salary of $300 per month. That was an amazing salary for young ladies in those days. Then anything we flew over seventy hours would be overtime. I never flew less than eighty plus hours in those days. I could do that because I was so junior and could not bid and 'hold a line' every month and therefore would be –

'flying in the pool' on reserve. I also volunteered a lot – calling in, when home - begging for a trip. Crew Scheduling liked that and utilized me a lot – especially since I had volunteered for M.A.T.S. Charters which flew into the war zone in Vietnam.

Pan Am Crew did not stay in the Pink Palace itself – we had our own building next door. 'Pan Am Crew Only.' Quiet and peaceful and away from any noise. So when we had been checked in we sashayed across the main lobby and around the corner to our building where my room on the 7th floor awaited and welcomed me.

Once again we had made arrangements in the Limo to meet for dinner the next night. We would all spend the day in our own way, on our own time. Jaquee had said she was meeting a good friend of hers here and they had planned to spend the day on the beach, so I was welcome to join them. I thanked her and planned to do that. This lay-over hotel was the airline's most busy. It was usually every trip's first leg out and every last leg home. It also was everyone's entry back into the US – so it was – home.

My room faced the ocean and I watched fascinated as the sun gently kissed the horizon to sink out of sight behind a palm tree and on down, beyond the dormant volcano of Diamond Head and gently on into the sea. The palm tree continued to wave gently as though playing hide and seek with the setting sun and the trade winds. The sky was a soft velvet aqua and purple dome, stretching wide over the silver slate of the darkening Pacific Ocean that was whispering to the crashing surf.

I turned reluctantly away from the window, leaving it open to the sound of the sea and the gentle breeze. I continued tearing the rest of my soiled uniform off and stuffing it unceremoniously into the plastic bag lying in wait on the bed. I made out the list and threw the bag outside my door. Then I hit the shower turning it up as hot as it would go and letting that water run over and revive my groaning muscles. After a long time I emerged, poured myself gratefully into the welcoming bed - and slept.

I slept through breakfast and it was close to noon when I came out of a deep sleep to the sound of the telephone ringing. "Hello"

"Hi Gi – are you OK? We missed you at breakfast and it is now lunch time. No problem, just checking." It was Bob checking in on his new baby chick.

"Yes, Yes Bob - thank you." I said sleepily rubbing my eyes and focusing on the clock. "I'm fine, where are you, I'll be right down."

"We are on the beach and we have wine and a spare avocado and shrimp salad for you. Take your time. Come when you are ready." The phone went dead.

Less than half an hour later found me walking in mesmerized wonder, through the manicured grounds of the Royal Hawaiian Hotel, on the path leading to the beach. The path was lined with mangoes and tall elegant palm trees with coconuts waiting to fall at their feet. Heavy clusters of exotic sweet smelling flowers were abundant everywhere, and birds – some I had never seen before – darting in happy song and play, amongst the lush foliage.

I spilled out of this exotic beauty and found myself on the most exquisite beach I had ever seen. Its wide open expanse of golden sand curved gently in a graceful arc towards Diamond Head. The Pacific stretched forever out to the horizon. There were catamarans floating gently along, with guys singing to the rhythm of their strokes just over the far side of the crashing surf. People were walking along the shore, the warm ocean bathing their feet with gentle waves. Some folks were lying on the hot sand under an umbrella, reading or sunning and still more were swimming. It was a peaceful scene – no crowds, just gentle movement.

Someone jumped up and waved from a group of about ten obvious crew members. They were all relaxing on the sand a little way down from where I stood, under an umbrella of bright Cobalt blue.

"Over here Gi." It was Bob who came running over to greet me in a colorful bathing suit and boasting a soft tan on a body in harmony with the Hawaiian sun.

"You are looking a lot better than the last time I saw you. Did you have a good night's sleep?" He asked grinning broadly, while walking me over to the group.

"I did, thanks," I said happily, greeting everyone with a cheerful wave and introducing myself to the ones I did not know.

"We decided we needed to initiate you to the Islands since this is your first trip, so we are organizing a Luau for this evening. There are a lot of people here that will be able to join in and it will be a good 'meet and greet' for you and a lot of fun. You will get to know a lot of folks that you will remember when you get to fly a trip with them down the road." Bob said, making room for me on the warm sand.

I sank down onto my knees on the towel I had spread and took my beach cover off, revealing my new bright yellow bikini. Suddenly I was aware of a total silence around me. Startled I looked up to see everyone was looking at me. Some were smiling in approval – some not sure, and some looking quickly away when I looked up. I was suddenly very self-conscious and unsure how to react, not knowing what I had done to cause this response.

Fortunately Bob saved the day by quickly saying.

"Wow good for you Gi – bikinis are still fairly new here, but I have noticed that most of the new girls from Europe are wearing them – it looks good on you but you better lather up and get some oil on that exposed skin or you will burn to a crisp." He handed me the baby oil and moved the colorful beach umbrella closer to me.

Looking around I saw that the stewardesses present all had on bathing suits or modest two piece suits that covered their stomachs to the waist. Suddenly I had a flash-back to a pool day in training, when the training was not allowed to continue till six of us European girls had been re-clad in hideous, black oversized bathing suits - because we were wearing bikinis. I was mortified. I had forgotten all about that day when I packed for the beach in great excitement in San Francisco. I no longer even owned a bathing suit.

This is 1964 and bikinis had been an item in Europe for some time now, and everywhere I had gone in the last couple of years most young women had been wearing them. In the late 1950's, Catholic France, Italy and Spain had a problem when they first came out and banned them from their beaches. However, they had a crisis and were forced to back down when, I believe, it burst onto a film set in living color. James Bond produced Ursula Andress - exploding from the ocean 'almost' wearing a white bikini - in a scene from the film "Dr. NO." As far as I could tell, from then on every young woman in Europe was clad in one – I think that may have been in 1961 or 1962. Certainly all my airline life.

I pulled my wrap around myself and sincerely apologized if I was offending anyone – but to my amazement they all cheered and indicated they were fine with it. I should make myself at home and enjoy the afternoon. Then they poured me a glass of wine brought off the airplane and handed me an avocado shrimp salad out of the Captain's cooler. I related to the phrase - my cup runneth over - I apparently was a trailblazer and proud of it.

That night we had the most amazing and wonderful Luau. As darkness fell the whole beach was transformed into a magical place - illuminated with hundreds of flaming Tiki torches. The guys had arranged for a group of local Hawaiians that our navigator knew well to come over. Some in grass skirts, some in muumuus, but all came by and helped us make it magical. They brought their local instruments with them, and so with the flaming light of the tikis and burning hot coals in the sand – we had a Luau.

Bob had found another new hire stewardess, Angela, from Seattle, who had just transferred in from the class before me. This was her first Hawaiian lay-over also. We joined arms, mesmerized - swaying to grass skirts and the intoxicating music. How could anyone beat this experience? We learned to eat teriyaki salmon, sausage, steak, Mahi Mahi fish, conch, and the local delicacy of savory purple porridge called poi – with hesitant gusto and then – with gay abandon.

As the liquor based punch continued to flow - we learned to dance the Hula.

We were in love with the people, the music and the islands of Hawaii.

"Aloha" - the Eagle was flying high into the soft azure of the Pacific sky.

CHAPTER 13 -

ALASKA - LAND OF THE MIDNIGHT SUN

I loved Tokyo and got to fly this same pattern several times over the next months. On one such trip I had just finished a three day layover in that city when I was unceremoniously rerouted. I was awakened from a deep sleep by the loud ringing of the telephone. It was crew scheduling reassigning me to a trip on Pattern 63 - line 94. Basically I was being rerouted to fly this morning's flight from Tokyo to Anchorage - pick up at 0500.

My bedside clock stated it was 0432.

I jumped out of bed with my equilibrium reeling. I had everything ready to go - my uniform had been returned from the cleaners and was hanging in the closet - my suitcase was packed because the pattern I was on was due to leave for Hong Kong at

1600 this afternoon.

The scheduler asked me if I could possibly make the pickup time - they were really sorry but a stewardess was very sick and the flight was full so they desperately needed a replacement or the flight would have to cancel.

"I think I can make it." I said - my head swimming while tearing off my night shirt. "Tell the crew I will do my best." I hung up and jumped to wash my face and clean my teeth. My uniform was ready to step into and all I had to do was tame my unruly hair. I did a quick check of room and bath - checked myself in the mirror, adjusted my hat then left the room as quietly as I could so as not to wake any other crew members on my floor. I arrived in the lobby to find my crew patiently waiting in the crew bus - the First Officer pacing the floor of the lobby. The time was 0505.

The elevator door opened signaling my arrival in the dim, quiet empty lobby and he rushed over to help me with my suitcase.

"Hi - are you Gisela? Great let me help you - everyone is on the bus - go ahead and board, I'll take care of your bag." With that he swooped it out of my hand and ran it to the back of the crew bus. This done he jumped in after me, slammed the door shut and gave the driver a thumbs up. The bus lurched forward and into traffic already heavy on the Ginza.

The crew of seven already on the bus gave me a warm welcome and someone handed me a cup of tea in a paper cup. It was hot and sweet and just what I needed.

"Oh my goodness, thank you," I said in total amazement and looking around I saw that everyone had a cup.

"The front desk brought us the hot tea and we asked them to

bring an extra one for you," the Captain said cheerfully. "Just don't spill it on your uniform 'cos we have no way of fixing that now." The atmosphere was upbeat and friendly even at this early hour, and I felt myself fit right in. I was sitting next to the First Officer who had slipped into that vacant seat and slammed the door. He introduced himself as Gary and said that now that I had joined the team and everyone had introduced themselves, he needed to fill me in on some plans their crew had been making in Tokyo for their five day layover in Anchorage.

It seems that Joe - the Navigator had a friend that lived there and owned an airplane. I was tickled - talk about sailors having a girl in every port - these Navigators had a friend in every port! So Joe had talked with his friend before leaving on this trip and he had invited the crew to come with him to his cabin on a lake in the woods. The only way to get there was by plane. Four of the crew had decided to do that but there was one seat left on that tiny plane - soooo - would I like to join them?

I looked at him in disbelief - my eyes the size of saucers. "YES - OH YESSS - thank you I would love to go."

"Excellent - that will please Lisa who was the only other female adventurous soul to agree to come." Lisa squealed her delight from somewhere in the back of the crew bus. I was thrilled.

The flight to Anchorage that morning was full and it took the airplane a little while to cool down. It was summer time and it had sat all night on the hot humid tarmac. I worked the front of the airplane with Tom, the Purser, and Lisa who was working the galley. Most of our passengers were making connections to other places in the US and Canada, but we had a large group of Japanese Engineers travelling to Anchorage to inspect the progress that had been made there since the earthquake. The islands of Japan also were very susceptible to earthquakes and had sustained them over many centuries, followed by devastating tsunamis and they were interested in learning from us. Melissa, our Nisei stewardess that joined us at the airport, worked the back to care for this large group. She had spent her layover with her family in Kyoto and was tiny and very sweet. Many of our Nisei stewardesses were based in Hawaii and would join the crew there. They were a great asset to us on our Japanese flights like this one today.

The Nisei are second generation American Japanese and our Nisei stewardesses are the grandchildren, born after WWII to Japanese parents interned in the camps of California during that time of misjudged loyalties. They spoke fluent Japanese, and for this reason were invaluable to us in-flight.

We only had four first class passengers on this flight, so after our meal service was over I went and helped in the back where they were still quite busy cleaning trays away. It was on one of my trips back to the galley with several dirty trays that a very frail elderly lady stopped me and asked for the rest room. She was beautifully dressed and very elegant but not too steady on her feet when she stood up in the slightly swinging aisle. I walked behind her and when I got to the galley she turned to me and I pointed through the rear cabin to the restrooms. I went up and down the aisle several more times while helping passengers get comfortable after their heavy meal. On my way back to the galley after one such trip I looked up and saw that little old lady standing in the aisle staring intently at one of the restroom doors - head bent far forward and with her hand resting on the door handle.

I noticed that the sign outside indicated that it was empty so I went to her and said, "They are both vacant - let me help you."

She turned to me in relief and said, "If I open that door - will I still be on the airplane?"

I assured her that she definitely would, and opened the door for her with a smile. Flying was still so very new to most people but the elderly passengers I encountered were just really in awe of everything in-flight.

We arrived in Anchorage on a beautiful sunny warm afternoon. The sun dancing off the enormous peaks in the distance, the higher elevations still covered in snow. The air was sparkling unlike the humidity we had left in Tokyo. Fortunately I had had a chance to revise the crew tag on my suitcase so it arrived here with me and not as previously marked to Hong Kong. We all went to our rooms to shower and change and then those of us going on our trip the next day arranged to meet a little later, for dinner, to finalize our plans.

The next day dawned also sparkling and bright with a slight wind that was warm and soft coming from out of the south. The three pilots joined Lisa and I in the lobby and we all climbed into our crew bus that was pulled up in front. We threw our small Pan Am tote bags into the back and jumped in - Joe in the driver's seat. We had packed a tooth brush and a change of clothes, a parka, socks and shoes more suitable for the outdoors. As little as possible because the airplane we planned to meet was very small and could accommodate six people including the pilot, but it could not handle much luggage.

We drove into the airport gate and around to the perimeter road that would lead us to some hangers and the General Aviation part of the airport. Our Pan American airplane that we had brought in the night before, was sitting proudly alone, in front of the terminal taking up all the apron in front of the giant windows. It had an army of personnel running around and over it like ants around their Queen - getting it ready for a noon departure.

The road lead us away from the terminal and around the end

119

of the runway with its approach lights guarding the tip of the runway like soldiers at attention - to the far side of the airport and a set of three medium sized hangers. Several small one and two engined airplanes were half in and half out of their giant doors, getting ready for the busy work day. These small aircraft were the work horses of Alaska where roads were few and often impassable through that state's mighty wilderness. Personnel and supplies were very often needed in inaccessible wilderness areas of the state. Especially now - in summer - which, this far north is very short, and every minute without snow and ice was a gift and utilized to the utmost.

This was indeed General Aviation and it was a busy place. A small single engined airplane sat out front of one of the hangers and caught our eyes immediately. It was painted bright red and it played with the sunshine that was flickering and dancing all over its shiny wings. A man came out of the open hanger door as we approached and waved a greeting. This was Nathan - Joe's friend and our pilot and host.

Nathan was a stich. A large, burley out-doors man that blended right into this wild country like a glove. You could tell he spent much time in the out-doors trying to tame the land that he loved. He was so happy and so excited to have us accompany him to his little hide away "man cave."

After all the "Hello's" and introductions had been made he introduced us to "Ellie." Ellie was old but she was beautiful - well-loved and extremely well taken care of. She was Nathan's pride and joy. She could take a pilot and five passengers BUT nothing else. Nathan was usually on his own or with one other friend when he went to his cabin, so there was always enough space for anything they needed. Today we would be sitting with our tote bags in our lap - or they would have to stay behind.

Ellie was extremely functional - she could land anywhere on land or water - she even owned a set of skis - Nathan informed us proudly, although she had her surfing equipment on today, the floats resting right above her wheels.

Nathan opened Ellie's door and pushing three metal steps into place, bade us board without further fanfare. We did so with much joking and good humor - the guys settling in the front of us girls who elected to take the two rear seats. Elliot, a friend of Nathan's came out of the hanger to help us load. Nathan settled into the pilot's seat, shoehorning his bulky frame into position with some difficulty and much teasing. Finally, Elliot slammed the door, removed the chucks and stood waiting for Nathan to give him the signal to spin the prop. He did so and we were on our way.

The single propeller bit into the morning air with gay abandon as the tiny airplane bumped its way to the end of the runway. We were inside like sardines in a can - Lisa and I hugging each other tight, arms entwined, shoulder to shoulder.

"OK - everybody ready?" Nathan said looking around our eager smiling faces - as he got clearance from the tower for take off. He pushed the stick forward and the engine roared. Ellie tipped eagerly forward in anticipation - and finally the little plane burst forth and danced down the wide open runway stretching out ahead of us. In no time at all - it seemed, to those of us used to flying in big jets - Ellie bounced in delight as the wind gently connected with the underside of her wings and lifted her into the heavens.

I felt the three pilots tense a tad as the earth fell away beneath us - a totally unconscious thing all pilots anywhere in this world seem to do, when they are passengers - and not in control. Lisa and I smiled at each other knowingly - both sensing the momentary tension as we banked slowly to the west and into a horizon filled with amazing mountain peaks bathed in sparkling sunshine. It looked like one of those pictures you are taught to paint at a lesson you have signed up for - in a church hall. The stark dark mountains with snowy peaks against a bright blue sky and wispy clouds afloat here and there.

This was the picture Lisa and I had sitting so far back - we could not see the ground or Ellie's bouncing wings as we flew through choppy air - the wind reverberating off those mountain walls. The mood and conversation was upbeat and fun as the pilots exchanged "tall" airline and fish stories for the duration of the hour long flight.

Suddenly, Nathan sat up and focused his sight directly forward though Ellie's thrashing propeller.

"There it is folks - we have arrived," and he proceeded to tip the airplane's nose down. We all leaned forward to see what he was talking about and right ahead of us was a large expanse of shimmering, sparkling sun bathed lake, surrounded by thick pine woods that climbed slightly around the edge to meet the stark mountain walls on each side. The lake was long and continued through the mountain gap to form a wide green valley at each end. Nathan throttled back when we were about 100 feet above the water and glided Ellie gently down until she kissed the water with a giant splash. She skimmed the length of the lake to where we could see a small cabin peeking out of a thick grove of giant fir trees. A jetty was built out into the lake and Nathan cut the throttle and turned towards it coasting to a gentle stop at exactly the right spot so that he could jump out onto a float and throw a line around a piling. This was obviously a well-practiced feat as the big man delivered the task with remarkable ease.

We piled out of Ellie - grateful to be able to stretch our cramped limbs, and stood in total awe of the breathtaking scenery that surrounded us on the slightly bouncing jetty. I felt myself tense in total delight - feeling the size of an ant in this spectacular venue.

How amazing is this world. How could any person confronted with this exotic beauty not take pause and admit - there HAS to be a GOD.

****

We entered the stark little cabin which was totally charming inside. The Great Room consisted of heavy long oak beams running from one side of the room to the other. It housed a torn up couch and easy chair pulled up to a cozy fireplace. In one corner was a sink with a long handle to pump water from the well - a long oak counter top leading to a dilapidated iron stove. Old iron pots hung from big hooks from a beam in the ceiling along with a hanging lantern. On the other side of the room were four twin bunks - one above the other. Under the window, facing the lake, was the dining table with a bench on each side and several lanterns sitting next to a large container of matches - waiting for the kiss of life.

The far wall, directly across from the entry door welcomed you with the most enormous Moose head I had ever seen hanging in a place of honor over the fire place and a big bear rug lay before the hearth. Every spare inch of wall had a trophy hanging on it - be it fish or fowl or deer. They all gazed down at us solemnly - as we invaded their empty, silent space.

We spent a simply charming afternoon leisurely exploring around the cabin and as the afternoon sun began to set - the days are short in Alaska - the guys built a big fire down by the lake and two of them went up on the pier with fishing poles and bait of corn, to see if they could catch our dinner. We sat around the fire on old tree stumps that had over time, been gathered and placed there to sit on. Nathan stood on a rock watching Joe and Gary get their lines ready to cast out. I was wondering what he was doing standing there with hands on hips smiling broadly - when Joe suddenly jumped up in excitement and started pulling at his bent rod and line and started to reel it in. He already had a fish - and not just a fish but a giant Pink Salmon. Gary was so intent on watching Joe that he was not paying any attention to his line dangling in the water without any bait when suddenly it was almost jerked out of his hand - a large salmon had hooked himself on it thinking there WAS bait on the hook because his buddy had found some on Joe's line.

This was a very funny scene and we all jumped up excitedly and ran onto the pier to join them - when Nathan suddenly waved his arm and told us to look at the lake. We stopped in our tracks and turned to look where he was pointing. The entire surface of the lake was alive - a solid mass of large, wiggling, jumping fish as far as the eye could see. It was the most amazing spectacle I had ever seen - it made you want to jump in and walk to the other side of the lake on their backs.

Gary laughed delightedly and after securing his giant fish on the pier said, "Nathan you did not tell me to bring my Jesus shoes with me on this trip - and I am not believing that I just caught this big fish without even baiting the hook. My fishing buddies back home will be driving me to the Emergency room when I tell them - worried that I am having a 'turn' of some kind!" We all agreed - no one would believe what we were seeing in this amazing place.

That night we tucked into endless helpings of delicious fresh Pink Salmon cooked over an open fire somewhere in the heart of Alaska. Later, we got our sleeping bags off the beds in the cabin, and stretched out under a canopy of a gazillion stars. We lay there speechless in awe as we watched the sky turn to fire and The

Northern Lights came alive in living color streaking endlessly across the heavens.

Lisa and I were zippered into a sleeping bag together - hardly able to breathe and back to back - because of course, there were not enough sleeping bags to go round. We were lying closer to the lake than the guys, and we had dozed off – as they had. We were all happily exhausted from a wonderful day capped off with wine and beer found in Nathan's store room.

I suddenly became aware in my light sleep, of a warm damp sensation over my face, and I laboriously worked my hand out of my tight enclosure, to scratch my nose. I opened my eyes and found myself cheek to soft warm muzzle with the most enormous creature I had ever seen in my life. That moose had obviously come out of the dense forest to drink from the lake and had tripped (fortunately not literally) over of all of us lying there prone, in his space. His ginormous "hat rack" completely obliterated the night sky and I squirmed in panic and squealed into the confines of my sleeping bag, jerking Lisa and the rest of the group out of their slumber.

"Stay still - don't move," I heard Nathan command very quietly from a few feet away. "Nobody move - play dead - he will lose interest."

I peeked at this giant form through my shaking fingers, hardly daring to breathe - Lisa as tight as a drum behind me. Finally, after what seemed like hours but in reality was a matter of ten or so minutes - he snorted in disgust and scratching his hoof in the soft dirt - turned and walked slowly to the water. He stood in regal stance for several minutes - as though proudly surveying his domain - then lowered that incredible head to the cool waters of the lake. We all lay still - mesmerized. The moose drank his fill in his own good time and then slowly turned and walked along the edge of the lake to a gap in the trees - and disappeared.

It is an experience I will never forget, and even now - fifty plus years later I get goose bumps of delighted terror, remembering it. Needless to say we did not repeat the sleeping by the lake saga. The following night we slept inside the cabin on the bunks. Lisa and I shared one, the pilots took the other three and Nathan slept on the couch.

The following day we all went fishing in two small boats that Nathan had stored behind his shed. Lisa and I sat in the back of one and Joe and Gary did the rowing. The Captain and Nathan were in the other boat. The sun came up early - as it does in the summer in Alaska - and we had feasted on a wonderful breakfast of bacon, eggs and biscuits. Nathan had been well prepared for our visit. He had come out the day before and stacked the tiny ice box that was hidden under the counter, with goodies. It had no electricity but it had large blocks of ice - also brought in the day before. We had been totally amazed at Nathan who had turned out to be a really good cook - well versed with that primitive dilapidated looking stove.

Now, full and happy here we were floating out on this amazing lake surrounded by the most exquisite scenery. The mountain peaks all around us and the dark dense forest full of wildlife stretching out on either side down the valley. Lisa and I were delighted to learn, that the only bait the guys had for this fishing venture - was corn. We had no problem baiting the hook with kernels of corn - and did so happily.

This floating fishing expedition turned out to be a hilarious fiasco, due to the fact that there was no trick to it. If a hook was hung over the boat's side - within two minutes a fish was on the hook. The first time this happened it took Joe by complete surprise and the fish jerked the rod right out of his unprepared hands and took it sailing off down the lake. Fortunately Nathan and the Captain were ahead of us in their boat and were able to "field" it as the fish shot past them.

Lisa and I could hardly control our laughter as these macho men that we entrusted our lives to on a daily basis, proceeded to turn into excited teenagers as they hauled in one giant fish after another. Then, as the fish flapped and slid down to us in the back of the boat, we would pick it up and when they were not looking - throw it back in.

The Eagle will never forget that amazing flight into the breath taking, unspoiled wilderness of beautiful Alaska.

CHAPTER 14 -

MY WORLD – MY OYSTER

Upon my return home to San Francisco, I found that I was the only one there. I checked the schedules left behind by all my room mates and found that Mona would be back tomorrow night. The other two were gone for another week or so.

I enjoyed being alone. I re-grouped my emotions, my soul and my energy. Having grown up as an only child – being alone was a pleasure. I restocked the fridge with bread, cheese and eggs and bought a bottle of red wine. This was necessary since I had not achieved the knack of drinking water.

I was aware that Americans did this all the time with gusto – it was disgusting – I could not bring myself to do it. I wanted my water boiled in tea or coffee - or not at all. Also, all this ice in everything – it was frozen water. What was the reason for all that water – I could not get used to it. If I wanted something cold I would put it in the refrigerator, I did not want frozen water diluting my gin and tonic.

It would be wine with dinner – so very civilized - as I awaited Mona's return.

It was twenty four hours since my arrival back in San Francisco. I had done my laundry in the basement of the apartment building. I had dusted and vacuumed the apartment and bought a small bunch of flowers to decorate the kitchen table, flowers were a necessary item to our European psyche. I was rested and ready to go. It was time to call crew scheduling and tell them I was ready to fly if they needed me.

Before I got the chance, the phone started ringing as Mona burst wearily, but gratefully into the apartment entryway.

"Hello, this is Gi, can I help you." I said picking up the phone while waving a welcome at Mona.

"Yes, hello Gi. This is crew scheduling and I was wondering if you could help us out. I have a flight to Sydney that I cannot cover, leaving tomorrow night. It is a 14 day, pattern number 73. I know you only just got back but I need you and you are legal to fly it. Check in time is 1645 tomorrow afternoon."

"OK – yes, yes - no problem I will be there. Thank you," I heard myself saying and hung up.

Mona and I embraced warmly and she went into her room and a well needed shower, and I went into my bedroom to regroup and repack. She and I spent a wonderful evening together, sharing a home doctored pizza with lots of extra cheese and veggies and, of course, the bottle of red wine.

I left for Sydney, Australia the next afternoon, leaving Mona home alone.

I checked in for my trip a tad early, so that I would have time to check my mail box and generally relax before meeting my crew for the first leg to Hawaii and a three day lay-over. The flight then went on to the South Pacific island of Pago Pago. This little island was the capital of American Samoa and Pan American would service it twice a week. The flight to Sydney alternated with Tahiti - it stopped there on the days it did not stop in Pago Pago.

These islands had been found and touched by missionaries in the early 1800's – they had brought and delivered Christianity to these little patches of heaven in the middle of nowhere in an endless ocean. It must have been a mind boggling assignment – I cannot imagine how they fared in that era, with their heavy Victorian dress and moral code to match.

We touched down in the early morning hours and taxied in to a long, low shack of a building built of bamboo and palm fronds. I was absolutely amazed to find almost the entire island population waiting for us at the ungodly hour of 2:45 am, with loud, happy song, music and dance - behind the airport fence. All this merriment to welcome the locals home, and the visitors - to Samoa. This big jet was still an amazing spectacle to these people, so very isolated and cut off from the world's hustle and bustle. As a result they welcomed it with great excitement, joy and fanfare. It is however, very easy to understand how Amelia Earhart could get confused and lost out here. These islands are just a mere speck in this mighty ocean and a panic attack could easily happen if you are low on fuel and do not have the modern instruments on board to help you find where you need to be to get more.

The crew bus took us to the only hotel – The Intercontinental, owned by Pan Am and nestled right into the foot hills of The Rainmaker Mountain. I would now have four blissful days to explore this beautiful, unspoiled place, where heaven and earth met in perfect harmony. I loved meeting and talking to the locals at all these 'off the beaten track' places. You could learn so many amazing things about their lives and culture.

A rather unique custom on this island was amongst the families that had all boys and no daughters. They would take one of the boys and raise and dress him like a girl. Give him a girls' name and teach him to cook and clean and care for babies, just as if he had been born a girl. Many times when he was older he would revert back to being a man and found himself snapped up immediately by a young woman - because he was so handy to have around the house. I wonder what the missionaries thought of that idea.

The crew I had on this trip were very seasoned and had flown this pattern many times before – it went very senior on the bid lines. Sydney was a very desirable destination. As a result I found myself doing my own thing for most of the four days – which was fine with me. I realized very early on, that being a Pan Am crew member gave me VIP status at most places around the world. I would get help, advice or input at any time or anywhere I wanted or needed it. So I took myself to the Rainforest Park one day – the little museum the next, and then to just swim or snorkel off the coral reef and the many wonderful silvery beaches.

My sun tan was starting to blanket my pale Nomadic body again, and it felt good and healthy. Very often the Pan Am crew and other airline crews from QANTAS or Air New Zealand that flew to the islands, would be the only people on the beach. We would sometimes join them for various events, or parties on the beach – but Air New Zealand crews could be pretty wild and we usually gave them a wide birth – afraid to tarnish our stellar image.

Upon arrival in Sydney I could understand why it was so popular. It is a wonderful city, with much to do and offer visitors. After the crew had exposed me to The Royal Botanic Gardens and Zoo and introduced me to a Koala Bear, the senior stewardesses took me shopping with them. I learned where all the best places were to get your hair done, buy shoes or leather goods, the best spa for facials and massages and so on. All good information I could pass on to passengers if asked, and information not found in our Pan Am World Guide Book that we carried on board the aircraft. Then in the evening we would all meet and go out to one of the amazing restaurants around the harbor.

Sydney harbor at night. Oh my! Special indeed.

Our flight back would be direct to Honolulu, flight time close to ten hours. Our load would be quite heavy and I would be working the coach cabin. Our crew briefing at the Sydney airport had been casual and routine. We were not expecting any problems in flight, although it was monsoon season, but the Captain assured us we would be circumnavigating the few thunderstorms in route and they would not affect us at 30,000 feet.

I stood in mid cabin and watched through the window, as the passengers broke free of the gate and streamed across the tarmac to our airplane in two lines. One thin line was headed to the front airstair for First Class boarding, and the second was directed to the rear airstair – these were our Coach passengers. I looked down the length of the cabin and was so proud of the welcoming way we looked to any passenger getting on. Each seat had a pristine white pillow propped up - just so - against a light Pan Am blue blanket that welcomed each passenger to their seat. Everyone had a seat assignment and I was there to help them find the one on their boarding pass. Three seats on each side of the aisle.

I had been told to expect an infant and I had set up the baby bassinet and secured it to the forward bulkhead that separated Coach from First Class. These passengers arrived on board first and I directed them to their seats, assisting them with the baby while they got settled and stored their bags. Finally all the passengers were seated and secure and we taxied out to the senior Pursers' "Welcome on Board" announcement. She was informing everyone of our flight time and what they could expect to have for dinner and much later for breakfast. She stated that the Captain would come on the PA after we had reached our cruising altitude and give them an update and progress report. In the meantime please keep seat belts fastened at all times while seated. Then she wished everyone a pleasant flight, dimmed the lights and hung up the PA receiver. I finished taking my drink orders and secured them in the bar area drawer, threw the secondary latch and strapped in to my jump seat next to Caroline who was working the galley.

We took off from Sydney - banked left over the harbor and lifted up into a darkening sky. The massive Pacific stretched before us – an endless, moody, expanse of ocean that you can never trust or take for granted.

It was almost three hours since our departure from Sydney and the dinner service was in full swing. We were serving a cold soup called vichyssoise – we did this on many of our flights in tropical zones. We served the soup on the tray with the set ups of salads and desserts, and then carried the entrees out after we had collected the soup bowls. It made the service a tad longer, but who cares – we had ten hours to do it in.

I had collected most of the bowls in the cabin and was at the forward bulkhead serving the entre of beef bolognese with rice and

134

carrots, to the family with the baby. I had four entrees on my tray and was leaning over two seats to serve the mother of the baby in the window seat, when suddenly, the floor disappeared from under me. To this moment I only have a vague idea of what happened, but I found myself rapped around the gentleman seated in the aisle. I was prone on his lap with three delicious dinners blanketing both of us. Even the baby in her bassinet did not escape unadorned – several pieces of beef and a carrot cradled her ears and head.

I managed to unburden the poor man in who's lap I sat by getting to my feet and shoveling as much of the errant food back onto my tray. However the turbulence was not done, and the aircraft continued to lurch, bounce and shudder violently. I sat down in the aisle – the safest thing for me to do at that moment since no vacant seat was available. I apologized profusely and explained to the frightened passengers in my vicinity that all was well – we had just hit some clear air turbulence and it would be over momentarily.

Not necessarily so. At that moment the Captain came over the PA stating that we had hit some clear air turbulence and we were climbing to a new altitude in order to avoid it. Please stay seated with seat belts fastened. We will be back in smooth air shortly.

OK CAP so do it - I thought to myself. I have just explained that to people. NOW, PLEASE DO IT.

I crawled into the First Class cabin and found a seat in the last row of seats there and strapped myself in. No sooner had I done that than a bright flash of light zigzagged down the blue carpet in the center of the aisle, from the flight deck to the tail.

We had been hit by lightning.

The gentleman in the seat next to me grabbed my arm as the airplane continued to thrash up and down.

"Did you see that – what in heaven's name WAS that?" By now passengers were screaming and crying and the lady across the aisle from me was mouthing a silent prayer with her prayer beads in hand.

"I am so sorry sir," I said reassuringly to the man next to me, brushing a carrot and some rice out of my hair on to the floor. "We have hit some turbulence in a thunderstorm but all is well I assure you - the Captain has it under control and we will be out of it in just another minute." I smiled weakly and stayed sitting there, all the while decorated and still draped in beef bolognese.

It took five more minutes before we stabilized. It felt like five hours.

Suddenly the flight deck door opened and the Captain strode out in full uniform to survey the cabin and reassure our passengers. A tall well-built man with an imposing demeanor and four shiny gold bars on his smart black jacket didn't hurt the message his appearance was trying to convey. The effect was quite magical.

The cabin was a disaster. There was food, salad and strawberry shortcake somewhere on every passenger and bulkhead and ceiling. Most of the hats and coats stored in the open uncovered overhead compartment had been thrown out onto people's heads, and although badly shaken, no one was seriously injured. It took longer to clean up our passengers than it did to serve the meal.

The Captain strode unperturbed through the dishes and debris, talking and reassuring everyone around him. The passengers bought into his quiet, positive, unflappable attitude and calmed down, as he progressed through the mess and down the cabin. Some even helped us gather trays and dishes off the floor and two little kids turned it into a game. So much for our glamorous stewardess image. The Captain's image however, was paramount at this moment in time, and it did not disappoint.

Our three day lay-over in Honolulu was a God send. We relaxed and baked all stress out of our bodies on the beach and in the soft warm salty ocean. Rejuvenated and refreshed we had no problem with a full load of passengers for our last leg into San Francisco.

Upon boarding we helped them in the cabin gently store their departure leis in little plastic bags that we had on hand specially for this purpose. We placed the delicate flowers in the bag and then twirled the bag shut by the corners till it was like a balloon. This would preserve the flowers until the passengers got home.

The City By The Bay welcomed us back to the mainland as it would many times to come. It felt good.

The Eagle had found its nest and gratefully folded its giant wings.

CHAPTER 15 -

M.A.T.S. CHARTERS

Over time, the little European clan in the City By The Bay started to settle down to a comfortable routine. We adjusted to our long trips to the most amazing far away places we had, up until now, only dreamed about or seen in movies. Our flights were long, hard and demanding – but thanks to our brutal training, we were up to it all. We were proud. We were confident. We were capable. We were relaxed. We were having fun.

I was still trying to kick in to the fact that I was now actually living my dream. How can you top that. Elvis – eat your heart out, I have caught up with you – you have nothing on me now. We loved to come home to our beautiful San Francisco apartment, but we hardly ever found anyone else there upon our return.

We started to date and make friends – life was full but so much fun. My room mates and I passed like ships in the night.

We loved our San Francisco home.

Our phone rang three days after I had returned from my last trip. I had just come back to our apartment after a trolly ride down to the wharf and a little shopping spree in China Town. I heard the phone ringing as I passed my bedroom window. As expected - I had a message. I was happy 'flying in the pool' because I did not think I would EVER have enough seniority to hold a real line of flying. While 'in the pool' scheduling called me a lot, and I loved that. As a result, I got to fly very senior trips I could never hold on any line.

I dropped my packages by the door and headed for the phone.

"Hello scheduling, this is Gisela Wheeler returning your call."

"Yes Gi Hi – thank you for returning our call so quickly. We have a problem and were wondering if you could help us out. We have a M.A.T.S charter out of Travis Air Force Base – we have no one but you on our volunteer list to fly this tomorrow – could you please help us out. You would fly to Da Nang, drop the troops off and then fly to Singapore to overnight. It is a two day lay-over in Singapore and then 'dead head' back to Da Nang to pick up another load of troops back to Travis."

"Oh sure, no problem, what is the check in time – I will be there." I wrote down all the necessary information and hung up.

Military Air Transportation Service - or M.A.T.S Charters, were easy flying and a lot of fun. There was more food on those airplanes than I had ever seen in my life. Per military requirements we had to feed those soldiers every four hours. There was food stuffed EVERYWHERE. In every bin – high and low. We had to take care of our troops and send them into battle well fed.

I checked into my flight the next day at 16:40, met my Captain and crew – all volunteers. We were going into a war zone and the cabin crew were not insured. Amazing, happy, focused, special people. We took off from San Francisco with an empty airplane and the cabin crew flew as passengers - or 'dead heading' - to Travis Air Force Base in California en route to Vietnam.

Travis Air Force Base was wind swept and business like. They were waiting for us but it would take time to load the belly with all the equipment they would need on deployment, before the troops could board. When this was accomplished to the Captain's satisfaction, the guys streamed aboard without incident. I have had the privilege of flying many military personnel from different countries around the world, but I have to say, without a doubt, the American military is the most efficient, smart, polite, clean cut, clean smelling group of guys I had ever met. We piled them in and strapped them down, chatting and smiling the whole time.

Finally we were all set with a full load of Military might. The aircraft door slammed shut and we taxied into the unknown. It was late evening when our Boeing 707 airplane - this giant piece of machinery, heavily loaded with supplies and precious cargo, defied gravity and leaped into the abyss.

The giant Pacific Ocean stretched endlessly before us as we reached into the heavens and leveled off on our way to Vietnam. The air was calm and we sailed along smoothly into the night. We served a complete meal on a tray with salad and desert and an individual covered casserole dish of beef over rice with gravy. It looked and smelled delicious but a challenge to prepare. Each oven only held twelve casseroles at a time - our galley girl however, had done a great job of heating them just right and keeping them rolling out of the galley as we needed them. Result - our passengers tucked in with gusto. The mood was upbeat and our passengers were happy to talk and joke with the crew when they were served. Later, when the meal service was over and the trays cleared, our passengers curled up with their pillows and blankets. We dimmed the lights and the cabin was silent as some slipped into sleep.

We monitored the cabin constantly, checking with the little Pan Am flash light each of us had been issued for just such times. We would check to make sure our passengers' seat belts remained loosely fastened, because turbulence was always a factor on these long Pacific flights. We would serve water, coke, aspirin - or just sit and chat with those who could not settle. These amazing young guys had much to ponder at eighteen and nineteen years old and now finding themselves heading into an ever escalating war. Many of them remained awake and just needed to talk to someone – anyone – who would listen. We - would listen. We - made it our job to listen.

By the time we arrived at our destination we would know almost every one of them personally – their names, their families, their background, their hometown. On that sixteen hour flight we would all become family as we laughed, cried, held hands and comforted some of these brave young men, many of which we knew – we would not bring home.

Breakfast was a much more somber meal, as we got closer to our dreaded goal - in spite of the fact that the sun arose in brilliant pink and gold and sparkled over a glassy ocean far below, throwing a gentle glow over the eating men. This was not a day to celebrate with the rising sun however, and after the breakfast service we handed out magazines and a lot of writing material. A few of the guys had left sweethearts and wives back home, some of whom were pregnant. As a result many wanted to write letters and have us mail them when we got home. It also gave them something to focus on during that long flight into who knew what. Some had tears gently flowing as they wrote – emotions and nerves were very close to the surface now.

We did our best to divert the mood and make everyone comfortable. We handed out playing cards and joined in with some other mind or word games being played throughout the cabin, until we had to start preparing for our snack service shortly before our arrival in Vietnam.

The Captain had briefed us upon arrival for this flight that we needed to make sure everything was tightly secured for landing. We would have a great deal of trash and debris to deal with – more than usual, which was normal on a M.A.T.S charter – and we needed to take time to stow it really well. He said he would call us when we were an hour out, in case we had not had time to check in with the flight deck before that time.

When that crew-call came I realized what the Captain had been talking about. This being my first charter I had no idea what to expect. I suddenly became aware that there were large bags of trash everywhere, filling up the galleys and taking up space against the aircraft doors. Fortunately I was working with a very senior crew that had done this many times before, very often flying together, they worked like a well-oiled machine. The senior Purser even opened two of the overhead compartments holding the large, heavy life rafts, and expertly jammed some bags in there, as all the available cabin space to secure the trash was eliminated. Everything had to be secured, tied down and the doors vacated.

When this was accomplished to his satisfaction, the senior Purser went to the flight deck to let them know we were secure. Shortly thereafter the Captain came on the P.A. and made an arrival announcement – hoping that everyone had had a comfortable flight and to alert us of an unusual mode of landing and he did not want us to be alarmed. Our decent would be very steep and very rapid. This was normal for this airport and we should also be prepared to hear gun fire hitting the airplane upon touch down. This also was normal as the snipers would be busy

143

and waiting for us. Please also lower all the window shades at this time then, lay back and relax, we will be landing shortly.

The cabin was eerily silent as all this information was obeyed, digested and understood. We did a final cabin check as the flight deck called for the crew to take their seats. I turned in mid cabin to return to my jump seat and found myself gazing into the big, round frightened eyes of some of the younger guys, on my way to the back of the airplane. I strapped myself silently into my harness, next to Sally the second purser that I had been working with all flight and who had been very helpful in helping fill me in on how to work a M.A.T.S charter. We were both in full uniform including hat and white gloves as was normal for any arrival with Pan American anywhere in the world.

This, however, was no normal arrival, and as I felt the airplane tip sharply forward on its intense desire to connect with the safety of earth, I felt my emotions burst to the surface and I found myself crying as though my heart would break. I felt Sally take my hand and rap her arm around it, hugging it, and when I looked she too was in tears. It was a very emotional moment and both of us were caught up in it. These guys were 'family' – we knew everything and everyone they belonged to – and now they belonged to us and we did not want to let them go.

Our mood was suddenly shattered when the angle of the aircraft became even more steep and a bullet slammed into the door next to my feet. Then another, and then ten more. Then a terrible crash up front as a window shattered and things started to fly around the cabin in the sudden burst of air. The wheels hit the runway with an earth shattering crash and we started to roll, bump and swerve down the runway with the tail of the airplane waving back and forth. The cockpit applied hard, loud reverse thrust to the four jet engines and we slowly shuddered, groaned and shook to a violent halt. There was much noise and commotion outside and I realized that we were listing to one side. There also was the sound of gunfire although it now did not seem directed at us.

I jumped up and looked at Sally expecting to do an emergency evacuation. She shook her head with finger tensely poised awaiting instructions. The crew phone dinged over my head.

Sally picked it up and listened as the Captain instructed us to "SIT TIGHT – DO NOT OPEN THE DOOR we will call when it is safe to do so." The line went dead. A flight of helicopters was taking off on an early morning search and destroy mission and heading out in our direction. We needed to wait for them to pass over us and clear the perimeter of the airfield.

I suddenly realized that the gunfire from the snipers that had been shooting at us was now directed at the departing Huey's. They thundered overhead, their rotor blades digging into the heavy humidity and early morning haze, shaking the very being of our silent crippled craft. This band of pilots, as I would learn much later, were the so called "fearless crazy guys" that brought truth to the saying "flying by the seat of your pants."

These were the amazing men that manned the Bell UH 1 helicopters - commonly referred to as "Huey's" - that would change the face of the war and how it was fought. These guys would fly at zero feet towards the tree tops – at the last second jump over them and bank into where they needed to be, often in a hail of enemy gun fire. They would sometimes sit with wheels a foot off the deck, rotors screaming – to drop off much needed troops and supplies or pick up the wounded and dying, in split seconds of time before lifting off again.

These aircraft were the work horses of the Vietnam war – but the men that flew them were the silent – unsung Heroes. Sadly we would end up losing 5000 of these heroic men before the war was done, as they did their job – daily and with monotonous regularity against all odds – door guns blazing – skirting over the heavy jungle canopy into a wall of bullets in order to rescue what often was already lost.

Thirty years later I would run into one of these heroes, an amazing unassuming man. A great pilot who claimed he was just doing his job – and would do it again. I am proud to call him "friend."

The crew call rang again over our head and returned us to the task at hand. Sally pushed the button to answer the call, the receiver still in her hand from before. The Captain said to open the rear door – an airstair was ready and waiting – please deplane everyone as quickly as possible.

We opened the door gingerly, waiting for the door to click into position, worried that the door had been damaged enough by gun fire that it could release and inflate the slide when opened. All was well however, and the door opened to revel an airfield full of tanks, armored vehicles and instruments of war. Two portable airstairs were rushing towards us on the taxi way and uniformed men were already swarming all over the underside of the airplane starting to unload our precious freight. Another group was pouring foam onto our tires and undercarriage.

Sally and I fought to get ourselves emotionally under control, taking turns to run into the toilet – while the other guarded the open door. When the airstair was in place a young officer climbed up to welcome us. Four buses also arrived and the young officer indicated to start to deplane our passengers as quickly as possible and please ensure that we stay away from the open door. This meant that I would not go to stand at the bottom of the stairs as usual to assist in deplaning. So, we both moved one to each side of the door, safely tucked inside. In this way we could touch, hug and cry as these sweet young men started to file off down the swaying airstair and out of our lives.

One young Marine came to attention at the door, saluted and said, "Thank you Ma'am - on behalf of all of us on this flight, we thank you. We will not be forgetting your kindness to us and I hope to see you on the flight home." He came to attention again - saluted - and was gone.

The airplane looked very sad and forlorn as we drove off – sitting sort of sideways on the runway, listing with one wing tip almost on the ground, tires deflated, a forward window blown out and many bullet holes scattered around. The airfield had the look of a giant ant nest with the Queen in trouble and a million worker ants swarming all over to help her. The crew bus was as silent as a morgue – not only had we lost our 'military family' - but we had lost our ability to leave this violent place.

The Eagle was forced to fold her tired wings and patiently roost in a hostile land.

****

The cock pit crew spent the next two days on that airplane – working diligently every minute with the base mechanics to get the airplane airworthy again. The damage was mainly 'cosmetic' – no vital parts had been hit it was decided, after a thorough examination. The base was very well equipped for just such an occurrence and had all the spare parts necessary. Pan American provided the Government with this service frequently and as a result all necessary parts were on hand to facilitate a turn around as quickly as possible. Besides – we had a full load of passengers waiting patiently to be gone from here.

Most times the airplane was well enough to quickly get out of there and on to Singapore or Djakarta once the troops were off and the belly unloaded. There it could be fixed and refurbished for the turn around two days later. The more serious problems we were faced with on this flight happened every now and again, and were dealt with as quickly and efficiently as possible.

The Captain informed us at dinner that we need to be ready to go before first light. We would get a wake up call at 0300 pick up was at 0400. The airplane was being fueled and stocked right now, and it was only a ten minute ride out to it from here. Passengers would board at 0430 and we hoped to be airborne before sunrise, thus hopefully giving us a head start over the ever watchful snipers.

The crew bus found its way, as though by magic to the silent airplane, sitting moodily on the dark airfield – not a light in sight. I found myself immediately having a flashback to another time, another country also at war, when I was exposed to situations like this. The memory did not feel good - but I exited the bus along with my vintage crew, all of whom had done this before and were not in the least bit fazed.

The window had been replaced along with the tires. They could not however, match the paint on the fuselage and as a result we looked a tad pock marked – but no one cared about that. We were delighted to be released from the confined boredom of life at the local "Hilton" – a building hastily constructed to house any unfortunate aircrew stuck here on the base for maintenance.

We climbed the front airstair and the door magically opened wide enough to admit us - and then quickly shut again. A young Sargent welcomed us on board as we found ourselves in a dark cabin. The shades were down and the only light came from the glow of the emergency floor lights leading us to the back of the airplane.

"Good Morning folks. I hope you had a quiet incident free stay with us." The young airman said cheerfully. "The airplane is in good shape but please do not open the shades. Also please leave the doors shut until we open them from the outside in order to board. We will do that in exactly thirty minutes from now and I will come and check with you to make sure you are ready. We have about 25 wheelchairs which we will board first and I will help you along with some of our medical staff to help them get settled and to let you know of anything unusual they may need inflight. They will each have an assigned helper flying home with them, so you should not have any problems." He checked the clipboard in his hand and continued cheerfully,

"You will find a staff soldier from the kitchens here, in each galley, to give you an overview of what we boarded and where we have placed your food items." With this information duly delivered, he opened the door a crack, squeezed through and shut it again from the outside.

Our eyes were now adjusting to the dark cabin, so Sally and I made our way to the back of the aircraft along with Erik another Purser, and Linda who were working the flight from the back with us. We were made up of available crew members from the volunteer pool - hence a third Purser was utilized to make up our crew. Erik would act as the junior Purser in the back for our flight home, as Sally wanted to work the galley. Matthew our senior Purser and Annette were working the front.

The silence was deafening. It was eerie in the darkness. As though the world was holding its breath in anticipation of something unknown – no, rather something unexpected - to shatter it. We did our cabin emergency checks in complete silence with the help of our pocket flash lights and were ready when the Captain called to tell us to open the doors and turn on the 'low' ceiling lights. He asked Linda to come up to row 15 and board the guys from there back, till all the wheelchair people had been seated and accommodated forward of the wings, then we could fill in as needed. The airplane had been modified for these charter flights and the forward lounge had been replaced with rows of seats.

The file of young men boarding the airplane in complete silence started immediately, and they settled themselves quickly and without commotion into the open seats. These soldiers were different from the ones we had delivered. At first I could not identify what the difference was. Most were young, polite and all smiling broadly at us as they passed and took their seats in silence. Suddenly the line ended and the door was slammed shut. I worked the cabin helping to stow hats and coats and any small soft items that would be safe and fit into the overhead hat racks, as quickly as possible.

As I worked my way forward, I suddenly found myself amongst all the wheelchair folks. What a sad, heart wrenching sight that was – it took my breath away and I had a hard time not letting the pain of what I was looking at show on my face. How could those beautiful, strong healthy young men, turn into these broken, bandaged torn forms – some with only half a body – that now rested, belted with extra restraints, into our seats.

I broke free and beat my way to the forward lavatory and slammed the door. The light came on and it startled me so much I let out a cry – as though in pain. I stared at myself in the mirror and was shocked to see how bad I looked. Every drop of blood had drained from my face and tears were streaming down my cheeks. I took my gloves off, peeled a paper towel off the rack and dumped it into the cold water filling the sink. I HAD to restore color back to my blanched cheeks and get my emotions back in check. The cold water felt good on my face in that hot lavatory. I closed my eyes and slumped down on the seat. I had heard the engines come to life, one by one, right as I entered the lavatory and now, as I sat there with my face covered in a cold wet towel, with my hands in the sink of cool water – I felt the airplane move and start to roll. I was running out of time. Suddenly there come a quiet knock on the door.

"Gi, are you OK – can I help?" It was Annette. I think she may have caught a glimpse of my shocked, ashen face as I shrank into the lavatory. I stood – unsteady - unlocked and opened the door. The light went out and I stood there in the gloom looking at her with my hand covering my mouth, tears still filling my big, sad eyes. She entered the now swaying lavatory and gave me a big hug. "It's OK Gi – we have all been 'there' – it gets better after the first time. Come on I will walk you back to your jump seat – follow close behind me - no one will see." She grabbed my hand and pulled me out of the lav and down the dark bouncing aisle.

I felt the airplane begin to turn onto the runway as I fell into my seat. Erik grabbed the crew phone and called the flight deck to let them know we were not secure yet for take-off. The airplane slowly completed its wide turn onto the now brightly lit runway, and jerked to a stop. Then, once Annette was safely seated and strapped in next to him, Matthew who's jump seat was next to the forward door, took over and gave the cockpit the 'OK' to go.

The engines roared as the airplane, held in place by mammoth breaks, shook and leaned forward in eager anticipation of freeing itself from this stricken land. The breaks held as if some creature had the craft planted down with its giant foot – then suddenly that foot lifted - and now released - the airplane burst forward in unrestrained glee. We rolled and rolled and rolled at ever increasing speed until the wheels lifted us free of the earth. As this giant machine heaved itself upward, the cabin was filled with a ginormous roar of jubilation emitting in earsplitting chorus from every throat. This jubilation was sustained for many minutes and then someone started to sing America the Beautiful as the airplane labored to sustain its steep climb into the wide open sky of a breaking purple dawn.

While in my jump seat and listening to this wonderful, happy sound, I suddenly knew what was different about these young soldiers. Their eyes were veiled, tired and sad. So very sad. They had each gazed into the portals of hell and now felt guilt about living and thus, able to come home. Many of their friends will not. And yet others will return - broken and shattered, physically and emotionally - forever.

The young Eagle was reminded with great humility for a second time in its young life, how costly freedom is, and usually is paid for - with enormous treasure.

CHAPTER 16 -

AN UNEXPECED TAIL SPIN

L ife in America was exciting. The little clan of European aliens were starting to settle down and love their new life. America was so BIG and so different - and the 60's was a very exciting time to be in San Francisco.

Chloe and I found ourselves at home together one weekend, and she being Catholic, decided to find the local church. When she came home she had the most amazing tale to tell - but that will be told later.

After she left I continued cleaning up the apartment and doing my laundry, when suddenly the doorbell rang. It was about fifteen minutes since Chloe had left and I thought she had forgotten her key. I went to the door and flung it wide laughing in anticipation of seeing her embarrassed, frustrated face.

"Ollie."

The blood drained from my face and I could feel the room start to spin. The love of my life – the man I had put my life into a tail spin for – the man I had placed the entire Atlantic Ocean and a giant continent between us for – was standing at my door.

He reached out to steady me when he saw and understood my shock.

"I'm so sorry, Gi, I could not find your telephone number, otherwise I would have let you know that I was here." I stared at him for a long time in disbelief, trying to get myself under control.

"Come in," I finally heard myself say. He followed me into the living room and I waved at the couch – inviting him to sit.

"It's good to see you – you look great – San Francisco must be agreeing with you. Are you having fun?" He was rambling too, and I could see the tension in his soft brown eyes. I excused myself and went to put a kettle on.

Tea of course, would fix this. In the meantime I needed space to get control of myself.

Ollie, remained in the living room and I heard him get up and look out of the window. I brought the tea in on a tray "borrowed" from Pan Am and sat in the easy chair across from the couch. I poured his tea the way he liked it without thinking - the way I had done for two years out of my life.

"Air Canada recalled me two months ago," he said quietly with his back to me and still looking out of the window. "I am based in Montreal and live in a two bedroom flat with another pilot that lives in Winnipeg and commutes to base. He is not there much and it works well," he finally said turning to me. I nodded and handed him his cup. He took it and came and sat across from me on the couch.

The silence was so intense it could have burst an ear drum. I said nothing and my liquid eyes must have been the size of saucers as I gazed at him over the top of my cup. The tea was not fixing this.

"That's nice." I heard myself whisper finally, then "What else?"

"I bought a house for Louise and the boys. They are settled and live about forty five minutes from the apartment."

I nodded. They had been the reason for my departure from my family, my life and my job in England. He and his wife had been separated for two years when I met him – but they came from good, Catholic families in the mountains of rural Calgary in Canada, and divorce was not an option. Air Canada had laid him off and he had acquired a job in London with British European Airways and that is how we met. He had rented a house in Malaga, Spain and had managed to entice his wife to move there while he was working in London. He would go once a month to pay bills and see his three darling little boys – but – but – I had a decision to make.

I loved this man more than life, but I could not – nor did I want to – compete with three little boys. I wanted a real life – marriage – kids of my own. But, we were soul mates. We were amazing together. The way it was however, would never work long term – but how to deal with it. We were both too weak. There was no way I could leave him and he would not, could not it seems – leave me. We could try, but we would keep tripping over each other at the airport. Be scheduled to fly together or run into each other at hotels down-line, and that would never work. So how to solve this.

I solved it by applying to Pan American World Airways – not expecting to have them hire me – but they did and I put ten thousand miles and the Atlantic Ocean between us. But, now, here he was drinking tea in my living room in San Francisco.

****

"You are not going to believe this Gi," Chloe said in an almost hushed, reverent whisper on her return from church. "They had HEAT – the church was heated, and that is not all – they had bolstered kneelers in every pew." She was completely blown away. She came from a small town on the southwest coast of England, and her church definitely had neither. The idea that you would be warm enough to remove your coat during a church service was beyond her ken.

When I did not respond to her amazing tale, she looked at me closely as though sensing something was wrong – no different. "Are you OK – you look like you've been hit by a freight train."

Ollie had left, asking if he could come back tomorrow and take Chloe and me to the beach. He had rented a car and would bring a picnic lunch for us – it would be fun and we had not been to the beach before. I reluctantly agreed, not knowing how to say "NO." Not wanting to say "NO." So this would give me a little while to think this through. I was happy Chloe was here with me. I was numb. My brain was scrambled - a mess of shocked, confused emotion.

Chloe helped herself to some of the now cold, discarded left over tea, while she listened to the explanation of my mood and weird demeanor. When I was finished she sat quietly staring out of the window at the gathering dusk deep in thought.

After a while she said slowly, "OK. So what do you want to do? After the shock has worn off, how do you feel about it. Do you want to see him again?"

"Yes – NO."

"Excuse me – translate that."

"I can't." I wailed - and now I have a meltdown.

Several hours later – we would come back to the problem.

In the mean time I had had a long lazy shower and spent time curled up on my bed. Thinking about nothing and everything. Then we had a nice dinner. Chloe had made a shepherd's pie and we had downed a bottle of red wine. Now, being both full and mellow – we could then return to the problem at hand.

"You are looking and feeling a lot better, I see," said Chloe, emptying the last of the red wine into my empty glass. "So what is the plan?"

"Well" I said slowly, sipping my wine for courage. "How do you feel about meeting him and spending the day at the beach?"

"I would love to meet any man that can have this amazing effect on you, my dear friend. And secondly I would give my eye teeth for a day at the beach here in San Francisco. How very sweet could that be."

She raised her glass to toast me with the last of her wine and downed it in one gulp. And so the die was cast. I called Ollie at the number he had given me, and told him we would love to take him up on his invitation. We will be ready at 10 o'clock in the morning and meet him in the lobby.

He arrived on the dot of 10 o'clock in a bright blue Buick (his favorite American car) with the top down. He got out smiling happily and I introduced him to Chloe. I could see right away, she was impressed and glowed as this tall, good looking man made her comfortable with the cooler and a blanket in the backseat. He just had a way of making a girl feel like a Queen in any situation, and continued to fuss over her till she finally smiled her thanks. He turned to me and held the front passenger door open, inviting me to get in. Before closing the door he took my hand off the rim and kissed it – then ensuring I was safely seated, he slammed it shut and ran around to the driver's side and got in.

Half Moon Bay

We had a glorious day. Chloe loved it – she loved Ollie. I loved it – and I STILL loved Ollie.

Chloe left for Hong Kong the next morning.

I spent a long, sweet, soft day of truth, together with the man I had loved so deeply for a long time. We spent a lot of time just hugging and holding each other – silently savoring the precious moment we had been denied. We fixed lunch – the way we had done for years – laughing and enjoying every moment. Then, we spent the afternoon hungrily making sweet, passionate, wonderful, fulfilling love with each other.

It was dark when I got up, went into the kitchen and by the light of the street lamp on Gough - poured us a glass of wine. I handed the glass to Ollie and joined him on the bed. We stayed like that – in the dark – for a long time. Reality once again setting in and rearing its ugly head.

"I am going to file for an annulment," he said softly, taking my hand. We sat silent for many minutes while I absorbed that.

Then I said, "How does that work with three little boys eight, six and four."

"I don't know – but I do know, it will take a long time to find out."

Indeed.

The Eagle's heart is heavy. Broken - again - but much stronger than before. Now resolute in decisions made, willing and able to soar - finally free of any of the bonds that had bound it for such a long time.

CHAPTER 17 -

TIME MARCHES ON

A s a group, we continued to experience and enjoy new things. We also got a kick out of the fact that we thought Americans spoke English. How was it then, that every now and again we definitely had a problem understanding each other. Life was a challenge – but so much fun. Also, in spite of the fact that we were different and sometimes acted like "fish out of water" we were accepted, embraced and loved by all we came in contact with. As a result we enjoyed the "Viva le Difference" between us.

Suzanne arrived home as I was leaving on a double Bangkok via Guam, Manila and Hong Kong. I would be gone about three weeks. She and I just had time to exchange information she needed to know about her mail and what was in the refrigerator. She told me Mona would be back before she left again and she was looking forward to spending a few days of 'down time' in San Francisco and with her.

Our eight hour flight to Guam was full, challenging but a lot of fun. I worked the forward first class galley and everything was great. We arrived at the Naval Air Station Agana and were quite intrigued to find a small group of Naval pilots awaiting our arrival on the tarmac. I had been invited to sit on the flight deck for landing and was looking out of the window over the Captain's shoulder when we pulled up and saw them there, looking very smart in their pristine, all white uniforms.

"Do we have somebody of importance to Guam on board that they are waiting for Captain?" I asked totally baffled. Not being aware of anyone. We would surely have known about it – it would have been noted on the passenger list.

The three pilots on the flight deck exploded in laughter.

"Yes indeed my dear Gi – they are waiting to check out the incoming stewardesses," the Captain informed me while trying hard to hide his merriment. "Just disregard them when you get into the crew bus." The three of them continued to laugh heartily enjoying the moment as they prepared to disembark.

The crew bus was waiting, and we climbed wearily on board – ignoring the admiring glances of the eagerly awaiting Naval pilots. We checked in at the small Cliff Motel, which was the only hotel on the island. We had landed there for some years and it was all a normal routine. Pan Am had opened the Pacific islands to air travel on its way to the Orient years before when it was desperately needed in World War II. It built the US connection with the old Clipper Flying Boats at Midway, Wake Island and Guam and we had a military presence there ever since.

We checked in and 'crashed,' agreeing to connect at breakfast to make plans for dinner. We would be there for two days. I opened the door to my room and jumped back with a shriek of horror. The walls and ceiling were covered with tiny little 'lizard people' running every which where when I disturbed the silent empty room. I had never seen such things before and did not know what they were. Tristan, our chief Purser who's room was next to mine, came over and told me not to worry – when I go in and turn on the light and air conditioning they would all disappear. He was right, but I did not sleep very well, feeling that I was not alone in that room.

I woke up the next morning pulling the covers way up to my chin and just lay there perusing the room with my eyes. Several of the little lizards were already comfortable with my presence and walking around the walls and ceiling. I got up, gingerly checking the floor before putting my feet down and opened the drapes. The sun was up and quite a few people were already enjoying the pool. I got dressed and went along to breakfast. The Captain and Tristan were already there tucking into steak and eggs. A real military breakfast that reminded me of a happy time spent at the German - Berlin Templehof Airport in between flights at the US military base there.

"Good Morning Gi – did you sleep well or did the geckos keep you up all night?" The Captain asked smiling as he pulled out a chair for me.

"They take a bit of getting used to," I confessed and poured myself some pineapple juice as the rest of the crew arrived.

"We have an invitation to go to the Officer's Club at the Naval base tonight. They are having a party and would love for us to join them," the Captain informed us after we had placed our order. After some lively discussion the invitation was acknowledged and agreed to. Then, after breakfast we spent the day with half of our crew staying at the pool and the other half going to the beach. I went to the beach with Tristan, Jennifer and Albert the First

Officer who told me to be sure to bring my tennis shoes if I wanted to swim. I looked at him in surprise but said nothing as I went back to get ready. He was a very nice man and had a son almost my age, so I was sure he knew of what he spoke and I did not question it.

The Pacific Ocean was as clear as crystal and you could see all the way to the sandy bottom – but the bottom apparently had some problematic things to walk over, so tennis shoes of some kind would be in order. Albert set us up on the sand with an umbrella and beach towels, and then motioned to me that he was ready to get wet - and be sure to fasten your tennis shoes. We walked quickly together over the hot sand and into the crashing surf. It felt wonderful on our hot skin – the temperature was in the 90's and the sun had burned when we arrived on the sizzling beach.

I found it very difficult and uncomfortable to swim with my tennis shoes on and rolled on my back and lay there just floating, staring at the deep blue of the cloudless sky. Suddenly the surf claimed me. I had not noticed that the waves had pushed me back towards the shore and I had to swim back out again. This time I stopped short of going in deeper and put my feet down with the waves up to my chest. When my feet touched bottom it felt as though I had hit some rocks and when I looked down to check I found myself standing on mounds of long green cucumbers.

I jerked my feet upwards in shock, trying to figure out what in the world was down there under this clear, pristine water. Albert saw me thrashing around and swam over to me.

"I see you have found some Sea Slugs Gi. They are just very ugly disgusting looking creatures but they are blind and harmless and will not hurt you. This is why we wear our tennis shoes around here because they feel very strange to walk on in bare feet."

No kidding – GROSSSSSE.

The rest of the day was uneventful and pleasantly lazy, till the sun became too hot and we were afraid to burn. Besides it was time to come in and get ready for our invitation to dinner, music, dancing and merriment at the Officer's Club.

Right at six o'clock we all gathered in the lobby and the engineer drove us to the Naval base in the crew van. The Officer's Club was located at the far end of a cluster of buildings about half a mile from the main gate. Here we were met and greeted by a group of very eager young men looking vaguely familiar, dressed in their white uniforms, who ushered us into the building with great delight.

Dinner was a very lively affair with music playing, and it was not long before each one of us girls was out on the dance floor. It turned out to be a very fun evening, resulting in a new, challenging, learning experience for me.

The next day I was picked up early by three of the young men we had dinner with last night. They had come to give me a diving lesson. I was the only person on the crew to take them up on their offer which was sad, but I was fascinated with the idea and eager at the chance to learn. Besides, they could come up with all the necessary equipment, which worked for me because I had no idea what was needed. This lesson would be repeated over several of my future trips to Guam and I became good friends with many of the guys based there as a result. I really loved diving and would do it with other crew members at various other lay over stations while based in San Francisco.

One Monday afternoon while on a Guam layover, six of us were lazily floating aimlessly around enjoying the reef and coral. We were distracted and had inadvertently approached too close to the point on Guam where the Naval base cooks deposited all the kitchen trash into the ocean on Mondays at 2 o'clock, every week. Suddenly, out of seemingly nowhere, a dark cloud covered the sunlit water above us. A school of sharks had come for their weekly dinner. Fortunately, they were all totally focused on beating each other to the point and all that floating treasure to worry about us. We, however, high tailed it out of there in Olympic timely fashion and headed back to safer water. Very scary, but an amazing experience.

Our flight to Manilla was an easy four hours and uneventful. We did not lay over there this trip but went on to Hong Kong and Bangkok. In Hong Kong I went into the terminal with the crew for lunch at our favorite restaurant. We had two hours there and it was a fun break for us to get off the airplane. After lunch I wandered around one of the airport shops and fell in love with the cutest little round clock on a chain to wear around my neck. I had had a problem sometimes while working the galley. My watch would get caught on pieces of equipment there and I had noticed that many stewardesses wore cute little clocks like these on the airplane instead of a wrist watch.

I bought one for $10 and tucked it into my purse. Our free time was up and I heard them call our flight and hurried to the airplane. I promptly forgot all about my little clock until three days later when we were flying back to Manila and I took a break after eating my crew meal. I saw Jennifer pull her little clock out of her blouse to check the time and remembered that I had one just like it somewhere in my purse. I retrieved it and played with it for some time trying to set it but I could not get it to start ticking. I wound it – and shook it – and wound it and shook it some more. Finally, totally puzzled I took it to the flight deck to have Albert take a look at it. He also wound it and shook it and then took out his pen knife and pried it open. At that point - all was revealed.

My beautiful little round clock had no innards – the only thing that spilled out of the little round housing was a piece of fluffy white cotton.

I did get myself a little clock the next time I was in Hong Kong, but I made sure they wound it and set it and got it going for me, before I paid them for it. Also I was on a three day layover and had time to see if all was well with it – and it was. No further problem.

The young Eagle learned many things and gained much valuable information every time it took flight.

CHAPTER 18 -

THE MAGIC KINGDON OF SIAM

Years ago in England I had seen the movie "The King and I" with Yul Brynner and Deborah Kerr and had fallen in love with the story and the beautiful Kingdom of Siam. On my 16th birthday in freezing cold snow bound England, I had made a vow to myself that after seeing Elvis Presley in "Blue Hawaii" I would get there and to many other Oriental destinations I had dreamed about. Now, five years later I was about to land there, in the capital city of Bangkok. It was like a dream come true. Not only was I living my dream – BUT I worked for a Company that was PAYING ME to go there!

We stayed in the five star Siam Intercontinental Hotel on Rama Road which in those days was owned by the Pan American hotel chain of Pan American Intercontinental Group. It was elegantly set in the more than twenty acres of the Sra Paduma Palace gardens. The unique architecture of the building with its oriental pagoda style roof and the exquisitely tended gardens of vividly colored flowers, trees and vines was a sight to behold upon arrival. Here you were quickly swept away by the beauty and magic of Siam. I floated out of the crew bus and across the threshhold of this beautiful building, into another world.

Bangkok was the meeting place of two major Pan Am crew bases. This is the city in the world, where the East - New York, and the West - San Francisco met. The New York crews arrived in Bangkok on their Round-the-World flights westbound, via Europe, Africa and India - and the San Francisco crews met them there, on their Round-the-World flights eastbound, after crossing the great Pacific via Japan, the Philippines and Hong Kong. Then everyone turned around and flew back the way they had come. The Siam Intercontinental Hotel was a busy place.

The next morning I got up early and met up with Jennifer and Albert at breakfast. I was very excited and could not wait to get out there and explore this amazing city. Albert suggested that we book a Klong Tour with the concierge, since this was my first time in Bangkok. The other two had no trouble doing the tour again although they had done it before. Every time is fun and a new experience and so it was decided. We headed for the lobby and the concierge desk and found we were in time to take the first tour of the day.

We boarded a small van and found that our driver Joe, was an expert at maneuvering us through the morning traffic at white knuckle speed, having lived in this city all his life. I was astounded at the amount of congestion and snarls created in traffic this early, by people, animals, carts, bicycles, cars and scooters all noisily fighting for a small piece of the road. It was exciting and total mayhem.

After 20 minutes of all this excitement our little van stopped along side a very busy canal. It seemed as if the mayhem of the street had somehow morphed onto the muddy water of the canal. The Klong was a narrow waterway teeming with small watercraft of every variety, stacked up to amazing heights with their operators desperately imploring the lord Buddha to help them stay afloat under their loads of fruits and vegetables and wares of every kind known to man. Among the noise and bustle, some boats even had barbecues with delicious smelling smoke emanating from the different and unrecognized foods, wafting amazing odors into the clean morning air.

We stood – smiling our delight at the amazing sight before us – and ready to burst in and participate in this busy joyful scene. In order to do that our driver led us down a rickety set of wooden steps to an even more rickety looking dock to which was tied an old flat bottomed boat with a very cheerful guide sitting in the stern, doing his best to coax a spluttering engine to life. He waved a greeting and we got in and settled down in eager anticipation.

I was sitting on the outward facing side of the boat and looked down at the murky water. It did not look too smashing - and when our guide "Burt" saw my look of disdain, he hastily explained in broken English with much gesticulation that the tidal movements of the Chao Phaya River totally took care of cleansing the Klong everyday of sewage and waste. OOOH, RIGHT.

The engine sprung to life and we moved quickly away from the dock and immersed ourselves in the mayhem of the Klong, to be carried along in its bobbing midst. The Klong – a patchwork of chaos and colorful clutter under an umbrella of wide brimmed straw hats was in full swing of commercial business endeavors. Food and fruit and wares of every kind were being exchanged from boat to boat to Klong side shack – with gay abandon and money changing hands. I sat enthralled. These people were magic. They were so happy.

As we weaved our little boat through the throng of overloaded half submerged boats eagerly engulfed in their daily chores, we sailed past the many rickety, wooden shacks crammed along the bank of the Klong. These hung precariously it seemed, by a thread, on fragile wooden stilts with steps down to the water's edge. The families living there seemed to be a living continuation of the Klong itself. Armies of naked children happily played and peed and bathed and brushed teeth and defecated in this ginormous bathtub, while mothers did their laundry and washed their dishes. I had a hard time controlling my smile – I loved these people. I wanted to jump in and join the merriment.

Burt maneuvered us skillfully through all this wonder and on along to where the canal widened out and the boat traffic lessened. Here the shacks were a lot further apart with luscious vegetation in between. Suddenly, after rounding a slight bend we came upon a beautiful temple with a large pagoda roof and I wondered if it was one of the ones that we had seen while driving in to the city of Bangkok from the airport. The temples are called 'wats' and are very plentiful in this land of Buddha. There it sat now, its gold roof glittering in the brilliant early morning sunshine, its tall needle like spires reaching for the heavens. Monks in bright orange mantels swarmed about doing their daily chores while chanting to the rhythm of their work. Others sat quietly in deep meditation and others still had a group of children in tow. I did not want this moment to end. When it did I promised myself I would repeat and enjoy this tour again, maybe more than once on future trips to this magical land.

Little did I to know I would repeat it with my dying Mother and meet my future husband and the father of my children - within the year.

The next day Jennifer introduced me to the most amazing Thai silk shops that gave a great Pan Am discount and could make dresses, suits to measure – you name it - in twenty four hours. I was blown away by the colors and beauty of this amazing silk material. Over time I would have many exquisite outfits - for every occasion - made here to measure, in this beautiful Thai Silk.

I learned a fun way to take care of these wonderful outfits after they had been worn, from some more seasoned stewardesses at my base. It seems that you could gently wash them in mild soap and then - because silk is a natural product made by silkworms it is as natural as your hair - so treat it the same and rinse them in Hair Conditioner. They would come out and be as soft and beautiful as the day they were made.

Jennifer had been to Bangkok many times since her arrival at the San Francisco base five years before and was a treasure of information I would enjoy and remember long after this trip. She and I seem to have the same interests and we formed a lasting friendship. Through her I would enjoy many a trip to local jewelry shops, markets and stalls – the precious stones loose or in beautiful settings – were a delightful magnet for me.

The next day Jennifer persuaded me to go with her to a shop she thought I would find interesting. She wanted to buy some cutlery that she had seen and really loved. We shoe-horned ourselves into a local taxi and sped to an address she gave the driver. The crews called it "The Bargain of Bangkok," but it was really called "Starrys." The taxi dropped us off at the corner of the street and we soon saw the sign waving and shining in the afternoon sun.

We entered the dark portal and found ourselves in a warm lofty room surrounded by beautiful sets of wooden handled cherry and brass cutlery. There were many intricate, some very elaborate designs set up and displayed in beautiful satin lined wooden boxes. They looked beautiful, and very expensive. They were in sets of eight place settings – one hundred and two pieces, including tall iced tea spoons and twelve serving pieces. I was enthralled. The workmanship was amazing. I gingerly inquired at the price. The beautiful young sales person pulled herself upright and smiling, stated the price was twenty five dollars for the set with the box. Jennifer and I looked at each other – uncertain if we had heard the price correctly. Needless to say, we left with each of us happily clutching a heavy box and wondering how we would get it home.

For many years to come, every time I lifted the lid to this box I could smell Bangkok and the unmistakable scent of the Orient and those amazing days spent there that can never repeat.

CHAPTER 19

MANILA AND A MAN NAMED OSKA

The next day we left for Manila, stacking our precious cutlery boxes behind the last row of seats in First Class. I had been to Manila a couple of times before and of all of our destination cities – it is probably my least favorite. I was constantly reminded of the incredible gap between the 'haves' and the 'have nots' on our drive into the hotel from the airport. The city, situated in the middle of a beautiful bay sheltering it from the wide open Pacific had a very affluent group of citizens living there. Their vast elegant homes were built with high walls, iron gates and well-armed guards, protecting them from primitive shacks jammed in on either side. Pathetic plastic covers sheltering the fragile roofs and rickety walls from the elements - in stark deference to their affluent neighbors.

The Manila Hotel was old, elegant and beautifully placed at the end of a long wide boulevard lined by tall waving Palm trees. It faced the bay and was frequented by the cities' elite and well to do. Their beautifully clad and elegantly outfitted male offspring awaited our arrival in the spacious lobby on a daily basis. Reading the paper and lounging innocently around in deep easy chairs while checking out the arriving crew members – hoping to get lucky for a date. They also decorated the elegant pool area in record numbers. They were hard to ignore but many stewardesses enjoyed the attention and the opportunities they offered – I however was not one of them.

The morning after our arrival I was sitting at a small table in the pool area in a corner away from the pool and under the awning sheltered from the oppressive heat and humidity. It was early morning and I was the first Pan Am crew member to appear, although an Air France crew was having a crew party on the other side of the pool with much wine, noise, music and merriment. I was writing letters home and happy to be alone for a while. It was still early and my crew had not yet surfaced. I got the impression that the Air France crew had arrived late, joined another already there at the pool and partied through the night. I noticed that several of the local 'dandies' had joined them and were participating in the fray.

I was deeply engrossed in my writing – I was worried I had not heard from my Mother for about six weeks. That was unlike her – I got a letter regularly about every three weeks. As a result I was unaware of a man approaching my table – then pulling out a chair and sitting down across from me with a big smile on his round fleshy face.

"Good Morning my dear young lady – I see that you are not in a party mood, since you are sitting here all by yourself. Let me introduce myself – my name is Oska and I am very happy to make your acquaintance – you are?" And he forced a fleshy hand across my papers and under my nose. I looked up without moving. The plump, cheerful, sleazy Philippino man sitting across from me held his pose until I reluctantly put my fingers fleetingly into his hand and he squeezed tightly in greeting.

"I know most of the Pan Am young ladies – I have made a point of meeting and greeting and welcoming them to Manila for many years. Many of them have become dear friends. I have seen you here a couple of times but have not been lucky enough to make your acquaintance."

"Really." I stated without emotion or facial expression.

"OH Yes. You will find I make a point of welcoming every crew at some time during their stay. I can be of great help while they are here – I know many of the best and most desirable people in town and I of course am very familiar with everything that is going on – be it at the Yacht Club or the Market." With that he pulled a gold cigarette case out of his shirt pocket, placed a cigarette between his smiling lips and lit it with a cigarette lighter that could have acted as a flame thrower.

"Really." I said again unimpressed, while slowly gathering my papers into a pile.

"I can be of great help to you my dear – we will become good friends. I will introduce you to some very special people – you will love coming to Manila."

"There you are Gi," a voice boomed from the direction of the lobby. I jumped up in heart felt relief as Albert appeared around a pillar. "We are all having breakfast in the coffee shop and were wondering where you were. Good Morning Oska – how are you this lovely morning – I'm afraid I will have to tear Gi away as we have plans for the day."

"Oh that is too bad, we were just getting acquainted," Oska said obviously quite unhappy with this turn of events. I said nothing but gave Albert the most grateful of looks while shoveling everything into my Pan Am bag. "I will make a point of looking for you tomorrow before you leave," he said as Albert took my arm and steered me through the lobby door which slammed shut behind us.

We joined the rest of my crew in the coffee shop and they got a big charge out of the fact that I had been 'found' by Oska. He apparently is a well-known figure in the hotel and one everyone assured me to avoid if at all possible. He invariably had some scheme up his sleeve that he would try and get the girls involved in – none of them good, they assured me. I was so very relieved to have been 'rescued' from that sleazy man that I tucked into my breakfast eggs and buffalo steak with gay abandon.

I was lucky enough not to bump into Oska again on that trip, but felt confident enough now that I knew what to expect, that it would not faze me the next time we would surely meet – no problem.

Our flight to Honolulu was long but uneventful, even though we had a full load. We arrived in the crew customs area shortly after an Air France crew and I thought I recognized a couple of them from the pool party in Manila even though their flight had come from Singapore. I was really tired having worked the aft galley so sat down on the bench next to my suit case. It would be a bit of a wait while the Air France crew was checked for arrival into the U.S.

Suddenly there was a bit of a commotion further up the line.

A customs agent had jokingly swept his hand over the shoulder of a stewardess that he had just cleared, as she bent over to pick up her suitcase. Air France wore dark blue uniforms and he was teasing her about the slight powder on her shoulder, suggesting that she had a bad case of dandruff.

The casual easy going good humored chatter in the hall suddenly stopped as all eyes focused on this poor stewardess who seemed to jump upright as though she had been shot, quickly brushing at the offending spot on her uniform jacket. The fine powder refused to be brushed away however, and a female customs agent appeared as if out of nowhere and suggested the young lady follow her out of the hall. By now she was extremely distraught and started to cry while trying to gather her things together, still brushing furiously at her shoulder.

It had been gently stated, but there was no doubt at all that this was an order and not a choice, as the female agent took her arm.

The Air France Captain now tried to intervene and started a loud argument with the leading customs agent, but by now several agents had appeared and surrounded the rest of the crew and insisted they all follow the ladies out of the hall. Finally, after much commotion, arm waving and loud argument – some in French and some in English – they did as they were told and grudgingly filed out of the hall into an adjoining office.

We all sat in amazed silence as the scene played out and the doors finally shut behind the unhappy band. The chief customs officer appeared shortly thereafter with three new agents in tow.

"Ladies and gentlemen – I am so sorry for the hold up, but we are ready for you now," he said cheerfully taking his place again behind the counter. Thus without further ado, we all jumped up and started to line up ourselves and our bags for inspection.

We left the customs hall without incident, but it was a quiet ride to the hotel as we were all wondering what in the world had just happened as we relived the whole vivid picture in our minds.

Sometime later on a trip to Honolulu I would learn that the Air France stewardess had indeed been one of the 'party group' the morning I met Oska. It seems he had met up with her later that day – they knew each other quite well - and he had persuaded her to carry a small package for him to mail to a friend in the U.S. She had decided to carry it under her uniform hat and had accidentally stuck her hat pin through it before leaving the airplane. Hence the 'dandruff.' She had been paid $1000 in cash for the small favor – which was big money in those days and a temptation that could be hard to turn down.

I never did hear what happened to her regarding this, or if any other of her crew members were involved. In our crew briefings we were always warned not to do anyone any "favors" while out on the line, and that day, on that trip, it was a lesson learned in living color.

CHAPTER 20 -

AN INCONVENIENT LESSON

It was wonderful to be in-bound with three days to relax on the beach before heading home to San Francisco. I checked the 'crew list' at the front desk and found several of my friends to be 'in house' – some in and some outward bound. I made a few calls the next day and found four of them that were interested in taking a trip to the north side of the island with me, for a change of pace. The north side of the island had some interesting shoreline and GIANT WAVES. That is where you went if you wanted to do some serious surfing. It was also away from Waikiki beach and the only people you ever ran across were locals who lived around there doing a little fishing.

We set off early prepared to spend the whole day. One of my friends was dating a young man who was based there with the navy and had a small Jeep. He picked us up and off we went clutching a bottle of wine and a delicious conch salad for lunch. We drove clear across the island on some very rickety back roads, through dense vegetation and Pineapple fields as far as the eye could see. Jim was very familiar with these island roads – he had been based on the island of Oahu for two years and did not hesitate to find his route.

Finally, we drove up a slight hill and through a lush grove of Papaya trees and burst out on the top of a sand dune facing a wide empty beach. The road ended but the sand was hard baked here and we could drive the Jeep down onto it without a problem. We all piled out and spread our beach towels under several small palm trees grouped together between the sand dune and the crashing surf. The heat was already intense although it was still early morning but the soft wind gently blowing off the ocean felt cool and refreshing.

The beach was beautiful – way off the beaten track – wide open and deserted. Standing in the surf you could see forever. There the cloudless blue of the sky sank into an endless slate colored ocean somewhere at the gentle downward curve that was the end of the world.

Jim had brought his surf board and said that a few of his buddies might come and join us, and a couple of hours later two of them did - bringing their surf boards tied precariously between the driver and the passenger of a Honda convertible. They were very nice and a lot of fun and we had a wonderful day swimming, surfing and playing in the mountainous waves.

It was about three in the afternoon when Karen and I came out of the ocean together. I wanted to get my little camera that I had bought in Hong Kong on a previous trip and take a few photos of the fun we were having. We walked over to our little camp under the drooping palms, dripping salt water and laughing at something one of the guys had said. Karen went to her towel and grabbed a cup of water she had left propped up against the cooler and downed the silky liquid. I walked over to my towel to find my camera which I had left on top of my big black Pan Am uniform purse. I looked at my towel – picked it up and wiped my face and eyes in case I had sand and water in them and could not see properly. There was no purse!

THERE WAS NO PURSE. IT WAS GONE.

Everything was just as we had left it. The beach was deserted and had been since our arrival. There was no one in sight and no sign that anyone had been there. Regardless, my purse was gone and everything of critical importance to me was gone with it. I now had no passport. No green card or shot records and therefore no way of working. I had no camera and no hair brush or make up for tomorrow's trip home. Thank the good Lord that I was in bound and had entered and passed through the U.S customs and passport control, so would not need papers again until my next trip out – which could not happen until I had both a passport AND a green card in my possession.

Needless to say the delightful, fun filled mood of the day plummeted to a memory. The guys came out of the surf and helped us search the beach in case some critter had come and played with it and hauled it off somewhere. To no avail. We finally packed up and left, riding home in confused moody silence through miles of empty Pineapple fields without a house or shack in sight.

It was a very scary, difficult lesson to learn the hardest possible way. You cannot take your eyes off your important personal 'stuff' for any reason at any time. If you cannot secure it while out and about, leave it safely locked up at home or in the hotel safe. Trust no one, and nowhere is safe to leave them unattended. These important papers are worth thousands of dollars on the Black Market and the 'underground' makes it their job to acquire them via any means possible. I would find out years later when I went to renew my replacement passport, that the original had transported eighty-seven people into Great Britain over a five year time period. A successful haul for some cunning person living in the shadows - in Paradise.

The Eagle could not fly and stayed hunkered down in her nest for two long weeks nursing a depressed, fluttering, anxious heart.

CHAPTER 21 -

VACATION

The time I spent with 'clipped wings' in San Francisco was also traumatic for another reason that had nothing to do with my lack of paperwork. Upon my return home I had received a letter from my Mother telling me that she had found a lump on a rib under her right arm and was waiting for an appointment at King's College Hospital to have a biopsy done on it – but not to worry, it was probably nothing.

NOTHING – something like that was seldom NOTHING!

I read and re-read her letter. Why was she still waiting for a biopsy – she apparently had found it over a month ago. I was worried – this was Britain's National Health Service at work – she would have to wait her turn. On my acceptance to training with Pan Am almost two years ago I had been forced to circumvent that same National Health Service in order for me to make my class date. I had to pay for all services rendered as a Private Patient. Fortunately I was financially able to do that, or I would not be here flying my dreams. SHE needed to do the same thing now and get that biopsy TOMORROW!

I picked up the phone and called London.

She had her biopsy and it was malignant. She had radiation treatment over the next six months and claimed she was free of cancer. In the meantime I worked a trip to London as soon as I was able after acquiring a new passport and green card. The trip was long and hard and reminded me why I did not volunteer to fly them. Sixteen hours over the North Pole – very often with full loads and a stop for fuel somewhere.

I arrived in Wimbledon and found my Mother had lost weight but was in very good spirits and happy to see me. We had a wonderful three days together and we planned for her to join me on vacation. We got a whole month of vacation every year and I needed to take mine within the next few months. We planned a round the world trip starting with me picking her up in London. She wanted to go to Rome, Istanbul, Beirut, Bangkok, Hong Kong, Tokyo, Hawaii and San Francisco. All my favorite places that I had written home about many times.

On looking back, I am so very happy that we grabbed the bull by the horns and did this – because she kept a big secret from me that I would not know about until much later. The lump she had found was already a "secondary" - she had breast cancer and would need a mastectomy – which she adamantly refused. She would live four more years.

We had a wonderful time on vacation, staying in all our five star crew hotels at great employee discounts. She loved everywhere, but some more than others. One of her favorites was

Bangkok. She had several dresses made in Thai silk and bought a beautiful emerald ring. We went on the Klong tour and she was mesmerized by the colorful flowers and vegetables and the atmosphere and happiness of it all.

While in the hotel waiting for our tour bus, we met a very nice good looking young man also waiting for the tour. He was American and had on a black tee shirt, khaki Bermuda pants, black socks and sandals. His hair was very short and he was very clean cut and polite. His image is burnt into my memory because I was so very amazed at my Mother's reaction to him. He was so very obviously in the US military and my Mother made it her business to verify that in a heartbeat. She engaged him in conversation and found that he was in the US Navy on a small mine sweeper based in Subic Bay in the Philippines and deployed off the coast of Vietnam. He was on 'R and R' and very excited to take this tour, he had heard it was very much fun. He was quiet and shy and my Mother thought, sad, because he was all by himself. I'm sure this was not true at all but my Mother was hooked and thoroughly enjoyed keeping him close for the whole tour and engaged in conversation.

His name was Bill and he was very kind and personable and we thoroughly enjoyed his company. There was only one other person on the tour besides him and my Mother and I - but I could not get over my Mother's reaction to Bill. This was so out of character for her. She is so much a very conservative, private person who does not engage ANYONE in her personal space! For some reason, this young man had her attention, and when we left the tour he told us that his ship was leaving for Hong Kong the next day. We were leaving for Hong Kong two days later, and happily agreed to meet him there for dinner. It would take his ship two days to make the voyage – our flight only 3 hours.

My Mother loved Hong Kong. We spent time shopping there and enjoyed bartering for a few small treasures as memories to bring home. I was enchanted by the beautiful bright apple green Jade that the Chinese used to create exquisite things, including jewelry. I bought a Jade ring which I treasured for many years reminding me of this trip with my Mother - until it was stolen years later in New Orleans.

We climbed the mountain stretching high behind the city and surveyed the world below. The bay was full of colorful Junks and local water traffic busily coming and going as far as the eye could see in the harbor. We sat there on a plateau overlooking the city in a little cafe and watched the lights come on like bright jewels. The sun slid down behind the mountain and darkness descended like a soft blanket over the city - and on to the sparkling water below. After a while, we tore ourselves away from this heady scene - to meet Bill for dinner.

The next day we left for Tokyo, where to my Mother's delight she spent several happy hours looking at and selecting - Mikimoto pearls. She also loved the Imperial Palace and all the shrines and beautiful, immaculately tended gardens.

Finally we were headed for Hawaii and the Royal Hawaiian Hotel. I knew she would fall in love with this exquisite location and the island did not disappoint. From the moment she was greeted with a beautiful lei upon arrival, she allowed herself to slow down and relax in the magic of 'Paradise' after our long adventure.

This three plus week vacation was a very special time for my Mother and I. Some eighteen years ago, we had left our bombed and broken homeland behind with much excitement, but also with some trepidation, to entrust our lives and our future to an unknown entity. A country victorious in war and totally alien to us, with a language we did not understand. They have been amazing years of growth and fulfillment, and we had become very close as we both became British and we had shared much.

In Hawaii we enjoyed slow days on the beach, joined in on a wonderful Luau one evening in the sands of Waikiki with island music and dancing the Hula, followed by a day trip on the air shuttle to Kauai – the Garden Island. We were indeed in Paradise.

I spent another week introducing my Mother to San Francisco. She was enthralled – loved the city and the life I had created. However, I was not comfortable with what she was telling me about her health. Say it was a daughter's intuition – but I did not believe all was as dandy as she claimed. I felt that I needed to come home more often, and the only way to make that happen was for me to transfer out of my San Francisco base. Crew scheduling informed me that they did not have a trip for me starting the new month after my vacation and I had four days left in my vacation month, so I accompanied my Mother on her flight back to London, stayed and settled her back for two days and flew home to San Francisco.

I spent the next few days filling out paperwork to transfer to either London or New York, and got a response from New York within the week. I had had a chance to talk to my room mates, Chloe, Suzanne and Mona upon my return, and was amazed to find that they might also be interested in transferring. We could go together.

WOW – that was an amazing shocker I had not expected – but I think our families were starting to complain that we never came home. The City by the Bay had been an amazing and successful transition to America and a totally new way of life and living. However, if we were to be really honest – we were missing the old homeland and family, more than we would admit.

America had welcomed and embraced us and taught us much in the two years we had spent there – but for me it was time to reluctantly move on, and I was delighted to know that my room mates were willing to move with me.

I checked into my next trip – a double Bangkok and was given a note to check in with my supervisor. Not a good sign as a rule, but I was promised it was not a negative request. Kathie Hauk welcomed me with a big smile and bid me sit. She said she had received nothing but good reports on my performance since my arrival and was wondering if I would consider upgrading to Purser. I was stunned. I had been so busy and so happy with my lot, that I had never considered such a thing.

"Oh Kathie, thank you for suggesting that – I'm not sure I'm ready – or capable to do that yet."

"I think you are Gi – especially since I see you have requested a transfer. New York would welcome you with open arms and they are always short of Pursers – but I will let you think that over – today I have a totally different reason for seeing you." I looked up at her with a worried frown. She smiled reassuringly and said. "Nothing bad – relax. I am to tell you that you will be rescheduled out of Bangkok upon your arrival. You are to join a special hand picked crew to fly Their Majesties the King and Queen of Thailand home to Bangkok from Vienna, where they have been for a royal wedding. You will lay over in Bangkok for 24 hours and then 'dead head' to Vienna to pick up your crew and a specially converted airplane. Here is all the information you will need and your pass to Vienna via Frankfurt. Congratulations, this is a big honor – it seems the 'powers that be' are very happy with your work and have added you to the Company VIP crew list. You may get scheduled for special charters from now on going forward. For your information, you have also been cleared by the FBI which was necessary in order for you to do this. They probably know more about you than you know about yourself! So – again, congratulations on doing a good job, it has been noticed and is appreciated. Have a good trip." She got up and smiling broadly held out her hand for me to shake.

I left her office in somewhat of a fog. So much was happening to me so quickly. It was all a tad overwhelming. I looked at the large envelope in my hand and stuffed it into my Pan Am bag. I would look at it later – now I was late for my flight check-in. The crew was already in the briefing room. I entered, excused myself and gratefully sank into the nearest empty chair. My equilibrium returned and my heart rate became normal again as I was enveloped in a comfortable well-rehearsed routine.

Vacation

CHAPTER 22 -

THE KING AND I

We arrived in Bangkok in the late afternoon. Our flight had been long and hard with a full load of passengers, including quite a few children, which was unusual. Flying in those days was still a very big affair and quite expensive, so children were usually not included on the itinerary. I had worked the rear cabin and had spent much time entertaining them and also ferrying them up to the flight deck and back. After the meal service most slept for a time, but then to their parents great displeasure, many came back to life - way too soon, due probably to excitement and the strange environment they were in. We had worked on updating their Pan Am Passports given to them upon departure, so that they could track their journey on Pan Am – now and in the future. Two of the children already had a Junior Passport from previous flights and so we just updated them and provided the Captain's signature after their flight deck visit.

We cleared customs and passport control in record time and climbed gratefully into our crew limo for the long ride into town. It was hot and muggy and threatening rain but the limo was cool and quiet and many of us slept in its soft welcoming seats. Two days later I left my crew and flew as a passenger to Vienna.

The day before Suzanne had arrived at the hotel – she was my replacement on the crew. We had a lovely dinner together catching up on all our news. I told her that Kathie Hauk had suggested I upgrade to Purser.

She shot me a questioning look and said, "Vunderful – are you going to do it?"

"No, not yet – not while I am still in San Francisco. The base is so senior I would never get the groovy trips as a Purser that I can hold now as a stewardess. Maybe when I get to New York - I'll think about it." She nodded in agreement and the conversation turned to our possible transfer. They had openings in New York and were anxious for us to make up our minds and commit to a date. They needed our languages.

"Ze bid lines came right before I left on zis trip and I 'ave a really great line next month. I don't vant to lose dat. Maybe ve vait to go till ze new year. Also, I forgot to tell you - my parents are coming for Christmas"

"Works for me - next year will be fine. Why don't we wait and talk about it more when I get home." I too had picked up my bid lines in the crew room before my flight and I was very happy with my next month's schedule. We were also in October, coming up to the middle of winter in New York and with snow and ice on the streets it was not a good time to house hunt and move. We were still enjoying San Francisco and the west coast flying – there was no rush I told myself.

However, the die was cast. We would be moving to New York in the new year.

****

I arrived in Vienna in the late afternoon and met the limo waiting for me to take me to the hotel. I checked in and found a large brown envelope with a message attached to the outside of it saying to be sure to let Captain Lewis know when I had arrived. I called the Captain of our Royal flight from the front desk and introduced myself. He welcomed me and said the crew would meet at seven in the lobby for dinner, to please join them and we could all get to know each other and discuss tomorrows special flight. Then I left a message for the Purser. All this taken care of, I found my room, took a shower, ordered tea from room service and emptied the contents of the big brown envelope onto my bed. It had a synopsis of the lives and background of their Majesty's King Bhumibol and Queen Sirikit who were in Vienna for a Royal wedding.

King Bhumibol Adulyadej RAMA IX was the great grandson of the king of note in the movie The King and I. He was born in Cambridge, Mass. to a father who was a naval engineer and physician based there on orders of his brother the then King of Siam. This King did not have a male heir, so upon his death the throne passed to Bhumibol's older brother who met an untimely accidental death three years later

Bhumibol was educated and lived his early life in Lausanne, Switzerland. While there, he met and subsequently, married 18 year old Princess Sirikit a beautiful, vivacious member of the Thai Royal Family also being educated in Lausanne. They met at a concert and shared a love of music. He was eighteen when his brother died and and he inherited the throne and twenty one when he married Sirikit. They had three children, two girls and a son that would inherit his father's throne upon his death.

The King – a very slight, quiet, reserved man was passionately in love with Jazz. He was an accomplished musician, playing the piano, clarinet, saxophone, trumpet and guitar. He had performed with the Preservation Hall Jazz Band of New Orleans, then with Benny Goodman, in concert and at his home, also with Les Brown and His Band of Renown and several others.

He had been very much influenced by Louis Armstrong, Sidney Becket and Benny Carter and in 1950 he founded a band of his own and played on the Thai radio stations and at Thai universities composing anthems for each of them. He was an accomplished composer and some of his compositions were recorded by the well-known US bands he played with, and they are still played constantly and proudly in Thailand. He composed a total of forty nine songs and music, the most popular of which was "Candle Light Blues," "Love at Sundown" and "Falling Rain."

At a dinner given in honor of the Royal couple while visiting in England, Queen Sirikit was asked jokingly by a fellow guest, if she was really the King's "only" wife - which was unusual for a Thai king. She laughed and responded that the King's only concubine was his Jazz Band – he had no time or energy for anything more.

The King had also been honored with many awards for musical accomplishment. The Sanford Medal was awarded him by the Yale School of Music, and the University of North Texas College of Music awarded him an Honorary Doctorate of Music. He was also one of only twenty three people in the world to be awarded a Certificate of Bestowal of Honorary Membership on behalf of Vienna's University of Music and Performing Arts in Vienna.

As well as his musical accomplishments, King Bhumibol was an accomplished sailor and sailboat designer, winning a gold medal at a large international sailing event. He also is the only Monarch in the world to hold several patents. These were for water management products and facilities, some of which he helped build in water poor areas of Thailand. An interesting, accomplished man indeed, that put his engineering training and knowledge to work for his country and people. He was a very wealthy, popular, well-loved King.

I lay on my bed - read and absorbed all this information, enthralled and very excited to meet this amazing couple. I had heard that in spite of their Royal Thai heritage, they were a very "Western" couple due to both of them having been raised and educated in Europe. Both spoke fluent English, French and German.

I sipped my tea and contemplated all of the steps in my life that had brought me to this amazing moment in time. I could not believe that I had been picked to be part of a crew that would carry this cherished Royal couple back to their homeland. I was in awe but very excited and proud in anticipation of tomorrow.

I continued reading the contents of the brown envelope, and found a voucher for $20 to be spent on three pairs of nylon stockings. These must be purchased before checking in for the flight. Protocol for being within sight of the Royal couple insisted that it would be necessary to get down on my knees – especially if they were seated. My head may at no time be higher than theirs and as a result, my walking on my knees could, would cause stockings to rip – hence the necessary extra pairs. However, I needed to be sure and save one perfect pair for arrival and disembarking in Bangkok.

I lay back sipping my tea, absorbing all this information and letting it run slowly through my brain. I felt like I was floating in a parallel universe. Finally I smiled, got up, dressed for dinner and prepared to meet my crew.

Late the next afternoon we arrived at the airplane that was parked well away from the main terminal building, in a private corner next to a taxi way. A long red carpet led from a hanger out to the forward airstair. Several Media people were already there claiming their "spot" to photograph and report on the the Royal departure.

We parked our crew bags at the foot of the forward airstairs – the loaders could pack them into the forward "crew baggage" compartment in the belly - and boarded the airplane. I was one of the last of the ten crew members to enter the forward door and found myself in a traffic jam. The first to board had jammed up the entrance because they were so blown away with what they found upon entering the First Class cabin.

The airplane had been completely refurbished for this flight. The First Class Cabin had been transformed into a boudoir – with a queen sized bed and beautiful French dressing table. A full length mirror adorned the forward bulkhead to the right of the aisle. Exquisite flowers were everywhere, and soft subdued lighting completed the scene. Slowly, we moved forward, enthralled by what we were looking at. The next section was transformed into a beautiful French sitting room, with a couch and easy chair with a large table for dining between the two. Fresh flowers adorned the center of the table.

The next bulkhead returned us to a little more reality. The rear of the airplane housed forty-five blue First Class leather seats set with a crisp white pillow with the Royal Thai crest and blue Pan Am blanket for the Royal Entourage. We filed through all this luxury trying to decide in our minds how we would work this service to satisfy the high standards that Pan Am was known for, in the alien environment of thirty thousand feet for about sixteen hours.

The crew was split up. Our Senior Purser and two stewardesses were forward to serve the Royal couple and a Purser, myself and two stewardesses would work the back forty five First Class seats. We stowed our hand baggage and suddenly found a senior maintenance man sitting in the aft jump seat waiting for us. He was there to explain where all our emergency equipment had been moved as a result of the refurbished airplane. We had of course, received all this information on paper during our crew briefing in Vienna, but this jovial man was here to show us everything 'in living color.'

Suddenly, the back door opened and a service man from the commissary arrived to brief the stewardess working the rear galley – would she please identify herself. Brigitte, a German stewardess from Munich raised her hand and joined him with pen and paper in hand and a slight tense look on her face. The amount of food provided for that many first class passengers was somewhat problematic in the rear of the airplane. It all had to be counted and checked in, and then stowed. We also had a first class bar back there with beautiful crystal glasses, engraved with the Pan Am emblem on one side and the Royal Thai Coat of Arms on the other. The white Pan Am china also had the Royal Crest in the middle of each plate.

It was beautiful and we were ready.

I stowed my hand baggage and large black Pan Am purse in the overhead rack and behind the back row of seats and hung my coat in the back closet. This done, I went back through the rest of the airplane to familiarize myself with where everything was located and to get comfortable with the layout of the cabin. I met the Captain in the middle of my check, doing his 'walk through.' He grinned broadly, and asked me if I had my spare nylons handy. I paused and gave him a withering look – but he just waved, continuing down the cabin laughing at his own joke.

Twenty minutes later we boarded their Royal Majesties. King Bhumibol Adulyadej RAMA IX, his beautiful wife Queen Sirikit and their entourage. A mind bender spectacle that I can never – will never forget.

The Eagle trembled with excitement. Poised, with more than a little trepidation - yet confident and very much eager for flight.

****

We left amidst great jubilation from the crowd of well wishers on the tarmac to see the popular Royal couple off. The media getting many really good shots and photographs to enjoy and pass on to the world - for cash.

The Royal flight was long, smooth and very busy. We served a brilliant, exotic dinner, with caviar and all the trimmings, followed by a choice of rib roast of beef or lobster. All this served with endless bottles of Don Perignon and other amazing wines and liquor.

The Chefs of Vienna had also out done themselves with amazing pastries and deserts to round off the meal. As the wine continued to flow, the lively party became even more lively when to our utter amazement and delight, his Majesty arrived from the front of the airplane carrying a clarinet. Six other members of the entourage immediately jumped up and dug into their carry-ons and produced more instruments - and in the next heartbeat we had a "Jam Session" at thirty thousand feet en route to Bangkok.

We were all riveted in wonder and disbelief as 'the band played on.' It was hard to tear ourselves away from this amazing happy scene to attend to our duties for those passengers who were watching and enjoying this amazing spectacle from their seats all the while clapping and swaying to the music. They needed more wine or champagne or water or whatever – and OH Yes – the cockpit needed to be fed!

I sped up to the flight deck – passing through 'the boudoir' where Her Majesty Queen Sirikit was sitting in the easy chair reading the latest Vogue magazine. I remembered at the last second to fall down on my knees while traversing her presence on my dash to the cockpit.

She waved, smiling and said, "I do hope my husband is not interfering with your work – he has trouble sitting still on these long flights because he does not like to fly, and his music helps and distracts him. Oh, and please – I have told your friends working up here with us – you do not have to 'do' the knee thing here."

I wanted to hug her. She was so gracious, so beautiful and so 'normal.' I stood gratefully and thanked her. I asked her if there was anything I could get for her, and she said. "No thank you, I am going to try out that bed in a few minutes."

I left her and entered the cockpit. The mood up there was very relaxed, they were happy to see me but more than a little surprised.

"Hi Gi, how is everything going back there?" the Captain asked turning way round in his seat with a cheerful wave. "We figured everyone must be really busy 'cos we have not seen any of you for about an hour in spite of the fact that the dinner service has been over for quite a while. I just went to the bathroom and the galley was empty, everyone was working in the cabin. Does someone have a radio on in the back – I thought I heard music?"

I spent about twenty minutes filling them in on what was going on in the back and getting them settled with what they wanted to eat - from caviare to lobster. There was plenty of everything left over plus our crew meals. While the Captain ate his caviare, smoked salmon, pate froi gras and salad, the engineer climbed into the right hand seat vacated by the First Officer who donned his uniform jacket and hat, straightened his tie and left the cockpit to go and check out the 'party' in the back. He and the Captain may not eat the same thing anyway, so he decided he would wait till later and the Captain was finished with his meal.

When I returned to the rear cabin, he was thoroughly enjoying the mood and the music and his hat was no longer on his head!

The engineer and the Captain would come down and relieve him, taking turns from the flight deck to enjoy this special moment. And so it all went on for another couple of hours before the cabin finally went dark as all gradually faded out, and most slept. Their Majesties safely in their peaceful boudoir in the forward cabin.

The Royal Flight carrying Thailand's treasure was silent and dark as it droned on through the night sky towards the eagerly awaiting dawn. A welcome space and time, giving us the opportunity to prepare the galley and the cabin for breakfast and our arrival.

****

The dawn broke – very gently at first - in soft grays, blues and purple and then with emblazoned splendor as the sun burst forth across the horizon. I was taking my break in the cockpit eating the most delectable leftovers from the forward galley when that happened, and everyone jumped at the sudden brilliance flooding the cockpit. The three pilots immediately donned dark glasses in defense of the sudden bright light, and I left my hiding place reluctantly and returned to the cabin thanking them for their hospitality.

The forward galley was a hub of activity – preparing for their elaborate breakfast service. The delightful smell of fresh perking coffee met me upon opening the flight deck door. I mouthed "Good Morning" as I crept on past and through the curtained off 'boudoir' and the sleeping Royals. On my way down to the back galley, I picked up trash, empty glasses, newspapers and magazines and anything else blocking the dark aisle as I passed our sleeping passengers.

Those same sleepy passengers had a hard time 'surfacing' when finally awakened for breakfast an hour out of Bangkok. The rear bathroom with its boundless hot and cold water and exotic toiletries did a wonderful job of returning them to their formal impeccable selves, and we found that many had donned native Thai dress or uniforms when the shades were lifted and the morning sun flooded the cabin.

Breakfast in First Class on any Pan Am Clipper is always challenging, but this flight with 45 First Class seats was especially so. My crew however, was well seasoned and comfortable with Pan Am's VIP flying, and the soft three minute eggs and the eggs Benedict were served flawlessly and with flair as the Mimosas flowed endlessly in crystal sparkling in the bright morning sunshine.

Our arrival that morning in Thailand was spectacular, the airplane parking next to a military band playing and thousands of people including many Buddhist monks in bright orange robes, jammed the fence to get a glimpse of the Royal couple. The Royals did not disappoint. They came regally smiling, and waving down the red carpeted airstair – the King now dressed in a sparkling white uniform and his Queen in exquisite Thai silk.

It was an unforgettable moment for all their adoring loyal subjects waiting on the hot shimmering tarmac to welcome their beloved King and Queen home. Their Pan Am crew watched in awe as the band played on and then they silently snuck away to a waiting limo.

CHAPTER 23 -

A NEW YEAR AND NEW HORIZONS

T
he morning sun was turning the pavements of Manhattan into shimmering wiggly shapes as Chloe and I went apartment hunting in this giant metropolis of solid granite. It was the end of July and the city was melting in summer heat. Mona and Suzanne had gone home to Sweden for a couple of days and left the house hunting to us. They would join us later.

We had transferred to New York from San Francisco via London, so it seemed like a good idea for them to take a quick side trip home. Chloe and I had done the same but only stayed twenty four hours – we were anxious to find an apartment and get settled and acquainted with a city we had so despised upon our arrival for class over two years ago. The four of us had agreed that we would live in Manhattan this time and the two Swedes had said that they would trust Chloe and I to find something suitable that we could afford. Transportation would be no problem – we could take the airline buses to the airport from Grand Central Station.

We had been given several leads from our new base supervisor who had also given us the address of an agency Pan Am had used before to find apartments for transferring crew members. We had already walked these shimmering streets without success for two long days before and started the third day wearily but with a list of addresses. We had five days off from crew scheduling after our arrival to find something. The young lady at the agency had given us a really good street map and also recommended that we look a little higher up in Manhattan than we had done the days before. The apartments she had given us to look at started at E59th street and 4th Avenue which was a good deal further up than we had been with the list given us in the crew room. Most of the apartments had been too small for us or not in an area that we would feel comfortable returning home after dark, hauling luggage and in uniform.

The next morning we left our airport hotel early in order to avoid the heat of the day. We took the airport shuttle to Grand Central Station and joined the crushing hustle and bustle of Manhattan – paused and looked around smiling at the thought of living in this amazing city. This time we were not traumatized or shaken – this time we were ready.

The first apartment we looked at was on East 59th street. It was nice and had two bedrooms but they each had a double bed which would not work for us and the living area was dark and really pokey. What really tuned us off however, was the fact that it only had one bath room. That was not a possibility for four young ladies   It had a nice lobby with a twenty four hour security person on site which was wonderful - but we would not be living in the lobby. As a result we once again steeled ourselves to burst back into the crush of the crowded street and the shimmering heat, to move on to the next one on the list - E 72nd street and 2nd Avenue.

The hot pavement turned the street and traffic into watery shapes that floated by as if suspended in the morning sun. The heat enveloped us, as we stepped out of the lobby. It was 10:00 a.m. and the temperature in this concrete jungle was already in the upper nineties. Chloe sighed as she wiped her brow and her neck in frustration with a hanky she pulled out of her pocket. She claimed she was not sure she could handle this heat on a daily basis as the hot crowded street stretched endlessly before us. I agreed but said nothing as we finally entered the heavy glass doors to the apartments on East 72nd Street. Our agent had called ahead and so the immaculately uniformed person we met enthroned in the bright air conditioned lobby, greeted us with gusto - claimed he was Antonio and he had two apartments ready for us to look at.

Upon entering the lifesaving air conditioning, we waved weakly at Antonio and collapsed happily into two easy chairs that seemed perfectly placed to welcomed us. Here we caught our breath and regrouped our energy. Antonio was a total delight and bustled around to bring us each a glass of ice water he had sitting on his counter, while he told us about the building and the apartments we had come to see.

The first apartment was located on the fourth floor and after our recovery Antonio swept us into the elevator with great flair, while filling us in on what it offered and what to expect. The apartment was a lot smaller in size and space from what we were used to in San Francisco. We had noticed that the rooms in Manhattan were smaller and a lot darker – more walls, lower ceilings and fewer windows – and, of course, more expensive. The apartment was nice, two bedrooms with twin beds, two small bathrooms, a large well equipped kitchen but small living room.

We filed out of the apartment and Antonio swept us back into the elevator.

The next apartment was on the twelfth floor – one floor below the Pent house. Antonio unlocked the door and we entered a large living room with a good sized window on the far side. The two bedrooms were small – one with twin beds and the other with a double bed. Two bathrooms and a small but adequate kitchen with an octagonal shaped window with a view of the street far below.

Chloe turned and checked out the kitchen and the view, while I looked over the bedrooms. The one with the double bed was slightly larger than the other and its bathroom had a tub plus a shower – the other bathroom only had a shower. I turned to Antonio and said.

"Antonio would it be possible to exchange the double bed for two singles?"

"Oh, but of course Missy, that would be no problem – do you like this apartment? I have a couple coming this afternoon to look at it, so if you like it I will not show it, and tell them it is under contract."

Chloe looked at me with eyebrows raised questioningly.

"Could you give us a couple of minutes Antonio? We need to talk," I asked turning to him.

"No problem, little lady – I have to run upstairs a minute to check on something – take your time, I'll be back in a few minutes to lock up and take you down." And with a cheerful wave he left us.

Chloe walked to the window in the living room which looked out onto 2nd Avenue, then turned and threw herself onto the couch.

"What think you about this one – I like it, but how will we address the larger bedroom and bathroom with the other two. Shall we toss a coin for it?" She laughed at the idea and got up again to look out of the window.

"I don't care Chloe – our schedules seem to keep us apart in any case. We have never all been home at the same time - not once in two years. I really like the size of this living room - I love being up here on the twelfth floor and the idea of Antonio guarding the 'gate' below – is sweet."

"I agree," she said coming back out of the smaller bedroom. "I like the bathroom and the whole layout with this apartment – so I don't care either. We will give them the choice - since we are making the decision to take this apartment. We are aren't we?" She said with a grin turning to me.

And so it was agreed - if Antonio could change the bed for us – we will take this apartment.

We held our breath and braved the heat leaving the cool lobby and a happy Antonio to return to the rental agency. We sat down with Amy, our friendly agent, who was pleased we had found something we liked while she filled out the paperwork for us to sign. The rent would be $350 per month plus utilities which was quite a lot more than we were paying in San Francisco - but we could afford it, and the apartment was in a nice part of Manhattan. Besides, we were prepared for such an increase in expenses – we had discussed it at length before we bid to move. We had decided we would live in Manhattan and not Kew Gardens and we knew that would cost more but it would be worth every cent. Here we would be in a nice part of Manhattan, we would be safe and it was very convenient to everything of importance to us. We would have bus service outside the door down to Grand Central Station where we would connect with Airport transportation. It could not be more perfect.

Amy said we could move in the next day if we liked, and she would arrange for water and electric to be turned on right away. We happily agreed and asked if she could also arrange for telephone service.

"Sure, not a problem," Amy said busily writing everything down on a pad. "I will call you at the hotel this evening to let you know when to expect the telephone guy so you can be there in time to let him in. Antonio will have four sets of keys waiting for you."

Our friends and roommates arrived from Sweden the next afternoon. We had left a message for them in the crew room, and they showed up with a bottle of Pan Am champagne, donated somewhere down line - to toast our new home. We were moved in, happy - with drink in hand and so very excited to get started - when the phone rang...

Once again – time marches on and we were all set. Prepared and anxious to attack our new life and challenges unknown with positive thoughts - ready to face any and all new horizons.

The Eagle folded her wings and roosted content.

CHAPTER 24 -

A DIFFERENT PERSPECTIVE

E nergy, perspective and life itself is a completely different thing on the East Coast of the US from the comfort level that we had grown used to on the West Coast. Amazingly the same country – yet life could not be more different. We had become Americanized in an environment that was welcoming, easy going, slow moving with happy friendly people. Our new world and reality now, was fast moving, congested, frustrating, challenging and hot – to say the least. It would prove to be very different living in Manhattan – but exciting too, and we found ourselves being ready to embrace the challenge which we had been unable to do upon our arrival in America, more than two years before.

Pan Am crew scheduling utilized us almost immediately, which forced us to get "into the groove" and settle down very quickly. Traveling to and from the airport was a breeze and we thoroughly enjoyed the frequency of the bus schedules in Manhattan, from the apartment and then on to the airport at Grand Central Station. We quite enjoyed the bus ride down to lower Manhattan where the tall Pan Am building loomed in welcome before every trip.

The flying out of this base also was very different – no three day layovers in Hawaii coming and going. Now our first stop was London, Frankfurt, Lisbon, Paris or Rome. Tokyo, Hong Kong, Tahiti and Sydney and the lands of the giant Pacific were in our rear view mirror, exchanged for Beirut, Istanbul, Nirobi, Teheran, Warsaw and Bombay. An adjustment indeed – but we thoroughly enjoyed the new shopping opportunities our move had created. Mona came home very excited after her first trip with a beautiful new gold bracelet from her layover in Beirut. Pan Am crew have always been great 'shop-a-hollicks' and gleefully participated in the opportunities offered them around the world.

Paris offered perfumes, Rome teased us with leather handbags and gloves and Beirut dazzled us with gold. I enjoyed a monthly trip via London to get my hair cut at Vidal Sassoon in Bond Street who gave Pan Am crew a terrific deal. All quite different from Mikimoto pearls in Tokyo, precious stones and Thai silk in Bangkok and on to tailor made clothes or electronics in Hong Kong.

We adjusted quickly and I was approached before bidding for our second month of flying at the New York base, to upgrade to Purser. They were short with my language qualifications and could fit me into an upgrade class after my next trip. It was very tempting with a nice boost in pay which would come in handy now that we lived in Manhattan. My lack of seniority would not matter here and I would not have any problem holding a line of my choice. None of us were "flying in the pool" anymore. Once a year was a requirement, but other than that, we were able to hold a line.

Upon our arrival we were also introduced to a slight change of uniform – we got a new hat. Probably influenced by Jackie Kennedy because it was a cute, jaunty pillbox that would sit - way on top of our teased hair. Very cute.

I accepted the upgrade to Purser and was having fun exploring my new home town. Our experience here in Manhattan was so very different from our introduction to New York and America in general upon our arrival for class. That seemed so long ago now, as I found myself thoroughly enjoying my trips to the shopping areas of downtown, with the amazing number of shops, boutiques and restaurants to get lost in, in the tall maze of granite. The crush and hustle was no longer threatening – in fact I quite enjoyed joining in. We had come a long way from Kew Gardens and the Forrest Park Towne House.

After my Purser upgrade I had a bit of a challenge getting on and off the bus coming and going to my trips. I now had an extra piece of luggage to deal with that was quite heavy. My Purser kit. I now had to carry all my silver First Class service tools. My long twelve inch bladed carving knife with the long pronged matching fork – all the long silver serving spoons and on and on. I also was required to carry a cash float for our Economy bar service and Duty Free. We would accept all currency from anywhere around the world but make change in US dollars. It was quite a large gray bag that sometimes weighed more than my Samsonite suit case due to the silverware, my heavy In Flight Service Handbook and now my Announcement hand book issued to all Pursers. Our announcements had to be read verbatim and may not be memorized – that went for the language announcements as well. I packed my in-flight uniform shoes and my smock in there also, as well as my toiletries and a change of clothing in case my suitcase and I got separated.

Our crew bags had special crew tags and were loaded in a different compartment from passenger bags. But it did happen to me one time however, that my bag was lost, and I spent twenty four hours in the Detroit hotel wearing a white Pan American mechanic's jumpsuit made for a six foot two hundred fifty pound man – till it caught up with me again. Not very sexy and very cumbersome. As a result I learned to pack with caution and was never caught wanting again.

In November I had an African trip that I had not bid but was reassigned to downline. I had been to Nairobi a couple of times and loved the Safari Park - but Monrovia was new to me. We had five days there, and of all the places I have been, I think I enjoyed this the least. The people however, were wonderful, friendly and happy all the time in spite of the fact that they had nothing of value or luxury at all. Definitely a place where you needed to list everything we ate - very carefully. This was a requirement when we were downline in some places, and it was fortunate that this was so, because a First Officer had become sick with Cholera on a layover in Tehran. The cause was traced back to watermelon he had eaten in a salad. The supplier of fruit and vegetables to the hotel had injected the watermelon with contaminated tap water in order to make it heavier – thus more expensive for the hotel to purchase.

We landed in Monrovia on a bright sunny afternoon. I was working the back of the airplane and opened the door for the airstair - to deplane our economy passengers. We had a full load and it felt good to feel the warm fresh air on my face. A young man in the uniform of our caterer came bounding up the stairs with a brilliant smile of welcome.

"Hello Missy- Welcome to Monrovia. Can you please open the other door so we can start unloading your galley."

"Of course we can, but it will have to wait till our passengers are off because it will cause too much draught and we don't need them to feel like they are being blown off the airplane," I told him with a smile and retreated back into the cabin to take an elderly lady by the arm to help her down the stairs. He waved in understanding and disappeared back down the stairs and climbed into his truck.

When the passengers had all disembarked I did a quick cabin check to make sure nothing had been left behind, as a jolly band of airplane cleaners clambered on, chattering and giggling while brandishing brooms and buckets. My galley girl opened the other rear door and the young man with the big happy smile was standing there on the elevated lift to his truck, eagerly waiting for her to do that. He maneuvered the lift to attach to the aircraft door and jumped aboard, as we turned to start collecting our things to disembark.

"Missy, Missy, please – could you please give me a big favor?" I turned back to him puzzled. "Missy, please would you take picture – I have camera – please to take your picture. I give you copy." His happy face was now creased into wrinkled and childlike pleading.

I paused in my packing and returned to him as he was waving his camera. It happened often that people asked to have their picture taken with us, so I dropped my bag and joined him at the top of the stairs. He took several pictures of me with the tail of the airplane and the Pan Am logo. Then he asked Amy the stewardess working the back cabin with me, who had come back to get her smock and shoes, if she would please take our picture together – for his Mum he stated happily. Then he said "Now I take picture of you two – so much fun. You both stand right there - thank you so much – I make copy and send to you via Pan Am crew mail." He was so sweet, excited and somehow childishly innocent that you could not help liking him and doing what he wanted. We stood outside the door together and he took our picture. So Cute.

Four weeks later, I am in the crew room at Idlewilde International Airport in our beautiful circular building, checking in for my London flight which was delayed due to a mechanical hold that could become problematic time wise. Meaning if it took too much longer to fix, my crew would not be able to fly it – arriving at our destination we would have exceeded our legal time on duty. We were spread out in the crew room, on couches, checking mail, making telephone calls – personal stuff of no consequence - to bide time. A crew came blowing happily into the room, weary but happy to be home after five days in Monrovia.

Captain Lewis, that I had flown two trips with the month before saw me, and waved with more gusto than I would have expected from him, a quiet shy man - saying as he floated by, "Hi Gi – you look amazing on the billboard. Congratulations we were impressed."

With that, he grabbed his bag and was gone. A couple of his crew snickered as they passed me with my puzzled, open mouthed stare. I sat down on a chair trying to haul in my thoughts. What on earth was he talking about, and why the snickering. At that moment a new message came in on the telex machine and distracted my bumbling brain. "The crew of Flight One – delayed flight to London - should report to the airplane ASAP." We were ready to go.

I worked the back of the airplane and we had a lot of German tourists on board that had done a long, wonderful tour of Parks in the United States. Yellowstone and Yosemite being two of many. They were happy and excited and moving around the cabin to exchange pictures and information making our dinner service a tad troublesome because someone or other was constantly underfoot and out of their seat. As a result it was, maybe, four hours before I had a chance to check the mail from my crew mailbox. I took my seat on the aft jump seat and pealed through the paperwork. Several Manual and Announcement handbook revisions – odd fliers and an envelope with a post mark I could not identify. It was sent from a Lt William Scofield. United States Navy. Subic Bay. I was completely baffled. Who did I know in the US Navy that would correspond with me.

No one.

The phone above my seat chimed – the Captain warned of bumpy air for the next half hour. Be sure to have everything including passengers secure. I jumped up jamming everything into my Purser kit and slipped it behind the last row of seats. I made sure Erica, my galley stewardess, knew to secure the galley, and as I entered the cabin the Captain was making his announcement for everyone to remain seated with seatbelts fastened until further notice.

The remainder of the flight would be uneventful.

CHAPTER 25 -

LIFE LOVES TO TEASE

I had a wonderful two days in Wimbledon with my Mother - that we had jokingly re-named "Fred" years ago. When I was sixteen she had informed us that it really made her feel old when I called her Mutti or Mummy.

My response had been, "But you are my Mother - so what in the world shall I call you - "Fred?"

It was all in lively good humor and jest at the time - but it has stuck, and she has been called "Fred" by family and friends ever since. Even now sixty years later - we still refer to her as "Fred."

Now, she and her husband Clifford, were just getting back from three weeks in Rorschach, Switzerland on the banks of Lake Geneva, where they had a Summer home.

I loved that little old town on the southern banks of Europe's largest lake, shared by France and Switzerland. It is a picturesque little market town founded in the Middle Ages in 978 and today finds itself three and a half hours by train from the town of Geneva. We loved taking the Steamboat across the lake to the beautiful old Spa town of Giesbach – enjoying their natural pool and the amazing waterfall. We would dine and spend the night, enjoying all of their culinary delights. Then the next day, again by Steamboat, we would go on to the town of Interlaken. I loved Switzerland - this part of Europe is just plain magic. They had a great time and I enjoyed hearing all about it.

The next day I joined my crew on the continuation of Flight One round the World to eventually meet my old San Francisco crew base folks in Bangkok. This is where the San Francisco base and the New York base meet – kiss – turn around and go back on Flight Two round the World the same way they had come. It was a really fun reunion in Bangkok for me, and many of the crews knew each other. It was on the last leg into Bangkok while on my break on the rear jumpseat, that I found the letter from Lt. Scofield again amongst my manual revision paperwork. I opened it with a puzzled frown, having no idea who it could be from. It was indeed from Lt Scofield – but now I remembered him as Bill – the young man my Mother and I had met when we were on vacation.

He said his tour of duty was almost over and he would be leaving the Navy and returning to private life, living with his parents in Philadelphia till he found a job. He wondered if he could come to Manhattan and take me out for dinner some time. He could come up on the train – Philadelphia was only an hour away. I was surprised but happy that he remembered me and smiled as I put the letter into the pocket of my smock. I sat there for a couple of minutes thinking and remembering the Klong tour and our dinner in Hong Kong almost six months before. How did he know I was in Manhattan?

I finished my cup of tea and decided to go up to the flight deck and ask the guys if they knew where Subic Bay was. I got up and pulled the curtain back, secured it and then walked up the aisle and on through the First Class section to the cockpit, picking up trash and doing a cabin check to make sure all was well. I stopped to briefly talk to the other Purser who was serving champagne to a couple sitting in the lounge area, before going into the cockpit.

"Hi Gi – about another two hours to go - how is everybody back there?" the First Officer asked as I walked in and flopped down on the jump seat behind the Captain.

"Everyone's fine. Can I get anybody anything?" I asked enjoying the magnificent view out of the cockpit windows.

"Thank you, but we are all set – just finished eating and am as full as a tick. You look as though you have something on your mind however. What's up?" the Captain said cheerfully as he turned his seat to look at me.

"Well" I said hesitantly - a little shy now as all three men turned to look at me. "I was wondering if you guys have any idea where in the world is Subic Bay?"

"But of course my dear girl – I was based there myself for a short time – it is near Manilla in the Philippines. Why do you need to know?" the Captain asked, grinning broadly.

"A young American service man I met in Bangkok has written a letter to me from there, and I was just wondering where it was, because he said his ship was based in Japan."

"The letter came from Subic Bay – do you think he is there now? OH what fun Gi – what is his name – let's check." I looked at the Captain in total disbelief.

"Whatever do you mean?" I said jumping to my feet and hitting my head on a gas mask and head set.

"Well, we are close enough now, we could call Subic Bay – they could find him and you could tell him Hello – Jack give her a head set," the Captain said to our engineer while turning gleefully forward to the controls and started fiddling with the radio. I was in total shock and disbelief. This was not the path I had sought going into the flight deck. I panicked as Jack handed me the head set I had just hit my head on when I stood up.

"No Captain – oh dear no – PLEASE don't do that." I gasped as radio static flooded the flight deck.

Suddenly a bright, business like voice came over the radio and gave the call sign for the Subic Bay Naval Station, in the Philippines.

"Yes, Subic Bay – Good Afternoon - this is Clipper One in bound to Bangkok and we were wondering if it would be possible for you to locate...... Gi, quick give me his name," the Captain broke off turning frantically to me while taking his finger off the radio key. I was paralyzed – I could do nothing except hand him my letter. He grabbed it, checked the name on the front and pressing the radio button again said "Lt. Scofield, would it be possible to speak with Lt William Scofield?"

There was a pause and then the voice came back on and said, "Roger Clipper One – please stand by," and the line went dead. I sank weakly into the jump seat again close to tears of embarrassment. The mood in the cockpit however, was anything but morbid – in fact it was alive with excitement which had relieved the occupant's temporary boredom on a long flight. Jack put his arm around my shoulders as my hands covered my face – finally the static came back on and then a clear voice came back over the radio. "This is Subic Bay calling Clipper One – do you read me?"

"This is Clipper One Subic Bay – we read you loud and clear." "Yes sir – Clipper One – we have checked, and Lt Scofield is temporarily off base Captain – could someone else help you."

"No problem Subic Bay – thank you for your help – over and out."

"Yes sir, any time – sorry we could not help – over and out." and the line went dead.

I almost fell off my seat. The Captain of Pan American Clipper One en route to Bangkok turned to me with great disappointment written all over his strong, suntanned face as I turned and burst out of the cockpit shaking in unrestrained relief.

****

The next day I slept in a little bit and lay in bed reliving my embarrassment on the flight deck the day before. The flight crew were so kind and sweet to me on our way off the airplane upon our arrival in Bangkok, that I forgave them putting me on the spot like that. There had been nothing but excited good humor in what they had tried to achieve and we ended up all having a good laugh over it and my panic attack.

I got up when the phone rang – it was nine o'clock.

"Hello."

"Hi Gi, it's Jeff Lane – I checked the crew list and saw you were here. Are you coming down to breakfast – there is a whole bunch of us here."

"Yes Jeff – give me twenty minutes and I'll be down." We hung up and I dashed into the shower. It felt good to be back in the Bangkok hotel – I knew it well – it felt like home.

Half an hour later I joined Jeff in the coffee shop and he gave me a big hug. Most of the others had already left so it was just him and I. We had a long leisurely breakfast, chatting for a while over this and that and how I liked living in Manhattan now - when the conversation turned to flying. We signed our checks and got up and walked out into the lobby.

"Have you done any Monrovia trips lately?" he asked innocently not looking at me while staring at a suit in the tailor shop window.

I hesitated and then, looking at him wearily said, "No why do you ask?" He looked at me with a very serious demeanor but I noticed his eyes were dancing – no - laughing. "What has happened in Monrovia – people keep making the most peculiar comments, laughing and then running away before I can ask them what is going on. Jeffrey, are you going to tell me what is going on in Monrovia, or do I have to shake it out of you." I said menacingly, stamping my foot.

He smiled, took my hand and gently lead me to the hotel bar where he ordered a beer for himself and a glass of wine for me. I was beside myself with impatience but tried to remain 'lady like' as we waited for our drinks in a silence that you could have sliced with my Purser carving knife.

The drinks appeared before us and he handed me my wine, picked up his beer and toasted my health.

I thought I would burst a gasket which is not very 'lady like.' I did not feel 'lady like' and grabbed his hand.

"WHAT IS IT JEFFREY?"

"OK, OK, slow down. It is very funny – but you will not think so." He said finally holding my hand in his and smiling like a Cheshire cat that has just swallowed a tiny mouse. "Did someone take your picture in Monrovia on your last trip?" he asked smiling at my discomfort.

"Well – yes – why – the little commissary guy took pictures after we landed – why?" I stuttered. He was silent but his smile got bigger and bigger.

"WHY JEFFREY?" I was beyond control.

"Your picture is on the giant advertisement sign as you drive out of the airport – it is a great picture of you smiling and standing in welcome on the airstair with the aircraft tail behind you."

"Oh, OK – that's nice." I said hesitantly waiting for the other shoe to drop. IT DID.

"Yes," Jeffrey added slowly, "It is nice – the trouble is – the only thing that you have ON in the picture on the billboard – is your hat and your gloves!"

CHAPTER 26 -

A NEW HORIZON

The phone rang. I tried to ignore it because I had just come in from a long fourteen day trip and I knew it could not be crew scheduling. I was in the middle of trying to count my bar money from the airplane. I had an impossible amount of foreign currency – six different denominations and it was taking me a long time to do my paperwork and make it all come out right. I had about two thousand dollars worth of money sitting in front of me of which easily half was "funny money" and I really did not feel like answering the phone – but it kept ringing.

I finally got up and walked over to the offensive contraption. "Hello." I barked into the receiver.

"Hello, good afternoon, this is Bill Scofield – could I please speak to Gisela?" The hair stood up on the back of my neck and my stomach lurched.

"Hello Bill – this is Gisela." I said trying to pull myself together "Are you back in America?" Stupid question – he would not be calling me from Japan.

"I am Gisela, and I was wondering if I could come and take you out for dinner sometime soon. Would you be available tomorrow or Friday?"

"Oh, thank you Bill." I said pulling up a chair – my bar money forgotten. "Tomorrow would be lovely."

"Great, is there anywhere special you would like to go?"

"No – I will be happy to leave it up to you," I said my pulse racing.

"There is a train that gets into Penn Station at five twenty-five from Philly – I could be at your place by six. If that would suit."

"That would be wonderful Bill – thank you. I will let Antonio, our door man know to send you up."

"Terrific, see you then," and he hung up. I sat motionless in the chair, still holding the receiver aimlessly in my hands. Not quite knowing what to feel. I was touched that he remembered me and went to some trouble to find me upon his return to the States and civilian life – but it was a strange feeling to be dating again. I had had no inclination what so ever to start doing so. I knew however, that I must try – I would not ever be seeing Ollie again – that was my decision. I had jumped through so many scary hoops – alone – to make that reality happen. It was time for me to find a life. Move on.

The door buzzer went off at exactly five minutes past six the next evening and I was ready to start 'the rest of my life.' I was alone in the apartment – Suzanne would be here in a couple of days, but Mona and Chloe both had long trips and would not be here until after I am gone again - sometime next week. I heard the elevator stop and then my doorbell rang. I took a deep breath – checked myself quickly in the hall mirror, put a smile on my face and opened the door.

Bill Scofield stood there smiling with an adorable little bouquet of yellow roses in his hands, suntanned and dressed in a beautiful dark blue suit, crisp white shirt and tie – looking every bit my Mother's dream come true.

"Hello Bill – how nice to see you please come in," I said graciously accepting the little bouquet.

"My Mother fixed them for you from her yard – she picked only the best she told me, so I hope you like them."

"They are beautiful Bill, thank you – please be sure and thank her and tell her I loved them."

We went into the living room and I bade him sit on the couch while I went into the kitchen to find a vase and water. We had water – but no vase – a tall water glass would have to do.

"Can I get you a glass of wine before we go out?" I asked him upon my return.

"Great – thank you that would be nice. This is a really nice apartment. I'm impressed. You know," he said a little sheepishly, "I am job and house hunting myself. Depending on where I find a job will be where I look for an apartment. It is a little daunting coming back after so long."

"I understand Bill." I said handing him a glass of Merlot. "We hated New York when we first came – but we lived in Queens and we hated it. Manhattan is completely different, and the four of us are really enjoying living here now."

The atmosphere was good – I realized I was happy to see him again which quite surprised me. We sipped our wine and made small talk. He asked me about my Mother and I told him all about how and where we had finished our vacation after we left him in Hong Kong. Finally, he put down his glass, looked at his watch and said, "I don't want to rush you, but we have a seven o'clock reservation at The Sign of the Dove. Do you know it? A friend of ours said it was really nice, so I took his word and made a reservation."

"I don't know it – but it sounds lovely – I'll get my coat."

Seconds later we were going down in the elevator and a cheerful Antonio was hailing us a cab. It was a short fifteen minute ride to the restaurant but the traffic was heavy and noisy on E 72nd Street at that time of the evening.

The restaurant was beautiful with low hidden lighting, soft music and exotic plants everywhere. The maître d' ushered us to a beautifully set table in a quiet corner and handed us a long menu in a leather case, for our perusal. It was quite enchanting.

We had a wonderful dinner, the food was delicious and the service outstanding. We sat for a good while talking and catching up, lingering over a glass of wine - hating for the evening to end. Finally the waiter brought the bill and Bill's sunny smile faded and a very scary look crossed his face. I was really concerned because he had broken off our conversation in mid-sentence and he seemed to be in quite a state of distress.

"Bill – what is it. Are you all right?" I said, really concerned now. He looked up at me with almost tears in his eyes.

"I am beyond embarrassed Gisela – but I do not have enough money to pay this bill. Do you by any chance have any cash on you? I am so very sorry – I will pay you right back next week – I promise."

"OH dear Bill – no. I am so sorry I came out without my wallet. I just have a five dollar bill I always carry with me in case of an emergency – but I doubt that will be any help. What can we do?"

"I'm not sure," he almost whispered. I felt helpless and desperately sorry for him. He looked so pathetic and I could see that he was starting to perspire in his misery.

Suddenly – I had an epiphany. I grabbed his arm in great excitement. "I think I have got an idea that might work perfectly – but you have to stay sitting here alone. Order yourself another glass of wine – trust me - I'll be back as quickly as I can." With that I jumped up and very carefully and unobtrusively let myself out of the restaurant and hailed a cab.

It was less than twenty five minutes later that I slipped back into my seat beside him at the table. He jumped, startled at my sudden quiet return.

"What on earth – where did you go – are you OK?" he stuttered thoroughly shaken.

"Yes – Yes Bill I'm fine – here take this, it should solve our problem," and I slipped an envelope into his clammy hand. I had suddenly remembered my Pan Am bar money and went back to the apartment to get some of it. I had the cabby wait for me while I rushed up to the twelfth floor, grab the bar money that was in dollar bills, counted out two hundred dollars and rushed back down to him – making sure I had enough to pay that cabby also, when we reached the restaurant.

Life and fate can be strange. I almost always stayed in the crew room upon return to do my trip paperwork and the bar money. This is what we were supposed to do – but sometimes, if the last 'leg' was long or hard or we were really tired and the bar money had a lot of foreign currency to deal with, we would take it home and drop it off when we next checked in. As luck would have it that was the situation that fateful day.

We have laughed many times over the years about our date and dinner at The Sign of the Dove and shared it with many family and friends – but at the time it was very traumatic and not funny in the least.

We were both so young and naive – and Bill was still very much out of touch having been overseas and in service for three years.

That night the Eagle went quietly to roost, curling up and thanking Pan American for services rendered.

CHAPTER 27 -

SO - THIS IS NEW YORK

Bill and I started dating on my days off. He went on many job interviews in a widespread area while living at home with his mum and dad. It was a long challenging process and he became quite frustrated as the summer came to an end and winter started to creep into the picture. I was invited many times by his parents to come and spend time in their cozy home on Manoa Road in Havertown. I would get on the train at Penn Station in Manhattan and Bill would meet me in Philly. I learned to love his parents who were very kind and quickly made me feel like a part of the family. His Mother was very bright and very talented. She loved gardening was a gifted artist and cook and ran the house and kitchen with passion and precision. Bill's dad was the sweetest of men. He had given his all to the world as a successful salesman – now retired he loved his wife – was unbelievably proud of his two sons – of which Bill was the younger one, and thoroughly relished his Manhattan at six on the dot, before dinner every night.

I came home from a Moscow trip via Warsaw and Frankfurt on a Monday in early November and found a message saying that Bill thought he had found a job in New Jersey and was driving up from Philly the next day. Maybe he could come by and we could have dinner – he wanted to see what I thought of the opportunity he had been offered. Then he would drive on to be in New Jersey the next day to meet the CEO of the company.

I called and told him to go ahead and come in to Manhattan next day and I would fix an early dinner so that we could talk but then he could drive on to New Jersey and find a motel in a timely fashion. His meeting was at eight thirty Wednesday morning and I did not want him to appear tired.

Mona was home when I arrived on Monday, but left early the next morning for Rio. It was good to see her and we enjoyed a cozy evening together. She was expecting Suzanne to arrive on Wednesday evening and I was hoping to see Chloe on Saturday because I was leaving for London on Sunday.

I went to the store and bought pork chops, veggies, French bread, cheese and a bottle of wine. We still had plenty of salad fixings and flowers that Mona had bought, so I did not need to get any of that for dinner with Bill. I did some laundry, leisurely house cleaning and then took a shower. Dinner was well under way at five o'clock when I checked – Bill would arrive any minute.

The lights went out in Manhattan at 5:27 p.m. on Tuesday November 9th 1965.

I had just lit a candle and set the table for dinner when the world went dark. Not just dark – BLACK. Manhattan was black. I stood riveted in disbelief – this was no ordinary power outage – this was serious. The streets were dark – traffic lights were out, people were running in all direction in confusion. The only lights came from buses and cars on the city streets amongst much hooting and hollering. I was scared and worried. Where was Bill?

Bill had entered the brightly lit Midtown Tunnel to Manhattan in a normal flow of rush hour traffic at 5:25 pm. He would emerge into a city of total blackness. He would be one of the last people to enter the tunnel which was immediately closed to all traffic at 5:30 pm.

We would find out later that this mammoth blackout had plunged half a dozen US states and two Canadian provinces into total darkness – involving 30 million people.

In Manhattan 800,000 people were stranded on paralyzed rush hour trains – some underground, some on bridges or in between stations. Thousands of people were stuck hundreds of feet above ground - in disabled, stifling hot elevators. Passengers waiting to board airplanes watched in disbelief as runway lights dimmed and went out at major airports. The National Guard was called out to assist in any way possible. If you lived in Ontario, Massachusetts, Maine, Connecticut, New Hampshire, Vermont, New York, New Jersey, Pennsylvania or Rhode Island your world stood still in immobilizing blackness.

Bill adjusted his vision to the sudden darkness and made his way very slowly and with much caution through the maze of buses and cars and traumatized people, trying their best to help the police to direct traffic. He finally managed to make his way to our building and entered a pitch dark lobby with a small candle illuminating Antonio and his desk. Bill greeted him as he was talking to another gentleman about to climb the stairs.

"AH Mr. Scofield – good evening sir. This is a fine mess I can tell you. Missy told me earlier that you were coming – you don't by any chance have a flash light with you?"

"Antonio, good evening – no, I am sorry to tell you that I did not expect to need such a thing as that tonight."

"I completely understand sir, but I have to somehow enable you to get to the twelfth floor. I have a very small candle I can give you and this other gentleman that is going to the pent house, if you would not mind holding it while I find a light for it."

Bill did so and greeted the other man with a friendly wave, then he gingerly took the small, offered candle - and the two men entered the stairwell. Twelve stories was a mighty l-o-n-g exhausting way up that entire building - all the while clutching a small piece of candle that proceeded to get smaller with every floor climbed.

Finally they were on the twelfth floor and passing my door. Bill knocked on it and called out to me so that I would know it was him and I would not be afraid to open the door in the dark.

I opened the door and saw the two men standing bent over a tiny piece of candle that Bill was trying to peel off his burning thumb in order to hand it to his companion who was going one floor higher. Their faces were illuminated grotesquely in the small flickering light.

Suddenly – as if by magic – the other man whipped out a brand new eight inch candle from his pocket – lit it from Bill's thumb nail and disappeared back into the stairwell without another word.

We stood in the softly fading light of the blinking candle stub -

and blankly looked at each other in disbelief.

What in the world just happened?

Did that crazy "Mensch" actually have a brand new candle in his pocket – all the way up that building – the whole time watching as Bill maneuvered his tiny piece from hand to hand so as not to burn his fingers as he attempted to light their way up the pitch dark stairwell of that entire building!?!

OH YES - HE DID! This is New York – in case either one of us was in doubt!

CHAPTER 28 -

THE STARS ARE ALIGNED

The giant blackout over the northeastern seaboard was over quite quickly. Indeed, it ended in the early hours of Wednesday morning. Life returned to normal in a hiccup of time to the resilient New Yorkers, and we rolled right on into the Christmas season.

The city burst into light with holiday cheer. Christmas trees, Hanukkah decorations and happy music is everywhere. The ice rink at the Rockefeller Center was, as usual, in brilliant full swing, and my room mates and I participated in all the excitement with glee and gusto. Christmas in England, Germany and Sweden was a big deal, and we thoroughly enjoyed the mix of cultures that happened in New York.

We loved the mood of the city during this festive time and the rink at Rockefeller Center drew us like a magnet whenever we were home. What an amazing magical place the city had turned this cultural site into with the enormous, lighted Christmas tree dominating and the statue of Prometheus gazing down on all the skaters swaying and dancing to the music.

My roommates had all been dating since our arrival in America – I however had had no interest in doing so up to this time. I had dated several times while living in San Francisco when on layovers in the far east. Usually poor military souls that needed to temporarily escape the ravages of war. I felt so sorry for what they were going through. Many a time I would be walking down the street beside one of them when a car or motor scooter would backfire and I would suddenly find myself alone in mid-sentence. They would be flat on their face on the pavement behind me - a life preserving reflex.

I had tried dating once before in New York after our move. My date was a very nice young man I had been introduced to by a friend – but my heart was not in it – I felt like I was on a job interview. So as a result I was quite surprised at the way I reacted when Bill came into the picture. He was kind, reassuring and not pushy at all. We had experienced and done many of the same things, got along well and as a result, established a comfortable friendship. I was happy with that.

One night he drove over for dinner and while he was helping me with the dishes produced $600 dollars in cash out of the back pocket of his pants and said he thought we should get married. I laughed in complete disbelief.

"Are you trying to bribe or buy me - with money?"

He laughed too but a little sheepishly and said, "Of course not – silly. I've been thinking about this a lot lately. I love you. Very much in fact and I thought you could take this with you on your next trip to London and pick out a ring you like with help from Clifford and his friends." I was floored. This was a lot of money to me in 1965 – but I knew that my family's fellow antique dealers would help me find something amazing on Jermyne Street in London's St. Jameses.

I dried my hands slowly on the kitchen towel – turned and looked him straight in the eye. My brain was doing summer salts. He was serious and very nervous – looking like a panicked caged animal. We stood like that for what seemed like an eternity. I finally broke the tension.

"OK," and fell into his arms. It felt good. It felt right.

Clifford took me to see one of his friends that was an antique jewelry dealer who showed me some breathtaking rings. In England an engagement ring usually has a colored stone in it, and I fell totally in love with a beautiful Burmese ruby with a diamond on each side. The ring was an antique in a beautiful gold setting from a Russian collection and was probably at least 150 years old. The diamonds were cut in the old European style and did not have as many facets as the rings of today – but the sparkle was intense.

Bill and I elected to get married in London. It would be fun, and I wanted to get married in The College Chapel in Dulwich where I grew up. The only problem was that this was not a registered neighborhood church and so we had to request permission from the Archbishop of Canterbury to be married there to make it legal and binding. I filled out the necessary paperwork on a trip to London and paid the required fee. Three weeks later we got a beautiful certificate signed by the Archbishop himself – we set a date and we were ready.

Bill's parents would come from Philly and stay with Fred and

Clifford in Wimbledon. My aunt Ilse would come from Hamburg and stay at 5 Trinity Rise with Dick and Betty. Now – what about Bill and I. Well we fixed that too, no problem - I would sleep with my aunt Ilse in the spare room and Bill would sleep in the living room on the couch. On our Honeymoon night I would join him there. Whoooooopppppi!

Of course, as with any wedding – there was much planning and arranging to do. Always more difficult while 5,000 miles apart. Fred and Betty Brewer were an amazing team and had everything under control – I just had to concentrate on what to wear.

The last couple of times while visiting the Scofields in Philly – I was aware that Bill had doctor's appointments that sometimes made him late to pick me up at the station. The first time I said nothing, but the second time it happened I was concerned and said, "Bill – is everything OK - are you sick?"

"I'm OK Gi – trust me. I am very embarrassed - but under the circumstances I believe I owe you an explanation." We continued driving and he was quiet for the longest time.

I said nothing, but finally turned to him, totally puzzled and said, "What is it Bill – why do you owe me an explanation?"

As a result, I was totally blown away when he suddenly and without explanation pulled over into a Burger King parking lot and parked the car.

"Gi, when I was in Manila I er- frequented a certain bar. There – er - were – er – ladies there and I – er – must -er – er - have picked something up from one of them."

The silence between us was – deafening – no explosive.

Was he there when we tried to find him in Subic Bay from 30,000 feet on our way to Bangkok?!

"I am so very mortified Gi - I am so sorry. I have been going to the doctor for some time and he has been treating me. I am now safe – I told him we were getting married and he promised me that would not be a problem at all, physically, but I am still on antibiotics for the next six weeks and as a result I will be sterile for that entire time I'm on these meds."

I was silent. Trying to wrap my arms around this amazing new revelation. Finally Bill said, "Gi, please talk to me – say something – anything – what is going through your mind?"

"OK." I said and turned and looked him, "I'm not sure what to think – but I am sure that you better get back on the road and drive, because your Mother is going to wonder where we are and she will have dinner on the table. I am going to have to think this through. You are going to have to be patient and give me some space."

That night, alone in my bed in the cute little guest room in Manoa Road that Bill's mum had set up for me – I squirmed restlessly in the cool ironed sheets.

What did I think?

What I thought was – so what! So the man had visited with a 'lady of the Manila night'. Big deal. The man is not a monk. He has lived for three years in very traumatic conditions and needs to blow off steam. So he did that and got caught. Who am I to judge him. B-l-o-w – it – o -f -f. Move on.

And so I did.

245

***Our Wedding Day
Feb 1966***

Dick Brewer and me

Mr and Mrs Scofield

CHAPTER 29 -

TIME STOOD STILL

Our wedding was small, sweet and a total delight. I wore a short dress of soft organza with a cream lace over dress – a little pill box hat in matching organza, covered in the most beautiful shoulder length antique Belgian lace veil, lent to me by Betty's mother. It had been her mother's and was at least 100 years old. I was insistent I did not want a fancy, long white wedding dress – and this dress was perfect.

Dick Brewer walked me down the aisle of the little chapel to where Bill waited at the altar. It was all very special and very sweet.

After the service we all drove into London to the old Dorchester Hotel where we had a small wonderful reception facing Hyde Park with a three tired wedding cake made lovingly by Betty

Brewer and her daughter Carol. The beautiful mixing of all the families of importance in my life at this time was very special, and the band and the party played on into the night.

Bill and I shared the couch on our wedding night and for three days of our Honeymoon – we were young and the lack of luxury did not faze us in the least. We were happy and we wanted everyone else that was visiting from outside of the country to enjoy this special time with us. My aunt Ilse went back to Hamburg three days after the wedding, but Bill's mum and dad stayed for a week. It was their first time in London and Fred and Clifford had a blast showing them around. When they left Bill and I moved to Wimbledon. I had taken my vacation for the wedding and we got four weeks off every year.

Eventually, Bill and I returned to the US and moved into a little apartment we had found in Plainfield New Jersey. It was convenient for him and his job and it was an easy drive for me to the airport. It was fun and we had no problem settling down to married life. We fixed the apartment up with odds and ends cast off from friends and his mum and dad and it was really cozy.

I returned to work the second week of the next month with a trip to Lisbon – the trip pattern gave us three days in Lisbon and then we were to take a limo ride to Rota in Spain and fly a M.A.T.S. charter home from the Naval base there.

I checked in for my flight without incident – happy to be back at work. I was now a married lady – one of the first stewardesses at that time to be allowed to be married. The flight was lightly booked and we only had about forty passengers in economy where I was working. Amy was my galley girl and we had worked together several times before. On the crew bus she confided that she had been to a party the night before and was feeling a tad queasy. We laughed about it because she said she was happy that she would be able to hide in the galley and did not need to interact with our passengers – just me.

I sat next to her on the rear jumpseat for take off and she was asking me all about the wedding. The wheels lifted off and as we climbed I felt my stomach start to feel peculiar and do little somersaults. The higher we climbed the sicker I felt, and shortly before we reached 10,000 feet I jumped up and hit the bathroom. I stayed in there for the longest time and finally Amy came to see if I was OK. I did vomit a little, but I had not eaten before the flight so it was mostly dry heaves.

I washed my face in cold water and came back out and sat back on the jumpseat. Amy had started arranging her galley for the meal service and looked up when I came out of the bathroom.

"Gi what on earth is wrong - you are as pale as a sheet. Is there anything I can get you?"

"Amy no – no thank you. Do you feel alright, how are you doing ?" I asked weakly.

"I'm OK – not good, but OK," and she smiled as she turned the ovens on high. "It was a lovely party – let me get you some coffee and you sit – Angela has the cabin under control, she is still taking drink orders."

"You are right, we still have time before we need to start if Angela can do the drinks. Why don't you fix us both a 'double' Alka Seltza and we will sit back here and rest for a minute and wait for it to take effect."

"Good idea – we are both bound to feel better very shortly after that."

Well – she did – but I did not. The higher we flew the sicker I became. I did the best I could but I was basically a walking zombie. It was the most difficult eight hours of my life. I kept going over in my mind what I could have eaten and not coming up with a possible answer.

When the wheels hit the deck in Lisbon I was feeling a lot better, but elected to take life very easy at our hotel. Also eating very carefully, a lot of fish and fruit which is very boring – I am a red meat carnivore. My steak must still MOOO when it hits my plate – and steak tartare is still my favorite dish.

After three uneventful days we boarded a limousine bus and drove many miles over hill and dale on bumpy country roads to the Naval Base in Rota on Spain's south eastern coastline. There we spent a day at the beach, relaxing and drinking wine before taking a M.A.T.S. charter back to Norfolk in Virginia.

The wheels came off the deck and we sailed out over the Naval base and on over a calm expanse of Atlantic ocean. Before we reached ten thousand feet I was once again prone in my jumpseat and then heading to the Jon. It was my turn to fly up front on the way home, but I begged off, telling Alissa the other Purser to please work there instead of me. It was almost as if I had a premonition. This aircraft had no first class cabin or lounge – it was all economy and packed with crisp, clean smelling military guys excited and so very happy to be going home.

I do not remember much of that flight home – I am embarrassed to admit I was unable to pull my weight. Thank heavens it was not a regular flight with all our fancy meal services. Also, the smell of the cooking food was intolerable. As soon as we landed and checked out in the crew room I headed straight for the medical department in Hanger 14.

I explained to the doctor what had happened to me. I was very worried that it could happen again because in five days I had a long fourteen day trip on my line of flying – there was no way I could or would dare take that trip if this problem was not fixed.

The doctor was very patient and listened carefully to everything I was telling him. With a long pause, after thumbing through my file, he said matter of factly, "I see you just got married, Miss Gisela – may I suggest that you could be pregnant?"

I looked at the man as if he had two heads and was not using either one of them.

"OH NO doctor." I said emphatically – there is no way I could be that. My husband is on medication and he is temporarily sterile."

"Oh really." he said with a smile. "I suggest you take yourself to see this gentleman as soon as practical," and he handed me a slip of paper with a doctors name on it. "I am taking you off flight duty until after you see him and report back to me."

I did not know it then, but that would be the last flight I would work for Pan American for 15 years. Two weeks later it was confirmed that I was indeed pregnant and Pan Am gave me a pink slip of dismissal. Pregnant ladies could not possibly work in flight for Pan American in those days. Pregnant ladies have no business being on an airplane at 30,000 feet – according to them – besides, there is no way you could shoe horn yourself into that uniform.

My oldest son Mark was born to the day nine months later – he was a Honeymoon Baby.

CHAPTER 30 -

MY WORLD REARRANGED

This was a very scary time for Bill and I. Although we were blown away at the idea that we could be – no – WERE - pregnant, we also were thrilled. However, Bill had a beginner's 'newbie' job selling maritime paint - that he was working his way into and not making much money. It had very good prospects but it would take time. I however, had a great job making almost twice as much as him – and now I am the one unemployed.

I delivered my first son in a Roman Catholic Hospital run by Nuns in Elizabeth New Jersey. We rushed in panic out of the apartment after I saw water on the floor where I was standing in the kitchen. Bill called my doctor – a sweet calm fatherly man – who told us to go ahead and come to the hospital and he would meet us there. We piled into the car with my little overnight bag in tow and in our panic – promptly got lost. While Bill was desperately trying to redirect and find our way – I made everything worse with my contractions – which scared Bill to death. But now I decided – I had to throw up my previously thoroughly enjoyed country style, rib dinner. Which I did with great flair, after poor Bill came to a screeching stop at my loud demand while throwing my door wide open.

We finally arrived at the hospital where a tiny, little Nun dressed in a flowing habit, met us in the lobby with a wheel chair and ordered me to sit in it. She had to be ninety years old if she was a day and obviously in charge of everything – at least in her mind. My contractions were so intense by this time – I did not argue – and sat where I was told. Poor Bill arrived somewhere behind me carrying my little suitcase which this tiny person proceeded to swipe unceremoniously out of his hand while pushing me into the open elevator door.

"Go away – go home – this is woman's work – you have done yours – we will call you if we need you," this tiny being yelled at my husband, as the elevator door slammed shut between us. I was alone with a ninety year old 'hellion' in a black habit.

Mark William Scofield was born at 10:23 on November 22, 1966 weighing in at 8 lbs 14 ozs. and 22 inches long. This was ginormous for a first baby and the result was that his head was as flat as a pancake. He was gross – so very deformed looking that the nurse covered him with a towel while wheeling him out of the delivery room to the nursery. The doctor ran after her and managed to catch up with her and her hidden charge just as they passed Bill Scofield sitting anxiously waiting for news and ready with a big bunch of flowers in the waiting area.

The doctor lunged at the baby and yanked the towel off him

saying, "No – no – nurse – let him look, let him see his son."

Bill jumped up in alarm – dropping the flowers and gasped in horror when he saw the baby – feeling sure we had created a monster.

"Bill it's alright – don't get upset – the baby is fine, you have a strapping, healthy son. He looks a little the worse for wear, but he will be fine in a week or two. You have nothing to fear – he just had a bit of trouble making it into this world – he will be as cute as a button when next I see him." And he was – and still is.

Three days later when my milk had come in I sent Bill out to buy me a nursing bra.

He was terrified – where should he find such a thing – what size do I need and on and on. I was desperately uncomfortable and felt as though I was the size of an elephant. Not having anyone to ask – my family being 5,000 miles away and Bill's being in Philly I did not know what to tell him. I was a 34 B normally, but now I was enormous – I did not know that you just ordered the same size as you always wear and the bra company took care of it.

So in my ignorance and pathetic naivety I said, "Oh Bill – I don't know – try 40." So off the poor man went to the Maternity department at Sears.

The young lady behind the counter was smiling at my husband's discomfort but said in a business-like manner trying to put him at ease, "Yes sir I can help you with that. What cup size does she need?" There was a panic stricken pause.

"EEERRR c-u-p size?" he stuttered in disbelief. "I did not know you measured them with a cup."

Bill was a real trooper, loved me desperately and could not

stand to see me in such misery. He did his best to help but he arrived at the hospital with a bra that all three of us could have gotten in together and worn comfortably - it was that big!

I came home from the hospital and Bill and I muddled our way through parenthood. We were happy – we were poor – but life was a joy. My Mother sent us a large beautiful English pram to ferry our son around in and Bill remarked that his son was riding in a Cadillac but he drove a Chevy.

Bill worked for a paint company that made very good paint – not just in the Marine Division that he was in, but they also made house paint. After Mark's arrival we had found a darling little house in Plainfield that we could afford. We bought it for $14,000 and had a thirty year mortgage. The house was yellow on the outside but all white on the inside – so we decided to transform it with Bill's paint.

Our First House

Every room had its own color and the kitchen was my pride and joy. There we painted everything in high gloss – the walls were Wedgwood blue, the cabinets were silver gray and the ceiling was pink. It was a real conversation piece. In England we covered the walls with wall paper – but I could not find any in this American location, that I liked. Besides, we would have had to have it professionally done and we did not have money for such extravagance. In any case we loved to do everything ourselves, had so much fun doing it and we got a big discount on the paint. We did everything now at a discount – our whole life was on a serious budget.

Bill took the train every day to his office in Newark – it was just impossible to find a parking space there during working hours. Besides he enjoyed riding the train and reading the paper at the start and end of his day. He liked his job very much – but he loved coming home to us. So most evenings I would get Mark dressed and put him in his beautiful pram with the two big wheels in the back and two smaller wheels in front – and we would go to the station to meet "Daddy."

We loved being parents and enjoyed our dinner every night with Mark sitting in his little chair on top of the table watching us eat. Every second weekend we would spend in Philly so that Bill's mum and dad could enjoy their new grandson. They were over the moon happy, doting, grandparents. Life was good – life was fun and we were so happy.

A year later Bill said he needed to invite his boss home for dinner. He thought that he might be getting a promotion and his boss wanted to meet me. I fixed a really nice dinner and we had a great time. His boss was a very nice man and obviously thought a lot of Bill. He mentioned that we would have to do a little entertaining – taking clients out to dinner and so on - how did I feel about that?

Needless to say I had no problem with that, and before he left he told Bill that he was very lucky - I would be his 'secret weapon.'

Three weeks later we were transferred to New Orleans.

****

Bill went down to New Orleans to look for a little house that we could afford. We had managed to buy our cute little house in Plainfield with a little yard for Mark to play in and we were loathed to leave that in case we could not find anything in New Orleans. So Bill went down to look.

On the third day he called to say he thought he had found something – he was not sure we could afford it but planned to put a bid down on it that afternoon. He described it to me over the phone and it sounded really nice – and even a little bigger than what we had in New Jersey.

We got lucky – and with even more tightening of our belts, were able to buy it. So now we were all set and could move down as soon as practical. It would be sad leaving our little house in Plainfield – we really liked it there – but also leaving Bill's mum and dad would be difficult for all of us.

The house on Bissonet Drive in Metairie was a nice upgrade from what we had. It even had central air conditioning which we had not had before and had spent several hot summer nights camped, with a mattress on the floor in our basement, because it was too hot to sleep in our bedroom.

We soon settled down to life in the deep south. It was very different from what we had been used to. One by one our neighbors came to check us out and say Hello - several bringing pies or casseroles as gifts. We had lived more than a year in our little house in Plainfield and no one had checked us out at all. We did not get to know a single neighbor unless they had a complaint.

Life was tough financially – the house was a good bit more expensive and we lived month to month to the last twenty five cents. Bill left with our only car – sometimes for four of five days – and left me with Mark and a bicycle. I would tie him on the back and peddle to the local store a good three miles away if I ran out of milk or butter or something. I was not happy. Things were difficult and steamy hot in this city. The climate alone was a challenge and the culture shock was enormous. I did not like New Orleans.

One day my neighbor, Peggy, from three doors down banged on my front door demanding to know if we were ready for the hurricane. She ran a small Day-Care business at her house and Mark loved to play in her yard with the kids – so we had become friends.

"Ex - excuse me – the what?" I asked her thoroughly mystified.

"The hurricane in the Gulf - Camille - it's getting close and I thought I'd better come and check on Y'all."

"Thank you so much Peggy – but I don't know what you are talking about. Who – what is coming and what are we supposed to do about it?"

"Oh MY – Baby Girl you ARE from another world. This hurricane is a killer. It is in the Gulf and heading for us – they claim it will hit as a Cat 5 which is the worst it could be. You have got to get ready and tie everything outside down or bring it in. Cover or tape up all your windows fill the bathtub with water – go get toilet paper, batteries, candles and bread from the store. We may not have any electricity for a week or more – you have GOT TO GET READY."

I was astounded. Blown away by what she was telling me. That night when Bill came home I told him what had happened and he agreed, saying that people had been talking about it all day and telling him the same thing. I could see he was worried.

We had about 48 hours before the first heavy bands of wind and rain would hit us, and we did not have the slightest idea what to do first. Bill carried our outdoor table and chairs into the garage and secured the front and back yards. That night we watched the TV news and saw first-hand what everyone was worried about. There it was – Camille – as large as life in the Gulf with some winds up to almost 150 miles per hour – but what was almost as scary, was the fact that most Louisiana residents living in the city and near or around Lake Pontchartrain were leaving. The roads west were completely clogged with traffic which was at a standstill. That night we slept in fits or not at all as we listened to the falling rain and gusty wind.

Before day break Bill was up – he had decided during the night that we also should leave. It was the safest thing to do – he said he could not see himself climbing on the roof with one arm around me and one arm around Mark – as the waters crept ever higher and the winds howled. Besides I was pregnant again and I could see he was really scared – not willing to risk it.

As soon as daylight cracked we piled into the car clutching Mark and three little suit cases. We secured the house as best we could and left. We headed in the opposite direction from all the traffic which streamed at a snails pace out of the city. Bill drove to the lake Pontchartrain causeway – he thought we should head north if we could, and that was the quickest way to do that. We got there and found much commotion near the access to the bridge which was 26 miles long and directly north across the lake to Slidell. There was a small line of cars and trucks – some piled high with personal belongings and animals in crates. The rain was heavy now and the wind whipped angrily against the car. A policeman waved and hurried us along as we crossed the bridge threshold.

We were the last car to do so. The police closed the causeway behind us.

We drove as fast as we could in those awful conditions – no more than 25 - 30 miles per hour as the rain blinded us and the wind whipped the waves from the lake sometimes completely over our car as we moved further and further out over the wide open water of the lake. The bridge shook under us as we drove – we could not see the truck ahead of us anymore and we were both scared. I hugged Mark tightly to me in my lap – but he, with the innocence of a child – slept.

It seemed to take forever to get across the lake, but we made it a little after noon. The low lying land was already starting to flood. We drove on and stopped at the first Motel we came to. It looked clean and was slightly elevated off the highway. We got one of their last available rooms as the wind and rain howled and crashed around us.

It was five days before we were able to return. Camille hit the coast the next evening with a terrifying vengeance – destroying everything in its path and rearranging the entire coast line from New Orleans to Florida forever. It was devastating with much loss of life and property.

Our little house on Bissonet Drive had fared quite well. We were relived and happy to be home.

We did not have a washer or dryer – I washed Mark's clothes by hand – and my Mother had sent me a little washing boiler from London that she had had converted to US current - so that I could take care of washing my diapers. I boiled everything. Sometimes Bill would come home hungry and say.

"What's for dinner?" and pick up the lid of a pot on the stove and find a pair of his shorts or my bra – boiling merrily away. I would hang the clean blue-white diapers on the line in the garden to dry, the only problem was that the humidity would not allow them to dry. They would hang there several days and the birds would bomb them and I'd have to start over again.

I realized as I did quite often – I did not like living in New Orleans – life was stressful and hard with no car, and no family or friends close by. I would complain bitterly to my Mother when she would call me from London and she would get quite aggravated with me – calling me a spoiled brat. This in German was very strong and would have hurt - except I knew she did not, could not, understand – this was not London where there was a bus or train on every corner and you could walk to the local store. This was America and America is BIG and you needed a car to function here.

One day we got very sad news. My Mother's dear sweet Clifford in London had had a heart attack and they could not save him - he had been a very heavy smoker and that had been a detriment. She was devastated and I did not know how to help her. I suggested she come out to visit – she was overdue with that anyway. So she did but before coming I told her to go to her doctor and have a complete physical because after Clifford's death she had been so depressed and had let herself become so very run down. She did do that and it made me feel better about her coming out to see us.

She arrived two weeks later and we picked her up from the afternoon flight from New York which was her first point of entry into the US from London.

The first thing she did is open all the windows in her bedroom and throw the screens into the yard. Our windows were all screened against bugs and lizards and besides we had air conditioning. This was the Deep South. A universe unknown to her.

"Freddie – what are you doing – you cannot have those windows open like that, with no screens – you will let all the bugs in Louisiana in and the cold air-conditioned air out."

"I cannot stand it," she wailed pathetically. "It gives me claustrophobia to be shut in like that."

It took a while, but she finally adjusted. However, then she complained about quite another problem. She claimed that there were scratching noises coming from the closet in her room – it was keeping her awake and gave her the creeps. Bill checked the closet and there was nothing there that could cause any scratching – but she continued to complain about it. Finally Bill sat in her room till around mid-night one night in the pitch dark, and low and behold, there was indeed scratching coming from the closet.

The next day he tore the closet apart and found a trap door leading to the underside of the bathtub in the adjoining bathroom. The trap was designed to gain access to the underside of the tub should that be necessary for some reason. Well, as we now discovered, much to our horror – it was very necessary, because the entire underside of that bathtub was a rat's nest. At night the rats had been eating around the wooden trap door trying to gain access to the bedroom – hence the scratching noise!

After this excitement, everything returned to normal, and we all finally settled down. But after about three weeks into my Mother's visit the phone rang and it was Betty Brewer my Mother's dearest friend, who was 'house sitting' for my Mum in Wimbledon, while she was gone. Betty had picked up the mail and found a letter from the clinic that Fred had gone to before coming over. What did I think – should she open it?

"Of course Betty, please open it – I wonder what they want," I said emphatically.

The letter stated that a very important test had come back inconclusive and would have to be repeated as soon as possible. To please contact them for an appointment.

"Please telephone them Betty and tell them Fred is out of the country and she will connect with them as soon as she gets back."

Betty said she would - but said that was strange. I was a tad bit worried and wondered what that was all about too but said nothing to alarm my Mother.

My Mother stayed with us for five weeks and called to let us know when she was home safe again in Wimbledon. Three days later I got another call from her. This time she called and told me that she had arranged for the little Fiat that was parked in Calais in France – to be shipped over to me. It was being loaded onto a freighter as we were speaking and would arrive in New Orleans in six weeks.

The Fiat had 'left hand' drive and was kept in Calais so that Fred and Clifford could leave their British 'right hand' drive Jaguar in Dover when they wanted to go down to the summer place we had in Switzerland on Lake Geneva. They would park the Jaguar in Dover, take the ferry, then pick up the Fiat and drive down. It was a long way to drive from the French coast though France and Germany at the break neck speed you were forced to drive on the Autobahn. They found it too dangerous to drive sitting on the wrong side of the car especially if my Mother was driving down alone – so they had purchased the little Fiat.

While in New Orleans Fred had found out how cut off you are in America – if you do not have a car. It was a problem she had never experienced before. After five weeks of being house bound – except for weekends when Bill was home she realized that my complaints had not been without foundation. Suddenly I was not such a 'spoiled brat' after all – so she sent me the Fiat! I was thrilled.

Life settled down and became much easier for me. I could now go out and about and shopping if I needed to. Bill still had to do his rounds of the shipyards on the Gulf coast – selling them special paint like anti-corrosion and anti-barnacle for the ships they were building – but I was now not stuck home alone for days at a time.

One day I was out with Mark in his little stroller when we came upon a lady walking her dog. It was the sweetest little dog and very friendly and started sniffing at Mark in passing. Mark let out a scream as if his foot had been bitten off and I stopped in horror. I apologized to the lady and started to pet the dog who was very happy to accept the attention. Mark continued to scream and squirm in terror and I was beside myself. What on earth could I do. No child of mine was going to stay afraid of dogs – or ANY critter – come to think of it.

Bill was away for three more days and I stewed alone on my problem. I bought a newspaper and started to look at the advertisements and For Sale notices on the back page. Sure enough, it was my lucky day - my eye caught a notice advertising Puppies For Sale. NOT just ANY puppies – but Dachshund puppies! I had grown up with Dachsies. I could hardly wait for Mark to wake up from his nap, so that I could bundle him into the car so we could go and check out those puppies.

We arrived at the address listed in the notice. It was a small run down house a little off the beaten track on the edge of town, with a fenced yard in front. I lifted Mark out of the car and rang the doorbell. An army of dog voices responded loudly and Mark jumped in my arms. A lady came to the door in a bathrobe and hair curlers and opened it a crack. Just a crack because of the excited commotion around her slippered feet.

"Good afternoon – I'm sorry to disturb you but I have come about the puppies. I was wondering if I could look at one?"

"Oh Yea – hold on a minute while I get them all under control." She shut the door and very soon all the barking and commotion stopped.

The door opened again and she ushered me into her living room which was dark and poky. Heavy dark green drapes hung closed across the window, and every couch and chair in that living room was shredded and in pieces, towels or blankets covering them. There were dirty dishes everywhere and the air was hot and stale and smelled of smoke and somehow - funky - like a deep woods toilet. She switched on an overhead light attached to a ceiling fan that was turning lazily, moving that funky smelling air around. She grabbed a blanket and spread it on the floor. Then she turned, went into a bedroom and came back out with four wiggling screeching baby Dachsies and set them down on the blanket.

I looked at them and the house – the room – the lady – everything faded out of my consciousness except those precious puppies. I was mesmerized.

I bent down and sat Mark on the grimy blanket next to them and watched him squirm – not wanting to be there.

"It's alright Mark look – feel how soft they are – how sweet," and I held his hand out to one of them to lick. He looked at me – his eyes wide with wonder and then one of the puppies came over to him and climbed on his lap and nudged him in the tummy with his nose. His hand came down and gently touched it and the puppy licked it and then started licking his face with the energy of a puppy needing attention. Mark giggled, squirming in delight and tried to hold him – not in the least bit afraid now. I was beside myself with relief. This cute little puppy had found 'his person' very quickly and I was both relieved and pleased but he was a strange color – I had never seen one like it and I turned and asked the lady about it.

"Yes, I cannot explain it, but every time those two dogs have a litter there is one that color in the batch." The little dog was 'Silver' and cute as a button.

"My son seems to like that one and the puppy seems to like him – how much is he?"

"He be $75 – I give you a discount 'cos he be the runt of the litter and he be that funny color."

I wrote the lady a check which seemed like a fortune – but there was no price too high to pay for this end result, and so the three of us happily left the squalid house and headed home to ours. I was on cloud nine. The only thing that had been missing in my life for some time now - was a dog.

Bill returned home two days later and went into instant angry shock when he saw our new addition. He was not happy and did not approve – actually he was the most angry that I had ever seen him. A side of my husband I would learn more about as time went on.

Bill went on and on about the dog in spite of the fact that he saw how much his son and the dog loved each other. It was really special to watch their interaction. According to Bill we did NOT NEED a dog – they were dirty, an added expense and a liability that was unnecessary.

I just listened patiently to his rant and finally said, "Bill I hear everything you are saying and I agree with none of it. I am not raising a child in this world that is scared of a dog – NO – of ANY critter. Did you never have a dog?"

He admitted he had not had one growing up but continued his tirade which he ended with, "OK – so just so you know - you threw the ball and YOU caught it. I don't want anything to do with it," and with that he slammed the den door and disappeared into his 'man cave' - the garage.

The next day was Saturday, and while I was cooking breakfast I checked on Mark who was on the floor in the den. Sitting there next to him was Bill – they were both rolling around playing with – yes – little wiggly Oscar who was having a blast crawling and licking on both of them. I said nothing and continued fixing breakfast – but now with a big smile on my face. I had named the puppy Oscar after the very first dog I had growing up in England when I was seven years old.

Bill stayed in his garage 'man cave' most of Sunday, sometimes taking Mark – to 'help' - in with him. Right before supper he came into the den from there, carrying Mark sitting in a wooden dog bed he had built. He proudly set it down and Mark rolled off and Oscar jumped in.

"Mark and I made this – we thought Oscar might like it. Do you have a blanket to put in it? And what are you feeding him – don't we need to get some real puppy food for him? We should take him to the Vet for a checkup too." I was speechless and just threw myself down on the couch in disbelief watching this amazing transformation.

And so the days flew by – time marches on. We were so very happy.

Mark and Oscar waiting for Dad to come home - 1967

CHAPTER 31 -

A MIRACLE AND A TRAUMATIC LOSS

B ill and I had lived and worked in the far east for a goodly while. Not together – but experiencing similar things. If we were 'hung up' in Vietnam due to mechanical problems with the airplane, we would sortie over to the local orphanage – usually run by French nuns and play with the kids - or feed them – or just generally help out.

Bill's little mine sweeper ship would tie up somewhere safe, and he and his guys would go to the nearest orphanage and play football, baseball or soccer with the kids – then they would have a BBQ and feed them.

One thing we learned very quickly from the nuns was that the plight of little girl children was much greater than boys. Boys -

even orphans once they were at least six years old – were needed and important. They could work. Little girls were considered useless. As a result, by the time they were five or six – they were earning a living on the streets. In those days we did not know about HIV/AIDS - but we had at least eighty-six different varieties of venereal disease and before many of these precious children could reach the age of eighteen or twenty – they were dead.

When in Saigon or in many other cities in the far east – you could tuck half a dozen small children into your suitcase. They would run 'in packs' looking for food or pandering for change, on any street corner. Small five and six year old girls would be carrying a younger child in their arms. It was tragic. However, in order for any child to have a legitimate future with 'real' paperwork and a family willing to adopt them it would take time. Lots of time.

The children that had the hardest time were the ones that were fathered by some of our military troops. They were 'half breeds' and did not fit into any society - and were shunned deplorably by all.

When still living in New Jersey I had looked into a society from whom you could adopt just such children. It was called The Pearl Buck Foundation and was founded by a wonderful lady who had lived in China for many years. She was an author and as the daughter of missionary parents, she had seen the need for just such a society as this to help the orphans. I called them and asked for information, but unfortunately the cost was beyond our ability to contemplate. It was very expensive and I was expecting a baby myself and so dropped the idea. Before our move to New Orleans however, we would find another group called Holt International that was a missionary group based in Eugene, Oregon and we would file paperwork with them for an orphaned baby girl.

In 1969 we were living in New Orleans and Bill and I were excitedly awaiting the birth of our second child - we wanted our family to be born close together. I had no form of reference, having been an only child, but Bill grew up with a slightly older brother and they were very close.

Dale Robert Scofield was born at Baptist Hospital in New Orleans on March 2nd, 1970.

Bringing Dale Home - March 1970

My Mother's cancer had returned with a vengeance in 1969 – she was terminal, but everyone kept that reality from me because I was very pregnant when that was made known. Upon her return to London, she went back to Kings College hospital to be re-tested. The result confirmed our greatest fear – she had cancer. It was pretty much everywhere and they could do nothing for her. She was forty-six years old. She, however, wanted more than anything in this world to be present when I had the baby, so she prepared herself and her doctors for her trip to New Orleans. They advised against it – but she was a feisty fighter and insisted they help her.

I had had much trouble with this pregnancy – especially the further along I got. If I relaxed, sat or laid down, that baby would start doing tumble sets in my stomach landing on painful and inappropriate places and keep me awake all night. Then he would stick a hand somewhere between my rib cage and manipulate my ribs.

Finally I went to my doctor on a Friday - exactly ten days before my due date and said, "Good Morning Doctor – I would just like to put you on notice, that if you do not take this baby out of me I am going to do it myself." I was as serious as a heart attack!

Unlike me however, he thought that was very funny – but after examining me, agreed to induce it. Be here in the hospital at O dark thirty on Monday morning he told me. I was - with a spring in my step!

My Mother was on an airplane the next day. We went and met her at the airport and I took one look at her and I knew she was dying. Why had nobody told me? Why would they keep that a secret? I said nothing but later after she had gone wearily to bed, I followed Bill into the garage into which he had escaped the minute we arrived home.

"Bill, why would you not tell me Freddie is dying?" He looked at me in total disbelief.

"Honey – no – why would you say that?" And then when he looked at my face he said very quietly, "How did you know? We did not want to upset you, you were having so much trouble with your pregnancy. We did not want to add to your stress." He came round the counter and held me very tight. Are you kidding – she is my Mother, a part of me – of course I would know the minute I laid eyes on her.

Dale Robert Scofield arrived at 4:30 Monday afternoon with the cord tightly wrapped around his neck and his little face dark blue. Had I waited till term I would have delivered a dead baby boy. That was why he was being so difficult and creating such pain and discomfort to me – he was strangling himself on the cord.

My Mother was in heaven – she loved that baby boy and could not tear herself away from him, but she was frail and needed to get special shots that she had brought with her from London. So twice a week Bill took her to the Metairie Clinic on West Esplanade and they gave her the shots which were very painful but kept her physically on her feet. She was feisty and a fighter and was prepared and willing to fight for every minute she could stay on this earth. After the fourth week however, she told us to book her flight – it was time for her to go home. If she waited any longer she was afraid she might not make it back.

She left very reluctantly and with great sadness two days later.

****

It was less than six weeks after she left us in New Orleans that Betty called and said it was time for me to come. Fred was fading fast and there was not much time. Bill had just left on a four week business trip to Japan, so I bundled up Mark and Dale and got on an airplane to London. The three of us moved into Fred's house in Wimbledon and took over the opposite wing from Fred's bedroom so as not to disturb her. The house was very un-English having been designed and built by a Canadian contractor ten years before. This was why Fred and Clifford had loved it so much. It had a wide open floor plan with a ginormous Great Room in the middle with a wing of bedrooms off it on each side.

Freddie was so very happy and excited to see the boys – especially her baby Dale, and promptly insisted I park him on her bed. I, however, was in shock - she was a living cadaver. Betty had warned me how thin and frail she was – but this was heart-breaking to see her like that and I was pretty much traumatized for the first few days.

Betty and Dick Brewer were life savers. One or both came over to Wimbledon every day on the bus from Stretham – they did not own a car. I do not to this day know how I would have lived through that time without their help. The doctor came every other day and brought Freddie her morphine – the cancer was everywhere. She was made comfortable and content to wait it out. No other medication was given to her and Dale slept on her bed at all times. Every so often I would hear "Clonk" - it would be Dale – he had rolled off the bed onto the soft thick carpet and Fred would be fast asleep.

In between them both sleeping on the bed and when Dale was awake, I would leave him lying on a blanket on the floor by the big window in the Great Room. When he was born he had a Yeast infection that covered his entire lower body. While carrying him I had had fits of craving for Marmite and the Brewers would send it to me from London. Marmite is a potent Yeast extract and we would eat it on toast for tea after we came home from school. It is the English excuse for Peanut Butter. The Yeast infection on Dale looked like a burn and was very sore. I could not put anything on it – it had to dry and fix itself – so it needed to be exposed to the air as much as possible. No diapers.

He was very young, 10 weeks old, and not moving around too much yet, so it was convenient to leave him there on that blanket by the window, if Fred called and needed something. He was safe and not going anywhere – unlike Mark who was running all over the house and garden. Sometimes I would come back to Dale on his blanket and he would be smiling and waving his arms and legs happily while peeing up the curtains!

My Mother's cancer was progressing, and now it had hit the brain. She had some strange mood changes and temper tantrums that was totally unlike her and I was worried for little Mark. He loved sitting with her in her big chair while she read to him or they played a game when she was not sleeping. He understood that she was sick – but I did not want him to have this memory of her when she was having a 'turn.' So when Dick and Betty arrived one evening after we had had quite a loud violent issue – I asked Dick if he would please take Mark back to America. I had called Bill's Mum and Dad and they had suggested if I could arrange it, to bring him to Philly. They would take care of him till I got back with Dale.

A week later Dick Brewer left with Mark and took him to stay in Philly. I was relieved because life was starting to get quite complicated and just having the baby to care for made things a lot easier. It was extremely traumatic and difficult to watch my beautiful, elegant Mother dissolve into this walking skeleton with skin stretched over bone. My children would never know her – how much fun she was – her endless positive attitude and intense sense of humor. She was now having trouble eating, swallowing – even the broth I would offer her was waved away.

Some days if it was warm and sunny I would help Freddie to

come and sit by the open French door to the garden. She loved that and would sit for hours in her nice big comfy easy chair that I pulled up to the window for her and wrapped a big blanket around her boney frame. She loved her garden and all the birds and little critters in it. She had a squirrel that would come to the open door and eat treats she had put out for it on the little table by the lamp.

That was where she was when she died She was forty-seven years old.

The Eagle was an orphan now and suffered greatly over this loss that only time could heal.

Or not.

Losing a parent is a very special loss – unlike any other – she was the only one I had ever had and now she was gone – the years to come without her stretched like an abyss – endlessly into the future.

"Freddie"

CHAPTER 32 -

TWO YEARS LATER

It was now three years since we had registered with Holt International the adoption agency in the Far East for a baby girl to adopt. Because of that Bill and I had decided that we would limit our own children to two. Holt had connected with us several times since Dale was born and sent us paperwork to fill out and honor. As I had mentioned before – while in the Far East it was possible to acquire any number of orphaned children running loose on the streets – but to adopt, legitimately, so that the child would be legal in the U.S and have papers to prove it, it would be time consuming and problematic. The paperwork alone was endless and boundless, and we would need home inspections and our children would need letters from their pediatricians that they were mentally and physically healthy.

Unbelievably with that we had 'push back' and discrimination issues from our pediatrician. This man had nine children of his own and another one on the way, but he was giving me grief about our decision. In New Orleans it was not understood that even though we could continue to have babies of our own – why in this world would we want to adopt one from a foreign country. We would know nothing about it - and we would not even know what it would looked like – go make more babies!

I was emotionally spent. EXCUSE ME DOCTOR – when I deliver my own children I have no idea what so ever what that child will look like either – do you? I will NOT make more babies – I WILL adopt one that has more needs than you, in your ignorance, could ever imagine - with or without your help I will do it.

To adopt a child like this in the grand scheme of things, was like picking up a grain of sand off the ocean floor. It meant nothing, totally meaningless – the ocean floor is an endless, boundless expanse of sand. To do it so that they have REAL paperwork,- to give ONE child a LIFE and a real family would be priceless. So it needs to happen one child at a time – and we wanted to start the chain.

By now we had been 'pregnant' with this child for approximately three plus years – when suddenly – we received a letter with a tiny one inch by one inch picture of a baby. We were so excited we could not think straight. However, thinking straight would be an immediate requirement when we looked closer at the tiny face above a set of numbers in the photograph.

The little girl was black.

We did not care in the least what color our new baby was going to be – but it needed to work for that child's life as well as for ours. If we had still been living in New Jersey that baby would have been on the next airplane to us – but we were now living in the deep south where life in the late 60's and early 70's was very different. When we first moved to New Orleans Bill had a very hard time getting in to the ship yards of the Gulf shore, to speak to the powers that be so that he could sell his paint. He was a YANKIE and it took him over a year of constant contact for him to get to be accepted by the folks down there. How impossible would it be for a white family with two golden haired little boys, to adopt – which is a choice – a black baby in Dixie?

We were heartbroken, but for everyone's safety, were forced to turn her away. I was depressed and defeated. The whole idea was to give a child a safe, loving home with a family and a new life. Here we were given that opportunity and had to turn it down. It was devastating.

A few weeks later however, our luck changed. We got another letter.

This little girl covered the entire one inch by one inch photograph with her sweet face and wild black hair sticking out everywhere. We expected a half American half Asian child – little Kim was full blooded Korean.

My hand shook as I signed the letter – as did Bill, and we accepted this precious little being into our lives. The letter stated that she was nine months old and in reasonably good health, and would be placed in foster care from the orphanage upon return of our letter. Life stood on its head. We were beyond excited.

Kim Soon Hee was to arrive in the care of a missionary returning home to America. Her port of entry into the United States would be Chicago. Please arrange for pick up there.

Bill and I jumped through a million hoops to get ready, and on the big day of arrival we decided that he should babysit the boys and I would go to Chicago and pick up our baby girl – our daughter.

Bill and the boys drove me to the airport in Kenner on the big day. I had to be in Chicago at two p.m. so that I could be in place for the arrival of Korean Air Flight 32. There were about eight children arriving to be met by their adoptive parents. We all gathered nervously in the waiting area specially allocated for us new parents. Due to weather, the flight would be about 30 minutes late. We all shuffled around the room – got more coffee – went to the bathroom. Most of us had waited three plus years for this moment – we could wait 30 more minutes. BUT these 30 minutes were worse than the three years – thirty times longer!

Finally the airplane arrived and they deplaned the special children first. It was traumatic. Some of the children were older and scared and in shock as they held tightly to the hand of their companions. They came off slowly and merged into the mayhem of welcome. Then came a gentleman carrying a little girl wrapped in a big blanket half asleep.

I approached him and introduced myself and asked if this could be Kim Soon Hee.

"Indeed it is," the gentleman said and handed me my daughter with a big relieved smile.

"Congratulations, she is the sweetest little girl – she slept a good bit of the way so she will probably be awake from now on."

I reached out and took her out of the arms of the kind missionary that had taken such good care of her on this long flight. My world stood still. All the years of preparation, trauma and wait – now a memory.

KIM Soon Hee took one look at this wild woman with the white hair and ginormous big eyes and started to engage her lungs which were in fantastic shape. She let the whole world know that she was in dire peril and to please help!

I walked to my flight home to New Orleans to the accompaniment of a screaming baby girl that I could not calm down. She was in total shock – as was I! Finally about forty minutes into our flight – she gave up in complete and total exhaustion and slept.

At last I was able to examine my new baby girl. She was bigger than I expected – not heavier just bigger. Her little face was weather beaten and her little cheeks were red with a thick skin over them from having been exposed to a Korean winter while being worn on some caregiver's back when working outside. I gently rubbed my finger over her little cheek. It was like leather. I spent the remainder of the two hour flight just holding her and smiling at the world around me. I thought my heart would burst with happiness. She was beautiful – and she was mine.

Bill met me with the two boys in tow to check out their new sister. It was with much happiness, emotion and commotion that we drove home to Metairie and the rest of our lives.

The Eagle was happy again – feeling love, fulfilment and stability in its constantly changing world.

Mark, Dale, and Kim – on Kim's Second Birthday

CHAPTER 33

OCTOBER 1974

Our life continued happily on with three babies and a dog. Every day was a challenge in the deep south – a white family with two precious little boys raising a beautiful Asian baby girl. A first in New Orleans.

"Very cute – But who will she marry?" I was casually asked when parading her around the neighborhood. I was blown away. My daughter was nine months old – I did not care who she would marry.

"Why would you do such a thing. You could have increased your family with natural children."

How ignorant and narrow minded is that? We had apparently thrown a ball - and now we were running with it full pelt and loving every minute. Life was full, busy but much fun.

Also, thanks to the money that I inherited upon my Mother's death, we had been able to upgrade to a wonderful new, bigger house one block from the lake. We moved into Page Drive and settled down with everyone having a bedroom – the master bedroom being on the second floor with French doors letting out to a balcony across the entire front of this Southern style colonial house. We loved it and stayed there many years as it was close to all the best public schools.

It was here that I received a letter in October of 1974 from Pan American World Airways. I picked up the mail and looked at it in total disbelief. What in the world could Pan Am want from me.

In a nutshell, the letter basically stated that they were sorry that my employment with Pan Am had been terminated due to my pregnancy with my son Mark. The Union had gone to court in 1972, challenged that decision on behalf of the Stewardesses and had won. After all, no pink slips had been issued to 'pregnant' fathers. As a result, Pan American was happy to inform me that my job as a stewardess with them was secure and to please call Pan American at this number in Miami, to be reinstated as soon as practical. They were looking forward to my return.

I must have read and re read it six times. I sat down on a chair in my kitchen in total disbelief. In 1966 Pan American had forced me into 'mother hood and apple pie', and issued me a "pink slip" before my pregnancy status was even confirmed. Now I had three babies under seven years old and they were telling me I could resume flying as soon as practical. The world is truly – mad.

Two weeks later I called the number in Miami stated in the letter. A very cheerful Personnel Department employee was delighted that I had called, and informed me that all was in fact well and they would be delighted if I could return in time for the next class.

EEEERRRR NO – sorry but that was not happening any time soon.

I explained my situation and the employee said, "No problem. You just call us when things settle down and you are ready. We will put you on the list for 'Returning Mothers' and look forward to seeing you when it suits. You will be returned to your 'A' pay scale that was in place when you left. We now have a 'B' scale for new hire flight attendants – but that will not apply to you. Please call us any time and we will assign you to the next class here at the Miami Training Academy."

I sat for the longest time with the dead receiver in my hand. I could not believe what I had just heard. My job with Pan American was secure and they were waiting for me to return – as a Returning Mother.

Thank you Flight Attendant Union. I have not the slightest idea when that return could/might be – but a wonderful ace to hold in my pocket.

And I did. For ten more years.

****

In the meantime we were having visitors from across the Atlantic. Betty and Dick Brewer's son Christopher, Carol's younger brother, came over for a visit. He was seventeen and fell in love with New Orleans. We had a lot of fun showing him around. He was blown away by how advanced he thought America was compared to England – he LOVED the central heating and air conditioning.

One night shortly after his arrival we were woken up in the middle of the night with loud crashing and banging and yelling coming from the direction of his bedroom across the other side of the house from us. Bill and I went rushing over to see what was happening and found Chris thrashing around on the floor in his closet – in the night he had mistaken it for the bathroom.

The following summer Dick and Betty arrived for a visit. After showing them around New Orleans we took them on a trip to the beautiful Smoky Mountains and Gatlinburg. They loved it. Betty bought a beautiful little Clipper Ship made of delicately spun glass and a porcelain magnolia blossom, skillfully painted to look like the real thing. She treasured both her whole life and they were close to her still, in her bedroom near her bed, when she died - sixty years later.

We had a great time and just like Christopher, they loved everything American and could not believe how BIG America was. With their upcoming visit looming, we needed to make a decision about a new car. The old Chevy was not going to be able to accommodate all of us and we were worried it would not make the trip and stay in one piece. So we went car shopping and ended up with a beautiful new Oldsmobile wagon.

It was perfect and we went to pick it up one evening after Bill got home from work. It was located behind the main building of the dealership in a large parking lot and when we finally found it - it was not alone. Sitting right in front of the shiny vehicle was the saddest, filthiest ragamuffin of a dog. He had no hair and no teeth - not sure about one eye - and was as skinny as a rail.

My heart broke for him - but Bill shooed him away so that we could get to the car and put the children in it. I hung about for a little while trying to get the dog to come to me - but he was scared and Bill was calling me to leave it alone and get in the car. We drove off with me in tears and the kids upset.

The car was amazing - beautiful - a big upgrade for us, and it drove like a dream. We were definitely all set for our long trip to the mountains.

That dog however, I could not get out of my head.

We were home about five minutes - Bill and the kids were settled in the den watching TV. I packed a bag with dog food and water, a spare leach and my resolve. I climbed into my little Fiat and drove back to the lot. A slow soft rain had started falling and it was getting dark.

I pulled into the slot at the dealership that had held our new car and got out. I looked around frantically with a sinking feeling in my stomach feeling sure he as gone. My eyes swept the parking lot and finally locked onto a lump that had taken shape under a bush at the fence line. It was him.

I opened the can of dog food onto a plate and poured water into a small bowl as the wet mist started to become rain. I walked slowly towards the dog who suddenly backed deeper into the bush. I stopped - talking quietly, soothingly the whole time. I set the food and water down and backed off and then sat down on the wet pavement in the dimming light and falling rain.

We looked at each other across maybe fifty feet of concrete. Neither of us moved. I coaxed gently, softly - then silently just watched him. After a while I started coaxing him again and ever so s-l-o-w-l-y he started to crawl out towards the food - on his belly. I remained motionless and silent as he reached the food and inhaled the whole can in a millisecond. He climbed hesitantly to his feet and swaying drunkenly, drinking the water in the now pouring rain.

Very slowly I too, got up. We both looked at each other trying to figure out the next step in the darkness with the soft rain blurring our vision. I could tell the poor animal was very close to death - he stumbled and nearly fell and then sat down - too week to go anywhere. He would not let me approach him however, so I turned very slowly and in a soft voice begged him follow me as I made my way to the car. I opened the passenger side door which faced him, and slowly went around to the driver's side - quietly just talking to him. I sat and waited. It was dark now, the door lights illuminating the falling rain.

Suddenly a wet, smelly, black, dirty, scruffy body landed on the passenger seat next to me - exploding through the open door in a spray of mud and water. He sat there dripping water off a fur less body, looking at me with one blind and one soft brown intelligent eye, ears pricked forward in anticipation, as though he had done this all his life. We sat and smiled at each other as water dripped off of both of us in puddles on the floor.

Finally we drove home deep in silent conversation with each other. Bill was waiting - worried now that it was dark and raining hard. He had the lights on and the garage door open and I drove straight in.

He took one look at this poor bedraggled animal and said, "There is no way we can bring him in the house. He will have to stay in the garage - who knows what he might be infested with - we cannot risk the kids or Oscar."

I grudgingly agreed and took one of the large towels I had set out on the counter and gently dried him off. Then I set out the heavy blanket and encouraged him to sit on it and lay down. He seemed now like putty in my hands as I covered him with an old comforter his one big brown eye soft with gratitude. He knew he was home - and I knew his name would be Ben, after the 1972 horror movie "BEN" - with the child that had a pet rat called that. HE was my pet rat - who knows what horror had confronted him before I found him.

Early the next morning Ben and I left for the Metairie Small Animal Hospital. I had been taking Oscar there for the last two years and the staff greeted me cheerfully when I walked in. My vet, Jim however, took one look at the animal that accompanied me and threw up his hands in horror.

"OH MY GOODNESS GI - what in the world are you expecting me to do with that?"

"I hope you can 'fix' him" I said smiling broadly. He took the leash out of my outstretched hand and led Ben to the examining table.

"I don't know where to begin," he said helplessly. "Where in the world did you encounter this creature. I cannot even tell what it is - a dog - yes - but what, I don't know." He looked up at me in total disbelief - but his eyes held a bright twinkle of merriment. "OK - leave him with me - I will call you later with news and an update when I have given him a good look over."

"Thank you Jim - his name is Ben."

Jim called me at six o'clock that evening. He told me that Ben had had a bath and that they had treated his bare, furless leathery skin with some soothing oil and he was doing well and smelled good! He was friendly, had eaten well and seemed calm, content and sleeping comfortably. He was quite a young dog - maybe one but not more than two years old - however, the bad news was that he had very bad heart worm that would cut his life short. Sadly, they were also too bad to attempt the cure - he was too fragile and would not live through it. If I wanted to keep him he would have to stay in the hospital for a few days till they could stabilize his condition and give him all his necessary shots - or I could put him down.

Exactly one week later Jim called me from the Metairie Small

Animal Clinic and informed me that Ben had grown a soft black fuzz all over his body and they had determined that I owned a Black Lab - and he was ready to come home!

Ben was a wonderful character - loved dearly by all he met. The whole world loved and adopted him as a wonderful gift and addition to the Scofield family. Ben's world was suddenly happy, healthy and full of love - just sadly - too short. He lived for exactly one year and died peacefully in my arms.

He always remained a "vagabond" however - happy to be a domestic indoor dog during the day - BUT the minute it got dark - he needed OUT. He roamed and checked out the entire neighborhood - a silent, happy black shadow - returning home with the arrival of the first streaks of dawn. I would hear him coming as he passed by our bedroom window - the tags of his collar giving him away.

He and I had a special bond - he was almost human and we could emotionally connect in a way I had never experienced before with an animal. We were soul mates. One morning I heard him pass the window and Bill got up to let him in. I rolled over under the warm covers and closed my eyes smiling sleepily when I heard him bound down the long hallway to our bedroom. He always did that and then curled up happily on the floor on my side of the bed.

NOT TODAY.

Today Ben came flying down the hall in such excitement that he slithered and slid around the corner on his butt on the linoleum to our bedroom. Today he jumped up on the bed straddling my body, shaking with excitement - and dropped something on my chest. I jumped up screaming - thrashing around wildly, not knowing what it was. Ben fell off the bed in the mayhem and just stood there looking at me, his wonderful soft brown eye filled with hurt confusion. He had brought me the most wonderful present that he had found in someone's trash can and because he loved me so much - he had not eaten it, but brought it home - for me. Seeing him like that broke my heart and made me look around to find what it was - since it did not slither, have legs or run off. And sure enough, there in the corner of the room, lay a large piece of pizza pie.

A present - with love from Ben.

****

The kids were now at an age where it was time for us to take a trip to Germany and introduce them to family. I had not been home since my Mother died and then I did not go to Germany, so Omi – my grandmother, Käthe Sperling, and my Mother's sister, Ilse, had not met Dale and Kimmie.

We made plans with Dick and Betty Brewer to rent an old farm house in the Welsh countryside big enough to accommodate three families for two weeks. Bill and I and our three kids, Dick and Betty plus their daughter Carol and her two sweet girls Karen and Anita.

We flew on Pan Am to Hamburg and had a wonderful week there showing off our family to all and everyone in the know that we were there. Then we flew to London and met up with the Brewers in Victoria Station on our way to Wales.

There we had a blast and Karen and Anita - aged 9 and 7- were enthralled with little Kimmie and loved to take control of her on our many outings. The weather did us proud and stayed warm and sunny so the girls had no problem manipulating her little stroller on our ventures forth.

Dale, Anita, Kimmie, Karen, and Mark

It was on one of these outings through the beautiful Welsh countryside that we came across a darling little chapel created out of the local rocks and built into the steep side of a hill. It was very old as was the tall oak tree under whose giant canopy rested a cluster of dilapidated gravestones. Bill went over to look at one that was set a little to one side and was totally blown away when he read what was left of the inscription. The gravestone belonged to a child who had died in the 9th century.

Coming from a country that at best was just 200 years old he could not wrap his arms around that. Yes, Wales was O-L-D!

CHAPTER 34 -

SIX YEARS LATER

T he happy years of marriage to Bill and raising the kids flew by in what seemed like a heartbeat and right into a life changing hurricane.

We were raising a family in the deep south - an alien environment - totally alone. My Mother and my family in England were gone and Bill's Mum and Dad were in Philly. We had trouble 'fitting in' – we were different. We were Yankees. Bill with a foreign wife that no one could understand, and an adopted child of another race. Friends were hard to find. If I liked a

female that I had met – Bill did not like her husband. Dead end. All Bill's friends were at the ship yards and women were not involved in that friendship. His interests were totally different from mine and he spent a lot of time pursuing them, leaving me alone with the kids. Mine, and it seemed - everyone else's. Some days I felt like the old woman in the shoe!

He was adamant he did not want to join a church and I had to fight to get the kids baptized. Because of my background with the church I was determined they would be baptized – in any denomination – it did not matter - except Catholic. When they were old enough they could make up their own minds as to which church suited them – but baptized they would be.

Mark was baptized Church of England in the little chapel in Dulwich where we were married, on one of our trips back there, and Dale and Kim were baptized together, Presbyterian, by a Pastor Bill liked and we met at some party.

Life became emotionally unbearably stressful – I felt lost. Alone. Cut off. Broken. I had always had some problems with my lower back – but over time with more and more stress and no one to talk it out with - I was in big trouble.

Bill and I grew further and further apart. He spent all his spare time when not working at the ship yards at the YMCA playing basketball, or at our local club. He had turned down a management position – for the second time – with his company. He was not interested in "flying a desk" in an office when he could be out and about in the ship yards having fun with his friends. I stayed home with the kids, unable to join him in any physical activities at the club, because physically I was becoming an invalid.

Emotional stress can cause physical problems, and sure

enough, one morning I was unable to get out of bed and in excruciating pain. I was piled into an ambulance and hauled off to Baptist Hospital where I had back surgery by Dr. Llewellyn, a neurosurgeon on staff there. He was great – this was my central nervous system after all - but in 1976 it was still a big deal – unlike now. A friend and neighbor came to the hospital to visit me and was directed to my room. He came in and looked at the person in the bed and decided this was not me – and left. I was that unrecognizable. It took me almost a whole year to recoup my strength and my health.

Things continued to be unbalanced and spiraling downward - and in 1979 Bill and I divorced.

It was devastating, traumatic and life altering for all five of us.

In spite of the fact that we owned the house – bought outright with money left to me after my Mother died – money was always tight. Bill did not want to be a manager which would have given us a nice financial boost, but he also refused to allow me to get a job in spite of the fact that all three kids were now in school. This apparently would be some kind of a stigma that he felt he could not outlive.

Things got complicated now, because in New Orleans, due to 'Napoleonic Law' you had to live separately for one year before you could file for divorce - and Bill decided HE was not leaving. OK, so I went to the bank to get money for a down payment for an apartment for the kids and I to move into. After we had paid off the house we still had $35,000 left in our joint account till we decided what we would do with it. Under the circumstances this would now come in very handy to get us settled and for me to find a job.

Imagine my amazement when I discovered there was only

$1,800 left in the account. It seems my husband had taken it into his head to play the stock market. The only problem was – unlike his Mother who was a very savvy lady, played and did well in the market – he was neither savvy nor lucky and managed to lose it all. He also did not feel it was necessary to inform me of any of this.

The Eagle was forever changed by the heart wrenching happenings of the last year. Now, again, it needed to regain equilibrium and so paused a moment, standing very straight and still, on the tallest branch of a mighty Cypress tree overlooking the expanse of lake Pontchartrain. Being close to water always calmed and stilled a troubled mind. The gentle lapping of the waves fanned by the soft wind - eased the stress - all the while absorbing this new low blow. The Eagle was facing so many heavy, unimaginably heart breaking challenges – no money and no job were just two of the lesser ones of note.

Time stood - frozen.

Finally the mighty bird, smoothed its ruffled feathers and slowly – with grit and determination - spread its giant wings to test the breeze. There was confidence in their strength as the Eagle breathed in the fresh warm air off the wide expanse of water below - and then gently launched out over it.

****

After the divorce I got a job as secretary to the Manager of Nursing at Children's Hospital in New Orleans. The only thing that stood out during that time was the fact that I was held up at gun point at 11:30 during my lunch break in the parking lot, fifty feet from the front door of the Hospital. I had just unlocked my car and was about to get in when someone came up behind me and stuck a gun in my ribs.

I paused in mid action and heard the bullet click into place in the chamber.

"Don't make a sound and don't move or turn around," a voice said quietly behind me. I did nothing. I froze. NO my BODY froze – my brain was going a mile a minute. I had always thought that if such a thing were to happen to me – I would faint dead away. NO SUCH THING – your brain takes charge and as the adrenalin kicks in - you react exactly as you should, with intelligent resolve.

"What do you want?" I asked this pathetic creature without moving.

"Gimme yer purse and yer keys – and then git in the car" he said poking me hard in the ribs with the gun. A pause while I let that sink in, and then I slowly handed him both without turning around. I proceeded to take a long deep breath without moving and then said calmly.

"I will NOT get into the car." A pause – then, "SHOOT ME!" I dared him – feeling sure he would not risk drawing attention to himself being this close to the front door of the hospital with people going in and out and a security guard in the front lobby. I however, was not into being driven to his part of the "hood" to be gang raped by his friends – I would rather be shot where I stood.

"Go ahead – Shoot me." I repeated leaning on the open door of my car for support and closing my eyes in anticipation, a silent prayer on my lips.

Needless to say – nothing happened and I heard him hurriedly depart with my belongings. Two days later they burgled my house and stole everything they could carry. I had a wonderful black Labrador Retriever in the house called Sammie and she helped them a lot by pointing out all the points of interest. "Over there is the TV – Yes and if you turn right into the bedroom you will find all the jewelry - and the silver is in the dining room – no NOT that draw, silly – that other drawer!" She loved everybody and was happy to see them – it broke the monotony of her day. Problem was - I loved her.

Soon after this I got a job as Operations and Dispatcher Manager for a small airplane charter company called 'Jet America' based at Lakefront airport. It was a lot of fun and I loved all the cute young pilots that I sent out on trips every day in our Navaho and King Air airplanes. We were a family and I worried about them like a mother hen till they returned safely to base.

Pilots Party - Jet America

I had moved out of Metairie and now lived in Uptown New Orleans at Riverbend - where St Charles and Carrolton Avenue met at a giant turn of the river – hence the name Riverbend. The roof of my house was 16 feet below sea level and a tall levee separated me safely from the mighty Mississippi. I walked my dogs along the top of the levee almost every evening and enjoyed watching the traffic on the river and the atmosphere of the Big Easy.

It was on a walk like this along the top of the levee one evening, that I accidentally interrupted a drug deal. I was walking along enjoying the peaceful flowing of the mighty river bathed in the sun slowly sinking into the horizon and turning the sky into a brilliant pink and orange masterpiece. My two dogs were running way ahead of me excitedly reading every blade of grass they ran over as though they were pages in the Evening Paper giving them all the local news of the day – or even the week.

As I walked I was suddenly aware of a huddled group of maybe five men at the base of the levee on the river side. They were very engrossed in deep conversation and some gesticulating wildly as though in anger while others were stuffing small plastic bags into their pockets. It was not a happy scene and they suddenly became aware that they were being observed – by me. I noticed that one of the men – the one with his back to me that was waving his arms around and seemed to be in charge of the group, had what looked very much like a firearm stuck in the back of his pants. It kept showing when he lifted his arm in the air which pulled his shirt up to expose it. I increased my pace as they all fell silent and turned to look at me then started to fan out and begin to climb up the side of the levee in my direction.

At this moment I became aware that a long freight train had begun its slow trek along the rails at the base of the levee - way down by the street - and cut me off. I had hoped to call the dogs and turn and run down the grassy slope to Riverbend and the restaurant with the little outdoor tables full of people enjoying the evening – but that was now impossible. I tried to look unperturbed and continued walking – my mind going a mile a minute. The train whistle blew three long loud blasts of warning when it came to the path next to the Riverbend restaurant where people could access the levee. A warning seemingly directed specially for me since all five of the men had now made it to the top of the levee and stood across my path.

I patted the back pocket of my jeans and felt the comforting bulge of my tiny revolver which a friend had given me after the incident in front of Children's Hospital. My racing brain did indicate to me that the tiny Mafia Princess weapon would not be much help against these five strapping men - and had better remain my secret and stay put.

"Hi guys – beautiful evening to spend on the levee," I heard myself say – hoping they did not detect the slight quiver in my voice.

"It sure is," the one with a big belly and his shirt hanging out that I thought might be the ring leader replied gruffly.

At this moment I heard my dogs barking loudly and in unison as though excited. My eyes looked past the men who had their backs to the commotion – being totally focused on me. All five turned in unison following my gaze to see what the commotion was. The commotion turned out to be three joggers and a man on a bicycle. My dogs hate bicycles and was letting its owner know this with loud abandon.

"Excuse me folks," I said diving through a small gap in the group while their attention was temporarily diverted. "I have to rescue that poor man from my dogs."

With that I ran the fifty or so feet between them and me like a gazelle chasing a hare.

"You are a sight for sore eyes gentlemen," I said softly upon arriving breathlessly in their stunned presence. "Please pretend we know each other – enough Bingo and Willie – enough, good dogs – heel," I threw out to my excited dogs already collecting at my feet.

"Are you alright – are you in trouble – is it those men?" one of the runners said taking my hand as though in greeting.

"Right on all counts gentlemen – thank you – you arrived in the nick of time – and my dogs caused enough commotion that they were distracted enough that I was able to blow through them and get here in one piece." At this we all turned to look from whence I had come and saw the scruffy group of guys casually meandering their way back down the levee to the river where a small boat I had not noticed before, had been pulled up in the weeds and tied to a dead tree.

****

Time and life had progressed and I now had the money I needed to buy a new car. I had made up my mind I wanted to buy "all American" and decided on a small Chevy sedan that I had seen at the local dealer. It was inexpensive but big enough for me and the kids – so I piled them all into my old Fiat and off we went to buy my new car. It was very cute and shiny and the kids got a big charge out of the fact that they had to open the big glass door of the dealership so that we could drive it off the floor and out of the showroom.

I had no garage at my house and so parked the car out front. One morning I came out to go to work and I stopped dead in my tracks. There was no car parked in front of the house. I thought I was hallucinating – but no – there was no car. I walked to the corner next door to me that was a flower shop – in case I had left it around there last night because someone was parked in front of my house when I had come home, and I just did not remember. The street was empty.

I went back into the house and called the local police. They came and were very kind but not very hopeful that it would be found. They claimed it was a perfect "catch" for car thieves and it probably was already in a million little pieces parts that they could sell. They were right and the car never surfaced.

It was now 1982 and I was offered a job as Chief Purser with the Delta Steamship Company on the paddle steamer 'Mississippi Queen.' There were two "Queens" that based in New Orleans and traveled up the river as far as De Paul – the 'Delta Queen' was quite a bit smaller and older and the Mississippi Queen that was newer and bigger.

I decided to try it because I was considering returning to fly with Pan Am and this would give me a good feeling of timing with regards to my children. Could I be gone for days at a time. How would that work. As Chief Purser I would be in charge of hiring and firing the crew, the safety and comfort of the passengers and $10,000 of cash needed on every the trip. I would work eight weeks on and four weeks off as we proceeded up the Mississippi River. We would "choke a willow" by pulling over and putting the front gang plank ashore in order to visit Plantation Homes or different places of interest.

I loved the job – it was a lot of fun with different crew people in costume and a typical eighteenth century piano player beating the keys on the brightly lighted aft deck till all hours of the night. Our passengers partied, gambled and danced the night away as the big paddle wheel threw up shimmering water and foam from the river that sparkled and danced in the lights that had been strung all around the entire ship - as we glided along in the silent blackness of that mighty river.

I worked one rotation. It was a disaster - things were not going well with the kids who were living with their dad in Metairie. Their school work was affected almost immediately, bedtime was tearful and traumatic and there was no peace at the homestead.

Mummy could not be gone for days on end. At least - not yet.

Subsequently I found a job as Manager in the "Le Cafe" lounge at the oldest and most famous hotel in the French Quarter of New Orleans – The Monteleone on Royal Street. It did not pay much but I met a lot of influential people there, that could steer my life in any direction I wanted and were happy and eager to do it. I did not however need a new direction – I had one - it was going back from whence I had come, to Pan American World Airways. I just needed to be patient – and wait till the time was right.

Little did I know that my airline training from years ago would come in mighty handy one busy night. I was walking back to Le Cafe through the crowded bar of revelers enjoying a night out in the French Quarter after escorting one of my customers out to a cab. Suddenly, an elderly man – looking very much out of place in this environment, dressed in shabby tattered clothing turned away from the bar with a full glass of beer in hand and collapsed in a heap on the floor. As he whirled round and fell, his heavy glass of beer became a missile – heading for the ceiling and smashing somewhere out of sight – the escaping liquid baptizing some in a laughing group of revelers. The music was loud and the bar packed with lively folks from all over the world enjoying their time in the Big Easy - totally unaware of the sudden crisis. I jumped at the suddenness of the movement as did a couple of people closest to the old man. He lay there motionless, in a heap of dirty torn clothing - but no one went to his aid. The happy revelers thinking him to be some drunken 'bum' off the street - which he probably was – needing to sleep it off. Ignore him - which they did.

I ran over to the filthy scruffy heap on the floor and rolled him over. His face was dirty and deathly pale – he was frothing at the mouth and smelled of yesterday's liquor mixed with today's body odor. I yelled at the people closest to me to call an ambulance while I pulled the dirty shirt away from his throat and tried to find a pulse. There was none. I proceeded to start CPR. At this point one of the doormen joined to help me but I begged him to go meet the ambulance. I turned the man's greasy face to me and swished out his mouth but there was no obstruction – then I wiped his mouth with the corner of my jacket and proceeded to do mouth to mouth resuscitation. At this point a gentleman had disentangle himself from the onlookers and the mayhem around the bar and asked if he could help. I quickly showed him how to count and do the compressions while I continued trying to blow air into the man's lungs. It seemed to go on forever but in reality maybe only three or four – at the most - five minutes had elapsed before I heard the sirens of the Emergency units from Charity Hospital that were on duty nightly in the Quarter. The medics rushed in and took the situation over and out of my tired, aching, grateful hands.

A crowd had now gathered to observe the excitement, as I straightened up stiffly wiping my mouth on the sleeve of my jacket. I thanked the gentleman profusely for his help before escaping the cheering crowd - running like a cheetah into the closest Ladies Room. I sank my head into the first available sink and washed my face and rinsed my mouth with clean fresh water. Then I looked at myself in the mirror – reliving the whole thing in my mind with the crazy wild looking person staring back at me - then promptly threw up.

The old man lived to retell the tale to his buddies on the levee in the 9th Ward.

Soon after this I met a man at the hotel that made me a really good job offer, and I took it. It was to be Manager of an old German restaurant called Kolbs that he owned, on St Charles Avenue on the edge of the French Quarter and Jackson Square. It was established in 1899 by his father who stepped off the boat from 'The Old Country', with 20 Deutschmarks in his pocket and plenty of dreams, elbow grease and determination.

I wore my German Dirndl dress every day and created a Hofbreuhaus atmosphere every weekend. The restaurant served genuine German food and had a good name around town. We had a full house for lunch and also dinner every night and served much Wienaschnitzel and Bratwurst and twenty different varieties of beer. The building itself was one of the first in town at the turn of the century to have ceiling fans installed, and people would come from all over to see the extraordinary contraptions and pulleys that made them work. There were nine fans in total across the length of the restaurant and a mechanical nightmarish challenge to keep them turning. I held my breath every day when throwing the switch to turn them on.

Then in the Fall we had a giant Oktoberfest and New Orleans mixed the Quarter's Cajun music and Jazz with our Oom Papa band. It was loud and exciting as our guests gradually oozed out of our wide open doors and continued their dancing in the street as the night gently and totally unnoticed - merged with the dawn of a new day. A merry time was had by all in the city that never sleeps on the banks of the mighty Mississippi.

****

Finally in January of 1984 exactly 20 years after my arrival the first time, I was able to return to the fold of Pan American World Airways as a 'Returning Mother.' Time had, indeed marched on. We were no longer Stewardesses – we were Flight Attendants, and I now also had young men training with me in the first class of that year. The male Pursers that I had flown with in San Francisco had originated in the early days of flight as Stewards on the first aircraft to fly with passengers. Juan Trippe, our founder, was enamored and charmed by the Clipper Ships of old, and as a result created and furbished his airline with naval uniforms and naval jargon such as 'port' and 'starboard.' The airplanes also were called Clipper Ships and hence the name that would distinguish the Pan Am fleet of airplanes around the world with their call sign of "Clipper."

The male Pursers at that time had much seniority and were "grandfathered" into their roll. Almost all were based in either San Francisco or Miami and had flown the line for some years by the time I arrived. We had no male stewards in our classes in the 60's but each airplane had a metal image of an old Clipper Ship hanging on the forward bulkhead in first class. I have one of these hanging in my hallway today - a wonderful memory.

The Returning Mothers were quite a distinguished group of twenty ladies in a class of one hundred trainees, and we found ourselves very much sought after by the newbies who would beg us to study with them and constantly encouraged us to talk about our past days 'on the line.' We also differed from these new hires because each of us had at least one or two foreign languages to offer – required at our time of hire - which was not the case for these young people.

At graduation I was asked to give a speech about our experiences in class and training - "the second time around." I was honored to be picked to do that on behalf of our group and made it fun and exciting and poked fun at the fact the we were "old ladies" compared to the youthful new hires. I was very tickled to get a loud standing ovation when I was done. The whole atmosphere was so different this time around however – totally unlike the quiet, controlled and lady like atmosphere of my graduation in 1964.

We even looked different. Now our uniform was navy blue. We were however, allowed to still wear our old Tunis Blue uniforms if we had them, and the uniform center still had some – and so depending on where my flight was headed I would often wear mine to warmer climes.

I still have it hanging in my closet forty years later with my wings and the Purser stripes on the sleeve. To this day - the Eagle continues to fly - on wings of brilliant memories.

Returning to Pan Am – January 1984

CHAPTER 35 -

MORE NEW HORIZONS

an American World Airways was a lot different "the second time around" in January of 1984. The whole 'feel' and atmosphere everywhere on the property and in flight was different. While I was gone the airlines had changed a lot and there were many more of them all competing with each other due to the Airline Deregulation Act that passed in 1978. Flying had also become financially within reach of most everyone – it was no longer an amazing luxury enjoyed by only a few. It was now necessary and excepted transportation across the country or around the world.

The New Hire 'B' pay scale had also relaxed the requirements of employment. Languages were 'desired' but no longer a 'requirement' for employment – thus opening up the opportunity to many more local American applicants. Pan Am also no longer went around the world as they had done years before, to hire flight attendants speaking many languages and introducing different cultures. Being a large "round the world" airline this knowledge was really very important and a large comfort level to our passengers and crew alike. The problem did not rear its ugly head until years later and after much natural attrition over time.

Suddenly, we found ourselves unable to communicate with our passengers at 30,000 feet on our 'long haul' flights.

For example, if you are on a flight from New Delhi to Frankfurt and you have a full flight with many Hindi passengers and suddenly one of them is about to deliver a baby – or, heaven forbid, has a heart attack. What American flight attendant do you know that speaks Hindi that could help you communicate with that passenger in order to render aid, until the Captain can hopefully come up with a timely possible "fix" of where to land? Heaven help you if you had such an emergency out over the mighty Pacific Ocean where the possibility of landing anywhere was still many hours away. Even with a doctor on board our service was completely hampered because we could not make ourselves understood.

It would be the same with flights to Russia, Poland, Norway, Greece, Thailand, Japan - or anywhere around the world that our flights would take us. Our flight attendants with the treasure of communication was evaporating at an alarming rate. It could definitely be a matter of life or death. As a Purser my heart always skipped a beat when I picked up my flight paperwork down line with my crew of 'The New Pan Am' - wondering what I could run into while aloft.

I based in New York when I first returned because it was an easy commute from New Orleans. I shared a "crew pad" with six other crew members that commuted to their flights as I did. I would come in the night before my scheduled trip to be sure that I was in place for 'check in.'

Another BIG event had happened since I was gone. Pan Am had no domestic service and this became a problem. We flew into only the "Gateway Cities" coast to coast, and were at a great disadvantage to other carriers like Delta or United that had domestic connection service. As a result Pan Am acquired National Airlines in 1979. Mergers such as this are always problematic but this one was very bitter on both sides, and for the remainder of Pan Am's 'life' till its demise in 1991, the crews emotionally remained either "Orange" or "Blue" depending on their airline's colors. National was Orange and Pan Am was Blue.

I flew with many ex National flight attendants out of New York and I must say that as a Purser flying a trip from New York to Rio via Miami – it was a total delight to have them on board. We served dinner from New York to Miami – this was (for Pan Am) a short haul service before the 'long haul' leg to Rio.

Pan Am was not used to 'short haul' flying – we could not seem to gather ourselves together unless we had AT LEAST eight hours of flight time. BUT for the National flight attendants this was a walk in the park – so I was tickled to death to have a National crew aboard, because we could knock out an awesome dinner service in three hours flat with time to spare on that first 'leg' to Miami.

Then I would show them how the World's Most Experienced Airline got its stellar reputation – with service second to none – on its long haul flights around the globe. I would show them how it was done on our next leg to Rio and show them how much they would enjoy doing it. They would arrive in Rio tired and weary – but Oh so proud to be a part of Pan Am's image that till then they had been programmed to hate and despise. I thoroughly enjoyed turning our Orange girls Blue.

And so the Eagle slowly regained confidence and technique when spreading those giant wings and launching out over still unfamiliar territory.

****

In the Fall of 1984 I decided that I would like to transfer to our new crew base at Dulles International Airport in Virginia. The brand new airport served both Baltimore and Washington DC. The airport at Dulles was gigantic but the crew base was smaller, more rural, and I wanted out of New York. I had found a really nice apartment in a house in Herndon, Virginia, a few miles from the airport. It was very pretty country with rolling hills and lots of trees – and the Potomac River – its waters crashing down over giant rocks at the aptly named Great Falls. My apartment was on the second floor of a private house and I had stairs down from the kitchen to the back garden where I had my small BBQ grill. I would grill out summer and winter – even when my grill was under two feet of snow.

I loved it there, and it was here that Pan Am introduced me to the Training program in Miami.

One day when I was checking in to my flight to Paris my supervisor called me into her office.

"Gisela – I have been asked to run an offer by you that I hope you will accept. We are starting to hire and train many new flight attendants in the coming year and we desperately need people like you to help us out with this. We are still growing and have ordered new airplanes. Would you be willing to take a twelve month Special Assignment to our Training Academy in Miami?"

I looked at her as though she had three heads. Linda H. Kelly was the Director of In-Flight Services at Dulles International. So far, we had had a little interaction with each other, but I had only known her for maybe two months since my transfer into her base from New York. I did not think I had any credibility with her – we did not really know each other yet, and she knew nothing of my work or performance. Or did she?

In total puzzlement I said, "Linda, thank you – I'm completely off guard. Could you give me a little more info about it and let me think it through."

"Of course – no problem, connect with me when you get back and I will fill you in on what we need and you can think about it."

My flight to Paris was reasonably quick - only four days - and uneventful except for one strange funny happening on the way there. The flight was quite full on an Airbus with a crew of seven ex National flight attendants. About four hours out of Dulles we hit turbulence - it was after our meal service which was good, but it meant everyone had a full tummy of chicken, peas and rice. Amongst the passengers was a tour group - very well known to most seasoned flight attendants - as problematic. This particular tour group was usually on their way to Rome - this one - via Paris. They are always loud, demanding, obnoxious and full of kleptomaniacs - and this one was true to form. They would take anything off the airplane that was not tied down. Knives and forks, china and glassware, anything in the way of hand lotion and Eau de Cologne in the bathroom - and of course - our pillows and blankets.

When the Captain turned on the seatbelt sign they were not happy and we had to get quite tough with them to keep them tied down because they were in a "visiting mode" all over the cabin. We too, had been told to secure the cabin and sit, till they could find us smoother air.

The bouncing around continued however and now some were

getting scared and others were getting air sick and throwing up. We did the best we could under the circumstances but the call buttons did not stop. Our spare air sick bags were starting to run low and I was very concerned we could run out. Then, after about an hour or so we had found smooth air and as suddenly as it started the turbulence stopped and the flight continued without further incident.

Upon our approach to Paris I found we had a problem. We had collected so very many used, full sickbags from our passengers, and I had run out of where to put them - so we started to stack them on top of each other near the airstair door. For some reason, our airplane had had the first row of seats removed at that location so there was quite a wide little space there. It was wonderful luck and solved our problem perfectly. We filled that entire space up with the sick bags so that the cleaners could swoop them up as soon as they boarded - which would really help them a lot time-wise, in cleaning the airplane.

We landed without incident and stood at the forward door as our passengers deplaned. Finally, the line got to our problem group who were noisy and making snide remarks about their discomfort on this flight - when the leading young lady who looked a little wild and disheveled suddenly spied the sickbags piled up at the door, and with our pillow and blanket tucked snugly under one arm reached out and brazenly grabbed a bag and fled through the door into the terminal. Suddenly all of her group followed suite - each one grabbed a used sick bag and ran out through the door.

At this moment the Captain opened the cockpit door and saw what was happening and said to me under his breath.

"Well they are all very happy - what did you find to put in those little 'Goodie Bags' for them, Gi?" I had to go into the cockpit and pull the door shut - I was laughing so hard.

I got back from Paris a week later and celebrated Mark's eighteenth birthday with him in my Herndon apartment. He was finished with school in New Orleans and had come up for a visit. I was trying to tempt him out of there by introducing him to Virginia where I felt he had more of a future, job wise than in the deep south.

Mark's 18th Birthday

All the oil and natural gas industries and business had moved out of New Orleans to Houston, and the chances of finding good employment for young people was seriously diminished, so I was hoping to lure my kids out of the South as they finished their schooling. Mark was my first opportunity to do that and I was very tickled that he really liked everywhere we went in Virginia – especially the Potomac. We went many times to the park areas by the river and he would climb and sit for hours on the giant rocks in the sun with the rushing waters of the Potomac River all around him.

My conversation with Linda Kelly had been temporarily moved to a back burner as I enjoyed my one on one time with my eldest son. I had five days to do that and we really enjoyed our time together.

At the end of the week I drove Mark to the airport to return to New Orleans. We had not talked extensively about him moving up to Virginia after graduation – I had just casually thrown it out there over dinner one night - but when he hugged me good bye at the gate he told me he had had a great time and loved the area and might like to come up and check it out some more. I was thrilled.

After leaving Mark I went over to the crew room to find Linda Kelly and check my mail. I had a London/Paris/Rome trip the next day and would be gone for a week and I wanted to talk to her about the training program. When I got to her office she was on the phone but waved me in and indicated that I should close the door and then sit. I did so, and when she hung up the phone she was all smiles.

"Gisela – I am so happy to see you – did you have fun with your son, and is he still here?"

"He has gone back - but thank you, yes, we had a great time –

he really liked it here and I am hoping to maybe 'drag' him out of New Orleans. That is very hard to do – the city and way of life is very addictive if you have lived and grown up there." We sat and chatted back and forth for a little while more, before she turned the conversation to why I had come.

The training program in Miami was starting to kick off with gusto and they desperately needed hand-picked people from different bases to go there on a 'Special Assignment' program to participate in many different ways. I would be taken off 'flight status' for the length of my assignment, or if it was going to be longer than twelve months I would have to return to 'the line' for one month in order to stay flight qualified. Would I be open to such an open ended assignment?

It seems Linda Kelly had gone over my personal file with a fine tooth comb and checked with my past supervisors. As a result she and others, unknown to me, had decided that I would be a perfect fit. Hopefully I could be persuaded to join the training program and would be assigned to the Miami base by the end of the month.

Two weeks later I checked into the Doral Hotel in Miami – a stone's throw away from The Pan American Training Academy.

Once again the Eagle sought the soothing peace and tranquility of endless stretches of water to soothe and calm the mind. It found it overlooking an open stretch of Biscayne Bay and sat a long time watching the night sky rain diamonds onto the sparkling water below.

Much later – all sense of insecurity, trepidation and fear vanished as the sun rose slowly on the horizon and turned the sky into a brilliant orange and pink masterpiece.

CHAPTER 36 -

MIAMI

Miami was an unknown quantity to me. I had never been there. I arrived at the Doral Hotel, checked in and requested the front desk let Stephanie Hill, Manager of Flight Attendant Training know that I am in house and available at any time to meet with her.

Upon opening my door on the third floor of the Doral Hotel in Miami the orange light on my phone was blaring into the empty room. I set my bag down and walked towards it.

"Hello – this is Gisela Scofield in room 321 – you have a message for me?"

"Yes ma'am – Stephanie Hill left you a message to please join her in the dining room at six this evening for dinner." I thanked the operator and told her to please inform Mrs. Hill that I will be there. I showered and changed and ordered a pot of tea and settled down to read the notes that I had been given on the new hire training program. I would be one of many handpicked flight attendant crew members to participate in this program. I was to check in with Stephanie Hill upon arrival and she would give me my assignment.

I was at the Doral dining room a few minutes before six and was led back to a table set off to the side of the restaurant. Stephanie Hill was sitting there pouring over a fat file and notes spread out over the table. She looked up expectantly as I approached her.

"Hi - you must be Gisela, I'm Stephanie. Welcome to the training center - I am so very happy and relieved that you are here. I need you for a critical part of the program." Her handshake was firm as her eyes met mine in greeting.

We sat and had a really nice dinner - Stephanie was very easy to talk to and getting acquainted was comfortable and informative. She was very excited to start this new program and told me that she was hoping I would agree to be the Executive Coordinator for the training program. It was a BIG piece of the action and involved many non-training sections to be pulled together by me on behalf of the company. I needed to be calm and very organized and would have two people to help me as well as a secretary I would share with Stephanie.

Every six weeks we would have a minimum of one hundred new hire flight attendants arriving at the airport in Miami. I would need to meet, greet and shuttle them to the hotel. I would give an arrival speech and assign them rooms, as well as provide them with an overview with instructions of what would be required of them during the six weeks of training. I would give them a schedule and inform them that every week I would pay them per diem for their meals and give them a "cleaning voucher." I would be responsible for handling this chore and be responsible for the money. I would inform them of the daily dress code and ensure that it was adhered to. Basically, any non-training assignments and responsibilities would be mine to take care of - any personal problems the trainees had would be mine to handle - including dismissal. If a trainee is dismissed from the training program, I would be required to take care of the travel arrangements and accompany the trainee to the airport - off the premises and out of the program.

I sat silent - trying to absorb all this information. Stephanie ordered another glass of wine for both of us and looked up cheerfully.

"So, you see why I desperately need you Gi? This is a big responsibility but I will make sure that you have two good flight attendants on Special Assignment to the training program, to help you. You come very highly recommended you know - everyone thinks you would be perfect to handle this - and now that we have met, I agree."

I left the restaurant and returned to my room with my head spinning. I needed quiet space time.

The Eagle glided into its comfort zone. It needed time to roost near running, flowing water, to let it all sink in and gain the confidence and perspective that would be needed to fulfill that amount of trust.

****

Eight o'clock the next morning found all of us flight attendants chosen for Special Assignment to the Training Academy in a large meeting room at the Doral. We were waiting for Stephanie Hill to fill us in on the program and to give us our assignments. The room was full of loud chatter and much laughter as the occupants circled round introducing each other or recognizing old friends. The atmosphere was warm, friendly and very upbeat.

I too did the rounds and found several people I had flown with before, one of which introduced me to a fellow base mate of hers from San Francisco called Elizabeth Magri. Every now and again in life you get a strange feeling when you meet someone new. I got that feeling now – we would become close friends. We shook hands and made eye contact. It was the same feeling I had had in London many years before, when I met Chloe – we just "clicked."

Stephanie Hill entered the room and the noise was slowly turned off as though someone was turning off a tap of running water. We all found a table and a vacant chair and sat looking at our host with excited expectation. She did not disappoint and we hung on every word as she filled us in on why we were here. Our first class would arrive in six days from now – we had one week to get ready.

After lunch we all went over to be introduced to the Pan American Training Academy and our assigned space in it. The Academy was also well-known to many other airlines from around the world, who would send their pilots here for training in our state-of-the-art simulators. In-Flight would take up the entire second floor for training flight attendants. I was given a desk in a large open area across from the stairs that would be easily accessible to all. I was also given two wonderful assistants who were flight attendants, both based in Miami which would prove extremely helpful over time.

Elizabeth was assigned to an in-flight cabin training room and we would get together every minute we had spare at lunch and later at dinner to compare notes on everything from this assignment to our personal life. We found we had much in common. We were both returning mothers. had left our husbands and were divorced, and when our one-month assignment turned into five years – we set up housekeeping together in a small house in Kendall, that was owned by a friend of Elizabeth. He was a fellow flight attendant and lived in San Francisco but he was from Miami and owned this house and rented it out. It was small but fully furnished and in a very nice gated community with a pool. It was perfect for the two of us.

After six weeks we graduated the first class of 1985. We had started with 100 students and ended up graduating seventy-two. The first two weeks of training was always aircraft emergency equipment and drills – hence the attrition. If the students could pass the grueling first two weeks, they would usually graduate – unless some character flaw or other reared its ugly head. It was a lot of work and the days were long for both Lizzie and I. We would often come home exhausted and compare notes over a bottle of Merlot.

After graduation we got notice that at least eighteen more classes were planned – but twenty-one could be expected. We had two weeks off and each went back home – I to New Orleans and Lizzie to California - to organize our lives for such an extended stay in Miami.

Lizzie was the first to arrive back in Miami – mainly because she flew back and I was driving. We would need a car and before leaving we had each confessed that we would need to bring our critters with us for the duration – each of us had two dogs. She arrived back and settled in and I arrived back the day before we went back to work.

It had been a long tiring two-day drive for me – my Datsun 280 ZX sports car was packed to the gills with me, two dogs and all the "stuff" I thought I would need. We arrived at the house in the afternoon with the warm Florida sun bathing everything in a shimmery glow. Lizzie threw open the front door when she heard us pull up and came running out to help carry. I hugged her and as I did so my eyes went to the open front door - and I froze in horror. The door opened into the living room and there – in the middle of the couch which could be seen as if in a picture frame – sat a black cat.

My dogs were squirming in the car with excitement to get out after their long confinement and I was squirming in panic – knowing I could never LET them out and into this house.

"Lizzie!" I squealed in horror, my face white as chalk. "You did not tell me you had a cat – in New Orleans the cats always sat in wait under the bush where I fed the birds – I have always taught my dogs to hate and chase cats (never having had the pleasure of owning one) I dare not let them see yours. Oh dear lord – what are we going to do. I will have to find a hotel." And I turned to get back into the car.

"My dearest Gi – that is Nephie and she has absolutely no problem with dogs – come on in and I will fix us some tea. All will be well. No problem - in this environment animals sort themselves out just fine with no help from us – you will see." With that she grabbed my arm and turned to open the side door of the car. I stood with my back to it, in defiance so that she could not do it. We stood like that looking at each other – me with a look of total panic on my face and she - grinning from ear to ear.

Finally, I relented and we each took control of a dog and led it into the house. She had had the foresight to put both of her dogs in the fenced back yard so they would not get under foot on our arrival. Liz had my little Dachshund Willie, on a leash and I followed with Bingo, the Royal Standard Poodle. Lizzie handed me Willie's leash and went over and picked up Nephie who purred and stretched lazily as she sat down on the floor to make the introduction. To my amazement it was quite calm and my dogs seemed much more interested in the Corgi and shaggy Sheep Dog barking and scratching at the glass door excitedly waiting to make their acquaintance.

The next morning Lizzie and I drove off for a long fourteen-hour work day with some trepidation, leaving the animals in charge of the house. All was calm as we shut the front door – Nephie was still tucked in bed because the sun had not yet appeared in the eastern sky to welcome a new day. That night, driving home weary and a lot the worse for wear, settling in a whole new class at the Academy – I said to Lizzie.

"I am terrified that we will come home to blood all over the walls and your sweet Nephie in pieces parts hanging from the ceiling fan."

She laughed and said, "You worry too much." I prayed that she was right.

I hung back with a sinking feeling in the pit of my stomach – my legs total jelly - as Liz put the key in the lock and slid the front door open. Three dogs burst forth in excited greeting as we crossed the threshold into the living room and there - on the couch surrounded by soft pillows - was my Willie with his rear-end smushed against Nephie the Cat Person in peaceful contentment as though they had lived together since birth.

Sometimes life sends you a little nudge to remind you - there REALLY is a God.

Mother and Son Graduating together - 1988

CHAPTER 37 -

CHALLENGES WITH TRAINING THE "NEW" PAN AM

The trainees in The New Pan Am looked quite different from any I had experienced before. We now had no restriction on age and as a result our third class of the year included a mother and her son. He was in his early twenties and she in her late forties. They both did well throughout the training program and I was tickled to death to present them both with their wings upon graduation.

One of the things that had changed since my return was the fact that New Hire flight attendants would be presented with Silver wings upon graduation - they would acquire their Gold wings after they had completed their six months of probation.

I learned so very much during this time in Miami that would really help me down the road in years to come. Over time, it became a ginormous problem on-line that we could no longer communicate verbally with our passengers aloft. In the late seventies the Government had indicated that as an American company – we needed to hire Americans. Mr. President – we are an around the world airline – how is this possibly going to work going forward? Americans live in this amazing country that speaks nothing but English coast to coast, border to border.

It was during this time that I had to return to the line and regular line flying for a month, to stay qualified. I encountered this problem first hand on a long-haul flight to Tokyo out of New York. The flight was sixteen hours from New York to Tokyo on a Boing 747 SP. I had fourteen Flight Attendants on board – three had only been on-line for six months and six had joined us from National. I did not have a single Flight Attendant onboard that spoke Japanese or anything close. This would never have happened on my first tour with Pan Am. I spoke German and French with a smidgen of Italian and we had one flight attendant who spoke Spanish. None of which would work for a flight to the Pacific area of the world.

When passengers made a booking for a flight it was required that you be less than seven months pregnant in order to buy a ticket. However – people lie if they need to go where they need to go. And they did frequently.

Almost nine hours into my flight a young woman came out of the aft rest room doubled over in pain. My rear galley girl was taking her rest brake on the jump seat and caught her as she almost fell out of the bathroom. She laid her down in the last row of seats – fortunately our load was reasonably light in Economy and the last row of seats at the back of the airplane was empty. Those were our designated crew rest seats. The young lady was visibly pregnant and in deep distress. Karen made her comfortable, lying across the three seats on the starboard (right) side of the aisle, and covered her with a blanket. The passenger was Japanese and speaking very fast in Japanese between sobs, and Karen was desperately trying to decipher what she was saying.

The cabin was dark – most everyone was sleeping and I was doing a cabin check when I became aware of the slight disturbance, so I made my way aft to see what was happening. When I got there, I found the passenger very distressed, crying and obviously in pain. We could not understand a word she said and she could not understand our questions – we could not help her. On my way back through the dark cabin I had noticed a young Japanese man sitting up in the aisle seat about halfway down with his eyes closed but seemingly waiting for someone to return – the two seats next to him towards the window, had a blanket and pillow thrown aside on them as if someone had gotten up to use the rest room. I made my way back to him and squatted down in the aisle so I could speak to him quietly without disturbing anyone else. He jumped a little in alarm when he saw me there so I patted his arm reassuringly and I asked him if his wife was using the rest room.

He jumped up and turned around anxiously looking towards the rear bathroom saying something in Japanese which I did not understand so I gestured to him to please follow me. He did and I was relieved to find that they were indeed a couple and our young passenger jumped up and clung to her husband crying and talking very fast, gesturing and holding her belly. Finally, he made her sit down and turned to us frantically, gesturing that the baby was coming. I told Karen to settle her down and called the cockpit – explaining to the startled Captain the problem we were facing. There was a long pause and then he said.

"OK Gi – do the best you can – make an announcement on the PA and ask if a doctor or nurse was on board and if anyone speaks English and Japanese – we will see what we can do up here." The line went dead. I made the announcement on the PA trying not to scare the passengers as I was waking them out of sleep – but needing their help. Then I checked the cabin all the way aft behind the galley. I had only seen maybe ten or so passengers back there. That was usually the "party" area where passengers congregated to smoke and socialize and they would not be sleeping. Tonight – it was dark - only one passenger was reading and smoking - the others were all sleeping. I turned back to my problem and noticed a lady making her way down the aisle. I went to meet her and she said that she was not a nurse but was returning to the military based in Japan. She spoke some Japanese - and could she help. I explained my problem to her and took her to join Karen and our expectant mother. She told me she had two children of her own and even though she was not a nurse it was a comfort to find someone who could communicate with the passenger and understand what was happening.

I went into the galley to checked the passenger manifest to see where I had empty seats at which point the other Purser on my crew and three other flight attendants joined me to see if they could help. I explained what was happening and we decided that we would try and empty out the aft cabin by moving those passengers up forward to empty seats – not an easy feat as all the passengers up there had been happy to utilize them to bed down in. If we were able to do that, we could leave the young mother in the aft cabin with more privacy.

I had checked the back bathroom when I first came upon the problem and had found that there was water on the floor at the entrance to the bathroom and also on the carpet just outside, indicating that the passenger's "water" had indeed broken when she got there about an hour ago now. Our helpful passenger, Kathie, had informed me that she was unable to tell how much time we had before the baby came. Both the husband and wife were – understandably – very scared. Even with Kathie doing her best to translate, it was clear that the language barrier was making a difficult situation even more difficult – both for them and for us.

I went up to the cockpit to see what if anything they had been able to come up with and give them an update. Ken, the First Officer followed me into the flight deck – he had been in the upper deck in the crew bunks and had been called back to his seat. When the Captain heard me enter the flight deck, he turned around to see what news I had about the situation. I explained to him that we had found a passenger who could help us language wise, but I had not found any medical help as of yet. I talked the problem over with the three pilots – all were married and had children and all volunteered to help anyway they could. The Captain then said that he had been in touch with dispatch and they were trying to find a fix if we thought the situation could not wait till we arrived in Tokyo – six hours hence.

At this moment dispatch came back on-line to let the Captain know that he was given permission to turn around if he thought it necessary – Wake Island was 2 ½ hours in our rearview mirror - South East of our position. The US Military base had been notified of our situation and was making preparations for our possible arrival. He looked up at me inquiringly and I nodded acknowledgement.

"Rodger Dispatch – thank you, I think we need to do that," and he continued talking and getting a new heading, altitude and weather information as I hurried down the stairs to the aft cabin to give the news to the rest of my crew. When I got there, I found that they had done a good job of moving our reluctant, sleepy passengers, forward, and our little mother was now comfortably reclining in the aft bulkhead row with her husband sitting on the floor holding her hand comfortingly. Just then she had a contraction and I froze with worry – as her face creased in pain and she arched her back up in the seat. I pulled our helpful passenger

Kathie aside and asked her what she thought – how was it progressing? She told me that the contractions were between eight and ten minutes apart but were getting more intense.

I decided we needed to get a little more prepared for a possible delivery and pulled one of the 'walk around' oxygen bottles out of its rack and put it in a seat nearby. This done I asked her to explain to the young woman that she should remove her undergarments so we pulled the curtain across the aisle, arranged the row of seats with a clean blanket and clean pillows and put the backrests - way - back. Then we made her as comfortable as was possible and covered her with a new clean blanket. Then, for now, I left her in Kathie's care while I returned to the two hundred and fifty other passengers on board. As my crew and I were accomplishing that the Captain came on the PA to explain our decision to the passengers that understood English – but many did not and were upset and confused.

We could not speak Japanese and had no way of telling them - until I had an epiphany. Our passenger, Kathie spoke Japanese. I wrote an announcement out for her on the back of a sick bag and asked her to please translate that into Japanese and inform our passengers that we would be landing shortly on Wake Island due to a medical emergency and not to be concerned. All would be well - we would not deplane - and we would continue on to Tokyo as soon as possible.

We had about two hours to get our passengers and the cabin ready for landing and my in-flight crew were professional and swift in accomplishing that. We offered freshly brewed coffee, tea, orange juice or water. Also, crackers or nuts to anyone interested. Mimosas/Champagne and hastily concocted snacks were offered in first class. Gradually, our passengers woke and stretched sleepily, finding a sky that was starting to show the first glow of a breaking dawn when they opened their shades. We made a long gentle curving bank over a dark, moody still sleeping Pacific Ocean - into the soft eggshell light of a new day - while now flying East.

We had decided to wait till we took off again from Wake Island, inbound to Tokyo – to serve breakfast. We would have six plus hours to do that - very leisurely, which would make more sense than trying to serve our elaborate breakfast service in less than two hours. We also would have time to emotionally make up to our passengers for the delay and inconvenience they had been forced to endure. All good.

We landed on the tiny spit of land in the giant Pacific Ocean that was Wake Island to an emergency entourage. We pulled up to a hanger and when I opened the rear door an ambulance was waiting and four young military medics rushed on board complete with gurney and medical supplies. Our young mother-to-be was loaded onto it and she and her frantic husband were delivered into the ambulance and whisked off to the base hospital.

Thirty minutes later we were airborne to Tokyo – sailing into a calm soft dawn as though nothing earth shattering had just occurred. However, it had, and it left an enormous mark on me and my confidence to render the kind of first-class service to our passengers I had been taught to deliver in-flight.

The good news came one hour before our arrival in Tokyo. The Captain announced that our little mother to be had delivered a healthy baby girl. The news brought a salvo of cheers in the cabin.

The Eagle was uneasy – decisions made at a later date would cause some changes in the world of this mighty bird – a direct result of this experience and flight.

CHAPTER 38 -

MY WORLD IN THE ACADEMY

lizabeth and I thrived, learned a lot and loved our time training the New Pan Am in Miami. We found not only a new friendship that would last the rest of our lives, but also an amazing phenomenon – we could live together in total harmony with five totally diverse critters. It is an amazing trick for two people to live together in total harmony over time. It is not easy - no matter the sex - male or female. We left our animals in the house in the early hours of every morning and returned to them sometimes sixteen hours later without a single incident. They thrived on being together, and Liz and I thrived on an amazing relationship with all our fellow training team. This made the long hours non problematic – we were tired and we were weary but we loved what we were doing and we were very good at it. Also, every night we came home to a rousing, delightful reception of total love, wiggly tail wagging and many wet kisses.

It all worked great. When Liz had to fly with her trainees – I babysat. I did not have to fly for three years in my job of Coordinator for the Training Program except for one month every twelve, to stay qualified for flight duty - so it worked great. We graduated thirty-two classes in four years – it was an amazing experience, but before the final six classes, I was called to fulfil a completely different path.

I had mentioned my troublesome flight from JFK to Tokyo – via our unexpected landing on Wake Island in the Pacific and the fact that we could not communicate with our passengers – in the last chapter. The powers that be in the Training Program decided we had to do something about that because there had been quite a few such incidents reported. We all huddled in many meetings on the subject – everyone had an idea – but how to make it work with the International Union of Flight Attendants and also the decision makers for Pan Am.

Stephanie Hill, our boss and the Director of Training called both Liz and I to a meeting in her suite at the Doral one lunchtime. Upon our arrival we found four other Flight Attendants on Special Assignment to the training Academy already there. We all knew each other and the atmosphere was warm, friendly and upbeat. We waited expectantly to find out what Stephanie had in mind, and what she needed us to do.

When we were all seated on various comfortable chairs around the room, she gathered her papers into a pile and looked at us smiling. All eyes were riveted on her expectantly and the silence was intense. Just then the door to her bedroom squeaked as it was slightly nudged open and in walked two beautiful, fluffy, pedigree cats, in tandem – tails held high, waving regally – obviously the Queens of all they surveyed, on assignment or not.

They were headed for the sunny window seat, where the window was open and the sheer curtains were waving an invitation to come and enjoy the afternoon in the soft, warm, Florida sun. All eyes swung in the direction of this sweet intrusion while Stephanie jumped to her feet in embarrassed confusion, to scoop up and herd the pair back into the confines of her bedroom. Meanwhile, our room was bathed in delighted laughter. Those cats were so very cute and obviously so very much in control.

Stephanie sat down again after this little episode very embarrassed, and apologized profusely for the delightful interlude. She stated that she was on assignment for an indefinite time and she had no one to take care of these sweet cats. The only way she could work it out was to take them with her on assignment. We loved it - Stephanie - relax - they are a part of our team.

The momentum returned to why/what we were there for and Stephanie stated, "I know some of you have become aware of a very serious gap in our ability to give our passengers the service that we are renown for - and, also, the kind of service our passengers have paid for. Especially in the India - as in Bombay and New Delhi - market. Some European markets also - in the Eastern Block, like Russia and Poland - but India is a priority."

"I have handpicked you guys - the best of my training team - to go to India and hire one hundred applicants that have answered our advertisement, bring them back to Miami for training while you set up a crew base for them in Bombay and New Delhi."

We were silent while we absorbed this information.

Had IUFA (Independent Union of Flight Attendants) agreed to this? We had a serious problem in-flight regarding language and culture - but IUFA had so far managed to block any fix for this by hiring aliens - the way we had done for years - the way I had been hired - with Pan American being my Sponsor. They had not been onboard with this - so what had changed.

Stephanie said a lot indeed had changed. IUFA had agreed

that we could hire alien flight attendants that would fly certain routes - from their home base to a "Gateway City" such as London or Frankfurt. Then IUFA flight attendants would take over and fly into the US.

If we could live with this - they were OK with it.

We were definitely OK with it - when do we start - the sooner the better.

****

Elizabeth and I had some serious issues to overcome. She had two children and I had three - and of course - we had our critters to provide for. I however, had a much larger, embarrassing, inconvenient problem to deal with. My kids were safe – they were with their Dad – but I had a husband that I had married against my better judgement two years before.

He was a wonderful guy – intelligent, sweet and treated me like a queen. We had been dating for some time and he begged and begged me to marry him. I resisted – I cannot tell you why – he was 15 years younger than I, maybe that was why I hesitated. He was very mature for his age and we were perfect together, so I finally gave in. One of the worst mistakes of my life. Totally undiscovered by me – until too late – was the fact that he was a raging alcoholic. How is it possible that I did not find that out until I had tied the knot?

He NEVER drank in excess around me – we always had wine with dinner and when out in company he would have a cocktail or two – BUT NEVER to excess. Life became a living hell – he would start drinking at three in the afternoon and be bombed out on the couch by dinner time.

There is no way in this world that I would continue living like that – so when I took the training assignment, I gave him an ultimatum – he MUST dry out or we are done. Several more times I had gone home on my days off and there had been no change – so I filed for divorce and moved the beautiful antique furniture I had had sent over from London after my Mother died – into storage. I had taken a lot of trouble finding just the right storage company because some of the antiques needed to be held in an air-conditioned space. Just because a piece of furniture is antique, does not make it pretty or valuable – but all my things were very special. My parents had been Fine Art Dealers in London's St Jameses and the total value was approximately $30,000 so I could not store it just anywhere.

After accepting the assignment to "Train India" I found the perfect storage company and moved my whole life into it. My antiques, my clothes, all my personal items - and left my soon to be Ex - the house and his dog. The divorce was not yet final but within the three-week window Pan Am had allowed us, I had everything under control and could make plans to leave the US. The day we had our meeting with Stephanie, we all applied for our Indian visas which would take at least this amount of time to be granted.

Everything fell into place and soon we were on our way to hire one hundred flight attendants from India - a magical land deeply seeped for thousands of years in complicated history - which after the British occupation and Ghandi, blossomed into the 20st Century.

We landed in Bombay at four twenty-five in the morning. We passed customs and passport control along with the regular passengers - because this time we were not 'crew' and not in uniform. Then we had to fight the rest of our passengers for a taxi to take us to the Sea Rock Hotel that had housed Pan American crew for many years.

We settled in and two days later started the interview process.

The Bombay and New Delhi Operations had each given us a box of applications from people interested in becoming a flight attendant with Pan Am from all over India. They were amazing. They were the best we had ever seen. There was just one problem. One entire wall of our communal sitting room at the hotel, was stacked high with boxes. We had openings for one hundred flight attendants - but when we started looking at the applications - we found we had more than ten thousand - hence all those boxes.

In a heartbeat our six week assignment turned into six months.

Ten thousand - amazing - educated - well qualified young people that could not wait to don a Pan American uniform awaited us. We were humbled beyond belief, but totally understood.

It turned out to be one of the best and most memorable assignments of my career. The culture difference in many cases was quite a challenge. During the interview process we would explain to our applicants that they would be required to cook and serve meat on the airplane, also alcohol, and some had a problem with that. Many did not eat meat and had not been around any alcohol at any point in their life to date.

Another problem came up when we talked about the uniform and what would be required regarding hygiene on the aircraft. Pan Am required all ladies to shave their legs and under arms and this was quite a strange requirement we discovered, for some cultures around the world. When in Africa on a similar assignment a year later, we lost quite a few really wonderful applicants as a result. We had returned to our hotel after a long day to find several groups of angry parents awaiting us after interviewing their daughters. They were horrified at this idea - stating that "ONLY 'Ladies of the Night' shaved their bodies and they would never allow their daughters to work for a company with such a requirement."

We loved India and Liz and I were determined that we would

bring our children to experience it also. She and I called home and arranged for our kids to get the necessary shots and visas and after we had been there for three months the kids were on summer break from school and came out to stay with us. Unfortunately, neither of our daughters could come but my two boys came from New Orleans and joined her son, Scott, who had come from California. The boys hit it off right away and had a grand time exploring while we were working.

Two years later I would bring all three of my kids to both Bombay and New Delhi on my vacation.

Most of us made great use of our travel privileges while with Pan Am and I was no different. I introduced my family to many of my favorite cities around the world. They learned things first hand that you could not learn from any book and I believe it shaped them into the amazing, wonderful, successful adults they turned out to be.

The six of us flight attendants that Stephanie had picked for this assignment could not have been more different. We each came from a different part of the world and the US, but we hit it off immediately, and worked well together while having a lot of fun. Our days were long and challenging, especially when setting up the crew base facilities but we knew what we were doing - and we were very good at it and achieved much.

When the long interview process was over and the crew bases had been set up we returned to Miami to await the arrival of the successful applicants for training. Training India became a great pleasure for us and we welcomed them fifty at a time, to Miami and America with great glee. They were wonderful students - very hard working and diligent and we lost very few to Hell Week. Finally, when their Miami training was complete, we went back with them to India to make sure all was working well on the airplane and their home base.

The culture shock for them however, was intense. I could relate when remembering my own training in that alien Kew Gardens so many years ago. Here, the emphasis on meat and liquor in flight was a very alien experience for these wonderful young people.

Elizabeth and I flew a training flight from Bombay to Frankfurt. She worked the front end and I the back. We had quite a heavy load but our trainees were all doing well and the meal service was going without a hitch - when suddenly there was a loud crash of metal hitting the floor and a slight cry of panic. Commotion resulted and I moved as quickly as I could through my cabin without causing alarm to all my passengers who were looking at the forward bulkhead, from whence had come the crashing sound, in silent concern.

I arrived at the galley to find the curtain drawn and much commotion going on behind it. I pulled the curtain aside and found Elizabeth sitting on the jump seat, cradling her galley flight attendant who was in tears.

Elizabeth looked up at me as though she had won the lottery when she saw me, gratefully motioning to the large pan of roast beef decorating the galley floor - fortunately still in the pan - and said quietly, "Gi could you please check the roast and put it in the oven for us."

I did so and temporarily took over the galley chores, cooking the food orders till that sweet young girl could put herself back together and resume the task. The two flight attendants working first class with her were amazing and calmly carried on in the cabin as though nothing was amiss. They were all Stars and the flight progressed as though nothing had happened to its conclusion.

That night Elizabeth told me that everything was progressing smoothly until the galley girl had to put the roast in the oven. She was a very slight girl of twenty one and the roast was very heavy. She carried it from the container with difficulty, across the galley to the oven, and then turned in horror to Elizabeth - who was watching her - and fainted dead away. It seems that she felt as though she was putting her own grandmother in that oven! Culture shock indeed - but it had to be learned. Americans LOVED their meat even when away from home.

Pan Am India Graduates

Group Dinner at the Officer's Club in Delhi – Elizabeth Magri (far right)

They would fly Bombay, Karachi, Frankfurt and back and New Delhi, Frankfurt and back on the 747 airplane.

It was on one such flight after they had graduated and were flying alone, without one of us Trainers on board, that twelve members of class two were high-jacked in Karachi. It was Friday, September 5th, 1986 when flight 73, a Boeing 747 with a full load of passengers departed Bombay en-route via Karachi to Frankfurt Germany. Upon arrival in Karachi it was high-jacked by four Palestinian terrorists.

In a heartbeat, every one of those young people we had just trained in Miami turned into heroes that fateful day. Their bravery and clear thinking as a group saved many a life - but sadly took the life of their senior Purser Neerja Bhanot aged twenty-three. When the shooting started, she used her body, throwing herself across three young children that the terrorists had separated from their parents. By shielding them and thus saving their lives this amazing young woman sacrificed hers.

During the ordeal the terrorists had ordered the flight attendants to collect all passenger passports. They did so reluctantly but their calm bravery under these terrible circumstances cannot be understated. The terrorists were parading up and down the airplane waving their machine guns and grenades threatening to shoot everyone onboard. Sometimes holding the barrel of their guns against the heads of our wonderful flight attendants that had only been flying the line for a few weeks and threatening immediate death. In spite of this horror - they calmly collected the passports as ordered, but when they came to an American one, they slipped it quietly down between the seats and out of sight. Our intense training in far off America cannot claim this bravery under fire. This was an amazing team of young heros with savvy way beyond their years that kicked in when desperately needed.

Nineteen people died that terrible day, including two Americans. One hundred and twenty-seven people were injured - but many, many lives were saved due to the amazing bravery and professionalism of that young crew.

CHAPTER 39 -

SIX MONTHS LATER –
TRAINING WARSAW

Finally back in Miami, we settled right into our old routine at the Academy. Taking six of us out of critical functions at the Academy had been a real hardship on the rest of the training team. They were happy to have us back.

The first thing Lizzie and I did upon our return was to empty our mail boxes and we smiled in anticipation at some of our more personal mail waiting for us. While in Miami I had made arrangements with my bank to pay the New Orleans moving company that was storing my antiques every month. Thus I did not have to worry about it, should I be assigned overseas – which indeed happened. As a result, I was not surprised to find a card from them in my mail. I set it aside, electing to open the more 'fun' mail first – so it was maybe three days before I finally came across the card again.

I picked it up and read it. I read it again not comprehending its content – the blood draining from my face, my heart dropping into my boots. It was informing me that the Company was very sorry - but the building had burned to the ground and my entire unit (containing my life) was a total loss. I had not taken out insurance on it because they had assured me before signing that I did not need any - because they were completely and adequately, covered. However, now that the whole building was dust - any claim of mine was too far down the list to be honored.

I was sitting totally stunned on the couch, with tears streaming down my face and jammed tightly between little Willie on one side of me and Nephie Cat Person on the other - when Lizzie came in with a glass of wine in each hand. The two animals had been animatedly vying for my attention when I joined them there on the couch, but both had settled quietly to one side when they sensed my distress and racing heartbeat.

"Gi - what on earth is wrong. Are you OK? You look like the world just came to an end," and she ran to place the glasses on the table and then turned to me in panic. She appeared to me in a kind of floating, fuzzy haze.

"Gi - please talk to me – what has happened?" She cried kneeling down in front of me, forcing me back to the here and now.

Without a word - I handed her the card.

We spent the rest of the day discussing the news. I had terrific trouble wrapping my arms around the finality of my loss. My pictures, my memories, my treasures, my clothes, my life – all gone.

I fell asleep that night dreaming I was sitting at my beautiful

Edwardian dining table with the upholstered antique chairs, while looking at my Mother's exquisite Queen Anne china cabinet with its delicate legs and hand-blown glass. I loved looking at it while eating dinner and enjoying the display of treasures - her delicate porcelains and my step father's treasures from 11th Century Egypt that had been his pride and joy. He was an Art Dealer – but he was a Mason first, and his hobby had been reading hieroglyphics. He had spent many happy hours at Christie's and Sotheby's over his life time, collecting these and many other amazing artifacts.

After calming down and sleeping on the news, one thing was perfectly clear to me. Especially after connecting with an attorney in New Orleans who informed me that it was an "Insurance Fire" - a scam – and yes there was no money left for me to claim - but the owner was in jail. No point wasting time and energy or money in suing – the well was dry.

I However, KNEW as sure as eggs were eggs – that that man had NOT allowed my furniture to burn. While picking up my antiques and before they had finished packing everything up, he had drooled and raved at how he wished his brother could see them. His brother apparently had a moving business also – in Florida. He admitted that he had never seen any antiques of this quality before, and how proud he was to have my business and how carefully he would store everything for me.

To this day I do not pass by an antique shop anywhere in America without checking to see if any of my treasures are there for sale. Those two crooks moved my furniture and treasures across State Lines to Florida, and then set the New Orleans building on fire! There is no way in this world that I can be convinced that they torched any of it. They could see and would be aware of the value on the open market. I'm sure many people have enjoyed and bragged to friends about having different parts of it over the years – and I'm OK with that.

The Eagle absorbed the tragic loss in stoic silence at the very top of a tall cypress tree, fanned by the soft soothing, waves of wind rising off the rolling Atlantic surf. The giant bird forced herself to b-r-e-a-t-h-e one day at a time.

This would take time.

****

About a week after our arrival back at the Academy, Stephanie Hill asked me to meet her for lunch in the cafeteria. Our days were jam packed now that we had a new class in-house and we had to find time where we could to share information. I usually ate when I could – if I could – at my desk, so this was a happy break for me. I found her sitting at a little table in the far corner tucking into a sandwich while totally engrossed in an open folder.

"Hi Stephanie – can I join you here?" I asked with a big smile of welcome as I set my spinach salad and glass of hot tea on the table next to her. She returned my smile and closed the folder moving it to the side to give us both more room.

"Hi Gi. Glad you could swing 30 minutes with me – I have a new assignment I hope you will agree to work for me. Could not think of a better person to do it so wanted to see you as soon as possible. Even though we spend all day, every day in the same building it is really hard to get even 5 minutes together for one reason or another."

"I know," I said starting to tuck greedily into my salad. "What can I do for you? Not sure I have a minute to spare to shoe-horn anything else into the day."

"Good Heavens Gi – I am not about to suggest such a thing. You would have to come off what you are doing now. You will have to teach for a while and then follow your students home to Warsaw."

"POLAND?" I said looking up at her with eyes the size of saucers.

"Yes. We have hired 60 with the hope of retaining 50 and need you to open a base in Warsaw. Most of them speak German fluently and this will help you in the training when they have a little difficulty with English. They will be flying The Eastern Block of countries into Frankfurt."

I closed my mouth and lowered the fork full of spinach that I realized I had been posing in mid-air - back to my plate. I had heard that the German girls from our base in Berlin, were having trouble language-wise with some of the flying into Russia and Croatia. Many of the occupants of these countries were now financially able to fly and as a result our loads were getting heavy into Frankfurt – which had become a new obstacle for the Company.

' I applied for a Polish visa, and two weeks later I welcomed twelve - beyond happy, excited young Polish trainees to the Academy.

They had excelled and were the cream of the crop of young Polish applicants that we had found. Now they were looking at me with high expectations that I would turn them into Pan American flight attendants in six weeks, and as a result could therefore don that world-famous uniform.

I would repeat this three more times - graduating a total of four classes of Reginal Flight Attendants to the Warsaw station to complete the station with a crew base of fifty-five flight attendants.

I thought I had been so very blessed to be associated with the Indian group of trainees - because they were so very special- but these young people were of the same caliber – they were amazing. I checked them in and settled them down in to the Viscount Hotel, and later in the afternoon, introduced them to the Academy and our routine for the foreseeable future.

Training Warsaw was a true delight. The classes were animated, fun and full of excitement and delivered in a wild mixture of English and German. If they could not find the English word – they just produced it in German. Because the class was small, I was able to take care of most of it without help – except of course, for the emergency equipment part. While they were doing that – I went to Warsaw to start the ball rolling on setting up the base.

What an amazing, special group of people greeted me there, and for a whole week helped me do every little thing to make this a very successful project. I met two amazing ladies that would end up being responsible for our flight attendants at that new base. They had been with Pan Am at the Warsaw station for some time now, having come from other carriers such as Aero Flot and Polish Airlines. I sat with them for many hours going over our Flight Attendant Manual, introducing them to the protocol, uniform criteria, Standards etc. etc. etc. They would even join me at the hotel for dinner and then we would go into another 'session' of questions and answers, as well as about things and people they would need to know.

I loved Warsaw. I loved Poland and everyone I came into contact with. I knew this would be a very special, very successful addition to the Pan Am family and I smiled all the way back to Miami.

We graduated the first class intact in Miami, with a special little ceremony including music and Champagne - and then sent ten of them home to Poland. Two stayed behind for another four days of class, to graduate as Pursers. They had all graduated with Silver wings, meaning that they were on probation for the next six months.

357

One morning, shortly before graduation, when we were practicing our announcements, I handed out a little booklet created by a wonderful very colorful, energetic man called Dr. Joseph W. Bator that helped us with languages at the Academy. He was a linguist and had a wide experience in teaching languages – which, of course, we desperately needed. It was a little International Airline Phrase Book that he had created specially for our in-flight announcements. In addition it had basic, useful stuff - phrases, numbers and days of the month etc., in six languages - English, French, German, Italian, Portuguese, and Spanish. It had over seven hundred phrases covering all aspects of air travel and could be invaluable in-flight.

It was a bright sunny Florida morning and the class was in high spirits. They were delighted to get the little books and I asked them to please print their names and their base inside the front cover and then turn to page fifty- one. I had my book open to that page and just sat ready, waiting for them to settle and write their names.

I preceded to explain to them how useful it could be and how they could utilize it in-flight. When I looked up, I was amazed to see almost all of them looking at me with the strangest, most puzzling expressions on their faces. Some of them were frantically looking through the book.

I stopped and asked, "What is it – do you not see page fifty-one – Boarding; Flight; Arrival?"

Puzzled silence.

I got up and went down to take a look at the book that I had given them. Imagine my shock, surprise – no – TOTAL DISBELIEF!

The book looked exactly the same as mine on the outside, however, when I opened their book I saw that the Fly Page read :-

THE FIRST BOOK OF
GHOST STORIES

"Widdershins"

 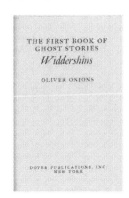

The inside of the "International Airline Phrase Book in Six Languages" by our Dr. Joseph W. Bator had, in fact, become - a book of "Ghost Stories" by a Mr. Oliver Onions.

A publishing nightmare. How could such a thing happen?

I sheepishly gathered them back in, and later that evening carried the entire box of five hundred to Stephanie Hill's Doral abode. It was one of ten boxes that had been delivered to the Academy. It was not a good evening - and I needed to break this strange happening to her – gently.

****

Nine months later we had a big elaborate ceremony in Warsaw celebrating all fifty-five of our graduates and presenting the first class with their gold wings. I was going to stay in Warsaw for the next six weeks to fly along with them and do check-rides and make sure all was going along as it should – in-flight and at the base. As a result, I thought it would be fun to invite my kids to come over and experience Warsaw - which I did.

Mark and Dale joined me there, arriving for the celebrations on the same airplane with Pan American's Director of Inflight Services, Hector Adler – a wonderful man who had apparently enjoyed their company. The three of them it seems, had partied in first class all the way from New York to Frankfurt and on to Warsaw - and exchanged much in the process. As a result upon seeing me, my boss delighted in teasing me mightily - claiming that he now knew more about the Scofields than I did, and would pass any pertinent information on to the FBI!

We had a wonderful time in Warsaw. The base welcomed my two boys with open arms and showed them everything of interest in that beautiful old city. They had a blast – I did not see my children for four days except at breakfast and the graduation festivities. My wonderful graduates pulled out all the stops and the boys returned home to America – very reluctantly – a week later. Each sported a new heavy-duty wool winter coat, (which they cherish to this day) and many amazing souvenirs bought with Zlotys in the special Government controlled market. Upon departure – they hugged me and vowed – they would be back!

They LOVED Poland. You cannot experience these things in any book – these memories are – priceless.

****

My experience at the Victoria Hotel, which was the first 'five star' hotel in the city of Warsaw - was somewhat problematic. Poland, at this time, was still under Communist control, and amenities that we take for granted were still luxuries in this Communist controlled land, and were limited. It was the dead of winter and the heat would go off in the hotel at night. Hot water was limited and did not come on again until close to noon. I FROZE in my bed. Ice cold showers in the morning after freezing in bed, did not work for me, when the temperature outside was below zero and you could write your name in ice on the inside of the window.

I connected with a couple of my flight attendants and explained my problem. I asked them to show me where I could buy a fur coat – I needed one to sleep in. They thought this was hysterical but took me under their wing and off we went – stealthily – to the Government market. A visitor could not do this alone – you had to be accompanied by a local resident. At the Market we walked around and past several "Dealers" that they did not like, until we found one that past their 'muster' – whatever that was. Here they showed me three amazing, beautiful Silver Fox fur coats that came all the way to my feet. I tried them all on and then picked the one that had the most room in it and that also was the most beautiful. It was awesome – the fur pristine and 'silver' all over and to my feet.

Having made my decision I now needed to pay the dealer and Piotr my protégé begged me to make sure that that was indeed the coat I wanted. He stated I needed to be sure, so grabbed one of the other coats off the table and held it for me to try on again. I was puzzled, but slowly put my arms in the offered coat and then as he slipped it on, he whispered to me to place the money into the pocket of this coat. I had made a deal with the elderly vendor, to pay him in American Dollars – but that was illegal – so now Piotr had created a perfect "fix." I handed over my $100 American dollars quietly, in an old envelope tucked in the pocket of the coat I did not want and handed the coat back to the delighted vendor. Then smiling happily I picked up the coat I wanted, slipped it on and reached out my hand. He shook it so hard and for so long I thought for sure he would shake it off – he was so happy, and I - was on cloud nine. In the States this beautiful coat would have cost me two to three thousand dollars.

I turned it inside out and slept in my bed like a baby for the first time in many nights – wrapped in fur.

The temperature continued to plummet with snow falling softly, blanketing everything in sight. Winter east of Frankfurt could be dire - you had to be prepared – and now I felt I was. Piotr and Grazyna, that had helped me with the purchase of my coat, now took me on a sightseeing trip of the Old Towne of Warsaw. Then, after a delightful lunch with hot wine in front of a blazing fire-place in a tiny Café we had found in the Towne Square, they led me back out into the blowing snow. The idea, apparently was to find a nice deep, crisp, pristine, snow-drift. When we found one around the Center's fountain, they begged me take off my coat. This done, Grazyna took it and proceeded to dump it into the snow-drift and rub it all over with snow. This apparently, is how you "season" a new fur coat so that it would not "shed" all over your dark wooly winter clothes and while hanging in your closet. It works.

The next day after my purchase I did a check-ride, warmly adorned - as were the natives of the country in which I was a guest - in fur. I flew with a crew from Warsaw to Dubrovnik and on to Moscow, as the snow continued to fall.

The airplane was a 727 and we departed Warsaw right on time at 1245 with 49 passengers and nine crew. The weather was of no concern. They were used to it. I sat in the last row of seats to the right of the back galley, inconspicuous and unnoticed by the rest of the passengers. The airplane had no first class – it was economy from front to back, and my six flight attendants did a wonderful job of boarding the passengers and settling them down for flight. These passengers had a lot of bulky hats and coats and shopping bags to stow in the cabin that maintenance had blown full of lovely warm air, while the aircraft sat waiting on the tarmac. They made sure the boarding door was quickly shut after the last passenger boarded - to keep the heat in the cabin. Then they also ensured that the passengers kept to their assigned seats. The crew had been briefed that with so few passengers, for the aircraft load and trim purposes, most would be assigned seats in mid cabin and forward of the wings.

Finally the paperwork was completed and the door shut for the last time as the three jet engines burst into life and our forward Purser started her boarding announcement in English – then Polish and finally in German because the flight had come from Frankfurt. During taxi, and after they were all seated in their jump-seats, I got up and quietly did a quick check of the galley. I had watched the galley girl do a great check of all the commissary items and turn on all the ovens in preparation for the lunch service. They had loaded the coffee makers and turned them on – everything was in perfect shape for take-off.

EXCEPT – one small tiny-winy item that could cause a

disaster - after take-off. Upon their final galley check – and I noticed that the four working the back cabin had all done one - they had overlooked the fact that the secondary latches on the ovens had not been set.

I quickly flipped them into position to secure the ovens and their contents and was about to take my seat, when I suddenly thought I could I make a point that they would NEVER forget. Although not a "safety" issue, this minor oversight could create a very problematic start to their day if they had a full load of passengers in the future. I turned back to the aft facing oven and counted the meals. We had forty-nine passengers and nine crew that had to eat. We had been catered with sixty passenger meals and ten crew meals. The ten crew meals had been loaded in the forward galley along with twenty passenger meals. I flipped open the aft facing oven and counted the meals in the aft galley. They had loaded twenty meals of chicken with carrots and rice, in each oven. The ovens were hot and the meals were starting to cook.

The Captain came over the PA system informing the passengers that we had been cleared for take-off and the flight attendants should please be seated. I hastily gathered ten meals out of the aft facing ovens and threw them into the forward-facing oven - slammed everything shut and jumped into my seat as the Captain released the breaks and the airplane burst forward.

Take off was smooth – in spite of the swirling snow. Airplanes always operated well in cold conditions and as the wheels lifted off the snow packed runway, I looked around to see the smiling faces of my flight attendants as they eagerly awaited the aircraft passing through 10,000 feet so that they could get up and start their duties.

The snow-covered houses and trees of the city of Warsaw were starting to fall away below us when there was the most earth-shattering crash in the rear galley. It sounded like the tail had fallen off and passengers began to turned around in dismay to see what had happened, while my flight attendants jumped up, looking at me - some letting out little cries of horror. I just sat very calmly smiling at the passengers and motioned to them and my flight attendants to stay seated. They could do nothing now except wait till it was safe to get up and take care of whatever.

It seemed like a lifetime before the Captain chimed and let us know that we were passing through 10,000 feet and it was now safe for the flight attendants to move around the cabin. My crew jumped up in unison and flew to the galley. What they found was the aft facing oven doors wide open and the entire galley covered in chicken, rice, gravy and carrots. A lesson learned and demonstrated in living color, and a minor oversight that would never be repeated again, as long as they were in this job.

We served free wine with lunch and our passengers were happy and enjoyed a lot of attention. The cockpit crew were all Pan Am - Berlin based American pilots - who got a charge out of the 'indoctrination.' They asked me over dinner in Moscow, what else I had in mind to teach on the trip back – and could they please help? There are always good-hearted comedians on every crew that dearly loved to play silly tricks on our new-hires – a right of passage they would claim. This however, had been a learning curve my sweet flight attendants would never forget, and a memory that they would smilingly pass on to anyone with whom they flew - which was the idea.

I loved the flying out of Warsaw, especially to Dubrovnik in the summer time. Some trips had a two day lay-over there and I found the town and the people, charming. The only fly in the ointment was the approach to that airport. The way it was placed between the mountains and the sea could make the approach quite problematic with cross winds coming and going in every direction. Fortunately, our pilots were very familiar with it and had all been flying in and out of there many times

I trained three more classes of fourteen each in Miami. I returned to Warsaw each time to finish it off. Training the two Pursers in my hotel room. It was an experience like no other and - like India – the memories of this time, I have treasured all my life. Their routes to the historical and ancient cities of Prague, Budapest, Vienna, Dubrovnik, Moscow and St Petersburg became my life for six months at a time - as my life became their life, checking them out into the high standards of the Pan Am in-flight family.

CHAPTER 40 -

A DARK LOOMING STORM

On Monday, July 25, 1988 at a giant Gala at The Biltmore Hotel in Coral Gables, our five-year training program at the Academy in Miami - finally came to an end.

We graduated the last class, number 32, at the Doral Hotel and Country Club at 5 p.m. with Champagne, music and much gusto and sent them blissfully on their way to their awarded crew bases. Then, we gathered ourselves together as ONLY flight crew members can – jumped into cars and drove to the Biltmore Hotel for OUR Gala Celebration.

We had Champagne on the Terrace at 8:00 p.m. and dinner in the ballroom at 9:00 p.m. To this day I do not remember it ending.

It was an amazing time - those five years. I was so very proud to be a part of it. Yes, it was 'The New Pan Am.' Not at all what

I had experienced and joined in the 1960's - BUT - Once Pan Am – ALWAYS Pan Am. SUCH a special entity. A family - a lifestyle.

We partied and celebrated that life that we loved so much and to which we were all so committed with the rousing rendition of a song. A song we all had created over the last weeks that we dedicated to Amie Peroz our Manager In-Flight Service Standards and Stephanie Hill's boss at the Academy. Amie was in charge of the program, and it was she that had connected with me in New Orleans at the end of 1983 - saying "I need you. can you please come back as a Returning Mother."

The song had four verses and was sung to the tune of "Leaving on a Jet Plane." with this chorus: "We're leaving on a jet plane - Don't know when we'll be back again - Oh Amie just tell us where to go." The lyrics were fun and it was a wild, joyous yet sad final night.

The Academy went dark. We all said our "Good Byes" and returned to flying the skies from our respective crew bases.

Lizzie and I parted company. She returned to California and I to Virginia. It was heart-breaking – not only for us, but for our critters. In those five years I had said Good Bye to my sweet boy Bingo and Lizzie had lost her fuzzy sheep dog Jenny – but gained a rescued Corgi – named Dannie. She also determined that we could not separate my little Dachsy Willie from her cat, Nephie, a black Siamese of great Royalty and named after Nefertiti – Queen of Egypt. They had become inseparable from day one – they were both elderly and needed to stay together. So I inherited her. I was panic stricken – I had never owned a cat.

Elizabeth was unfazed. "You have lived with one for five years," she stated laughing. "You will be fine, trust me – and them."

I did – and we were.

****

Upon returning to Virginia it was difficult to get back into a 'normal' pattern of life and flying the line. I found I needed a lot of 'down time' before I was ready. Fortunately we were all given three weeks to settle back at our bases and into a regular routine. The Dallas base had inherited a lot of European Airbus flying, so I found myself bidding the same short patterns to Paris, London, Frankfurt, and Rome - where I was only gone for 3 to 5 days. I left the long-haul 747 flying to all the wonderful new hires I had just trained that were based in New York, London, San Francisco, Delhi and Bombay.

I found that I was able to bid and hold lines I wanted which made life a lot easier for me. I flew what I wanted and when I wanted. Life was good. My kids came up to stay with me, and Mark had moved to Virginia near the Potomac River that he loved. Dale had also graduated from LSU in Baton Rouge, Louisiana. We had retired his #15 jersey from the 'line up' of the "Roaring Tigers of Death Valley" with much pomp and ceremony, and he had found a good job in Boston. My sweet daughter, Kim, had decided that she was going to move to San Francisco which was very special to me. We had introduced the kids to California when Kim was eight and she had really loved it. She found it amazing to see so many of her Asian countrymen in residence there - which she was not used to seeing in New Orleans - where so far, she was the only one. I was beyond happy that all three of my kids had elected to come out of the deep south where they had no future - job wise.

Lunch with my beautiful daughter Kim in San Francisco

The year of 1988 was winding down. Winter had come to Virginia and I woke up to snow covering my little BBQ grill in the garden at the bottom of the stairs from my kitchen. I brushed the snow off the stairs and carried little Willie down to do his business. I set him down in the snow and he looked up at me as though I had lost my mind.

Having lived in Florida for the last five years, it was as though he was saying, "EEEERRRRR - Mum, you have GOT to be kidding me – what is this, and what do you expect me to do with it? This mess comes right up to my neck and my very private parts are in complete 'deep freeze' mode. 'Dorothy' we are not in Florida now and I am not Toto!"

I chuckled to myself as I took my broom and cleared a small path for him to walk in, around the steps and on down the path. He very grudgingly did what was expected and ran back up the icy stairs, shaking himself dramatically upon reaching the kitchen.

Nephie, his black Siamese cat buddy, walked regally into the kitchen upon our return and like the Queen of the Nile checked him out from head to tail. Then, turning in puzzlement at his indignant, dramatic display - strutted over to the open kitchen door. There, she stood for a moment, surveying the frozen whiteness and sniffing the cold air. Suddenly, as if struck by lightning, she darted back into the warm living room taking a running leap on to the couch - with Willie right behind her.

The next day I checked in for my flight to Lisbon. My flight pattern had been rescheduled with an extra 'leg' to JFK. The flight to Lisbon originated out of New York and they needed a Purser. I walked into the JFK crew room to find my crew – but what I found was a room full of people wrapped in silent disbelief and horror, clustered around a small black and white television set. The TV was located in a quiet corner, furnished with cozy easy chairs and a couch – used by crews with delayed flights or rescheduled ones. As I approached this extraordinary sight, I noticed several people turn away from the group with tears flowing while running to the nearest telephone.

Totally puzzled and concerned, I made my way to the front of the crowd and could not believe my eyes. The entire screen of that television set held the picture of the smashed and shattered cockpit of our Pan Am 747 Maiden of the Seas, lying on the ground somewhere in the world.

It was 12/21/1988 and our Flight 103 from Frankfurt to Detroit via London and New York – had been blown out of a clear, bright, evening sky - shortly before crossing the Atlantic Ocean en route to New York. The blast succeeded in killing everyone on board, including 12 people on the ground in a little Scottish town called Lockerbie.

The reality and frame of that image, will remain emblazoned into my memory for as long as I live.

Everyone there was in total shock and not wanting to believe what they were watching in real time, as the excited voice of the narrator continued to report what was known - and with information he was constantly receiving from the crash site.

The Maiden of the Seas had majestically lifted into the heavens from London Airport on its way to New York, when at 31,000 feet above the tiny town of Lockerbie a prematurely detonated bomb, hidden in a suitcase in the forward hold, had blown the aircraft into a gazillion pieces. Pieces which had rained down and smashed with devastating results into 21 sleepy festively decorated homes on a dark evening - three days before Christmas. The large pieces were covered in waves of burning jet fuel. The carnage was unimaginable.

Much later, it was thought that the bomb - made of odorless plastic Semtex, hidden in a cassette player in a suitcase - had detonated a tad earlier than planned. It should have detonated over the mighty Atlantic Ocean, so all evidence would be lost as though that mighty bird had never existed. Instead it blew the pieces of our mighty Maiden of the Seas over 850 square miles of dark Scottish countryside.

It was seven o'clock in Lockerbie, Scotland - on the evening of December 21st, 1988.

Startled – I suddenly came back to the here and now. This information was going out over all the airwaves of the world. My family in New Orleans would see or hear of it and panic, realizing I was scheduled to fly and was somewhere in the system. It could have been me. I too turned and headed for the nearest phone – only to find I was about number ten in line. This all, before the technical era and knowhow of cell phones.

Everyone waited patiently in stunned silence for their turn to let their loved ones know that they were alright and safe. It was a terrible time for anyone wearing a Pan Am uniform.

The crash in Lockerbie was heartbreaking. Many of us had known some of the crew – but even if we didn't - we were family and this had happened to some of our own. We were all broken and sad and it was an unbelievable chore for those of us working flights that day, to stay professional and upbeat while facing our passengers. It was imperative that they not be scared or troubled should they have heard about the crash before boarding.

I remember it being one of the longest most challenging flights of my life. Not only did I have the passengers to deal with – I had a devastated crew to help stay focused on performing Pan Am's noted premium in-flight service, to a full load of passengers headed for Lisbon.

Life went on. Slowly, over time, we healed.

Or did we?

It was the beginning of an endless storm we all pretended was not looming on the horizon. The Pan Am family circled the wagons till we - just blocked the horizon out.

CHAPTER 41 -

AN UNEXPETED OFFER

O ne afternoon about a year later, when I was reporting for my flight to Paris, I had a message in my mailbox that my supervisor Linda, wanted to see me. So, I walked around the corner to her office. She was on the phone but smiled when she saw me and waved me in and pointed to a seat.

When she was finished, she said,

"Good Afternoon Gi – I was hoping you would have time to stop today before your flight. I see that you are early, as usual!"

"Hi Linda – yes, you noticed. I hate being rushed before a

flight – so usually try to be ahead of the game. It's good to see you, what's on your mind – nothing bad, I hope." I added smiling at her greeting.

"No indeed, my dear girl. In fact, I have an interesting offer I have been asked to talk to you about." I looked up in surprise as she continued. "Our crew base in Berlin is in need of a base manager. We know you have spent quite a bit of time there in the past and we were wondering if you would be interested. The 727 flight crew are all American, but the flight attendants are German. You are bi-lingual and would be a perfect fit, if I could persuade you to go."

I was stunned. This was the last thing I expected.

"My goodness Linda, I am blown away. Thank you."

"We don't want you to give us an answer right away – sleep on it – think it over. It would transfer you into Management which I think would be perfect for you. Do you like Berlin?"

"Oh my goodness yes Linda, it is a wonderful city – I know it well and have operated flights in and out of Tempelhof Airport many times with BEA. I met several of our crew members when I was training in Warsaw - and I really like the 727 airplane."

"Great. So I can tell 'the powers that be' that you will think about it. It would be a two-year assignment – and could be longer."

We sat for a little while chatting about this and that – my five years at the Academy and my experience with the Reginal group of flight attendants and how helpful they have been in-flight. About our families and how much my kids have enjoyed following me around.

I told her about the fiasco when my boys joined me in Argentina on a trip I flew, out of New York. My flight was scheduled from JFK to Miami and then on to Buenos Aires. They were to fly from New Orleans and join my flight in Miami. Fate reared its ugly head that day and we were delayed in JFK with a mechanical and cancelled. I connected with the boys and told them to get on the BA flight out of Miami, check into my room at our crew hotel and I would see them the next day. No problem.

I arrived at the airport in BA the next day weary – the flight had been long with a full load in First Class and Economy - and a tad worried until I spied the boys at the airport waving and very excited to see me. They joined us in the crew van and I asked them if they had had any problem checking into the hotel.

"Oh no Mum – we had a great adventure." Dale, who was fifteen at the time told me excitedly – while his brother Mark who was seventeen, giggled as he tried to innocently look out of the window.

"What on earth do you mean?" I asked looking from one to the other - as the rest of the crew fell silent, all eagerly awaiting his explanation.

"Well we got into a cab and told the driver where we were going and he said 'Oh you don't need to go there – I will take you to a wonderful hotel – very inexpensive – you will have a great time there.' Mum, he was so nice and friendly, and he took us to this little hotel across town."

I almost had a heart attack – but both boys calmed me down and said it was no problem - very interesting and safe - however, neither of them had gotten much sleep. It seems that the room they got was on the ground floor and was tiny with a large bed that was almost wall-to-wall. It had nothing else and it cost them $10. They settled down for the night but were constantly awakened by the sound of stiletto heeled shoes running past their room all night long. It was very busy and noisy.

The entire crew bus erupted in laughter. That taxi driver had dropped the boys off at a 'house of ill repute' that he was probably an 'agent' for – thinking he was doing them a big favor.

The Captain laughingly put his arm around me and said, "Welcome to BA – City of light and excitement!"

I was mortified, but the crew loved it and promised to help me show the boys round BA the next day. They did that, and to this day both of my sons have returned to enjoy that City as adults. My oldest son Mark even opened an office for his business in BA, and Dale claims he would have moved there to live, if given the opportunity.

Now Linda and I could laugh about it – but at the time I was not amused. She too has teenagers and we both parted laughing and sharing Pan Am kid stories.

My trip to Paris was pleasant and uneventful – we did not have a full load so I had time to chew over the amazing offer the Company was making me. I spent two days in Paris which I loved and then flew home via London. We had to stop in Bangor, Maine for fuel, because the weather was not good and we might have a long 'hold' in Dulles upon arrival. This also was wonderful because the Captain sent out a list asking us to add our names if we wanted to buy lobsters from the Bangor station. He planned to call ahead with the order and even though we would not get off the airplane while they did the fueling – the Station would deliver the lobsters to us on board.

I was in heaven. I LOVE lobsters and would take a couple of big ones home to celebrate my new assignment – which of course, I planned to accept.

I was so very blessed and could not wait to tell Linda my decision.

****

Three months later in the first week of November, 1989 I arrived in Berlin, to get acquainted with the base, the crews and to 'house hunt.' I checked into the old Kempinski Hotel - my old crew hotel on the Kuhrfuerstendamm - happily remembering the many times I had been there years before when I was with British European Airways. The weather was cold and wet with heavy dark grey skies – but my mood was as bright and my heart happy as if the sun shone on a warm summer day. Although not my birth place – which was Hamburg - I had learned to love this ancient city with history going back to the 1500s. It was also here that I had met Ollie.

The Kuhrfuerstendamm - called the Ku-damm by all who called this city 'home' - was a beautiful long avenue of Linden trees and was often referred to as the Champs-Elysees of Berlin. It had wonderful boutiques and shops, hotels and restaurants of every kind along its entire length starting at the Breidscheidplatz considered the center of Berlin. Here stand the remains of the old Kaiser Wilhelm Memorial Church built in 1891 for Kaiser Wilhelm - the first German Emperor – destroyed like everything else around it in the bombing Blitz of World War II. The western Tower was badly damaged and is all that remains of the original church and stands pointing skeletal fingers skyward as a memorial of that terrible time. A new church and tower were built in 1956 right next to it – the tower, a very modern structure not popular with many residents of this old historic city.

The first couple of days after my arrival I spent getting introduced and familiarized with the lay-out of our offices and the airport. We no longer flew out of Tempelhof Airport which was right downtown and which I had done with BEA. It was now totally unsuitable for modern aviation and unable to handle jet traffic – now we operated out of Tegel. Gone are the days when you landed in a propeller airplane – flying within inches of houses on each side of the runway and able to look right into people's living rooms. This was the "Jet Age" and we had progressed to the outskirts of town and Tegel Airport.

I had made friends with Jutta, one of the crew schedulers who had volunteered to help me find an apartment. I really liked her and gratefully accepted her offer. She was off on Saturday – the day after tomorrow – and so we agreed to meet at a small out-door cafe at the Breitscheidplatz where all the commercial arteries of the city fanned out   She promised to look in the Daily Newspapers and on the crew notice board for vacancies, and she would bring some street maps that might help us find our way around. She also marked off some of the nicer areas of town – near and around the Tierpark where we could look. I thought I would prefer to stay in the city as opposed to being in the outskirts and closer to the airport.

Saturday broke cold but sunny with small white clouds sailing across a blue sky. I was in a happy frame of mind as I made my way to the café at lunch time to meet Jutta that sunshiny day. We met and spread ourselves out at a corner table in the sunshine, but out of the wind. Jutta had found several adds that she thought might suit, and after a leisurely lunch we set out with a list of five addresses.

We spent a totally delightful afternoon checking out some good some not so good. One of the things I really wanted was my own bathroom. I did not mind sharing a kitchen BUT I really did not want to share a bathroom – PLUS I wanted unrestricted – hot water. We found only one small apartment that fit that criteria – but it was very expensive. Most apartments had a communal bathroom that they shared and hot water was on a meter.

Jutta said she would check the evening papers when she got home and call me in the morning with any new options to check out on Sunday. I thanked her and we parted. I needed to return to the hotel to check my messages and see if the Station had left me any paperwork to fill out for 'passes' and 'parking' stickers, effective December 1st, 1989.

Sure enough, I had a large folder waiting for me at the desk. I spent the evening filling out a mass of forms – two in English for parking but the rest in German, while ordering 'room service' and answering telexes from New York. I wanted to call New Orleans and talk to my kids, but could not do that till the morning, due to the time change. So, I took a long hot shower and went to bed and slept like a baby.

I got a call from Jutta while eating breakfast in the coffee shop. She had found four more possibilities for very suitable apartments in the Tierpark area. She will pick me up at the Kempinski at ten o'clock.

That works for me. I went back to my room to get ready and also to call my kids. All was well at home and so I went down to meet Jutta in the lobby. I found her talking to the concierge who gave her another possible lead. We set off for another full day of walking, talking and fun with a new friend.

The first two were in a really nice area of town but were too expensive and also did not give me my own bathroom. The third one however, was almost perfect. It was the one that Gustaf, the concierge at the hotel had alerted us to. It was a ground floor apartment in a beautiful old house at the very edge of the Tiergarten. I would have access to a kitchen shared by the owner, but I would have a bedroom and living room and my own bathroom with unlimited hot water. I would also be allowed to bring little Willie and Nephie cat person. The elderly owner loved animals and offered to babysit any time.

I was beside myself with happiness. I had EVERYTHING I

needed in an awesome location – and I could afford it. We said Good Bye to the sweet owner, taking all the necessary paperwork home to fill out. I could not wait to inform New York I was all set and had a place to live – we were right on schedule for December 1st, 1989. It was five thirty on Sunday afternoon November 7th when I ran happily back into the Kempinski.

When checking in at the front desk I was met with a barrage of super urgent messages. "Call In" – "Call New York Headquarters" etc. etc. etc.

The Concierge Gustaf, ran up to me when he saw me at the desk and said, "Fraulein Gisela, New York has been calling you all day – almost since you left this morning. Please let me know if I can help."

What in the world is happening? Thoroughly shaken I placed a call as directed to the number at New York Headquarters I had been given and waited patiently as the message went out across the ether.

An hour later – I sat – dejected and sad - no heartbroken, in my hotel room. I could not believe what I had heard from New York.

The Berlin Wall was 'coming down!' RETURN TO BASE.

Our crew base here had existed since the Berlin Airlift had ended in 1949. Due to the division of Germany after the war, only British and American airplanes were allowed to fly the 'corridor routes' across Soviet East Germany and in and out of West Berlin. That was Pan American and British European Airways.

I had been hearing 'rumblings' coming from the Eastern sector since 1988 that "cracks" were starting to appear in the Soviet Iron Curtain. The Hungarian, Polish, Czechoslovakian and Austrian boarders had been breached – were compromised – were cracking open. East Germans were racing across any border they could - to get out of harsh, restrictive, Soviet controlled East Germany.

Somehow – this rumor had been so vague, remote – unrealistic. BUT NOW IT WAS REAL.

The phone rang in my room. I looked at it blankly and did not move. I did not want to talk to anyone. It kept ringing. And ringing.

Finally, I lifted the receiver.

"Hello - hello - Gi – it's me Linda. Can you hear me? Are you there?" It was my supervisor in Dulles.

"Yes Linda – Hi, I'm here." I said dejectedly.

"Gi are you all right – I was so very upset when I heard the news. Are you coming back? Send me a telex with your flight number and I will meet you at the airplane. We MUST talk."

"Yes, OK Linda – thanks. I'm just a tad in shock at the order to return. I was all set – even found a great place to live. I will telex my flight number when I am confirmed." I placed the phone back on the cradle, settled back on the bed fighting my disappointment. I lay there contemplating this giant phenomenon.

I was a child in Germany when the division of Germany took place. My whole life has been changed forever as a result of it. All the blessings I have lived - are a direct result of it. As an adult I was exposed to the hardships of the people of East Berlin and the Eastern Sector of Germany living under the heavy Iron Curtain of Russia when I flew with BEA. Finally, this hardship is about to come to an end – should I not be dancing in the street? I should – but I was not and felt guilty about that. My selfishness seemed to add to my sadness.

The order from the Pan Am Building in New York had been.

"Return to base – the 'Wall' that the Soviets had built to control and divide Berlin into East and West is coming down and we will no longer be needing a crew base in Berlin. Berlin will now be open to the world."

Since the end of WW II when Germany was divided up into four 'parcels' by the Allies, the Soviets got the Eastern sector which included Berlin. However, Berlin was the capital of Germany and the Allies decided they each needed to keep a presence there. Russia did not like that idea and when the Allies refused to give Russia more "say" in the economic future of Germany, they decided to try and squeeze the Allies out by creating a 'blockade' of Berlin. They completely cut it off from all land access by road, rail or canal, thus the city could now no longer bring in what was needed to sustain it and its population of two million people.

The Allies refused to be forced out and created an 'air bridge' where they would fly the desperately needed supplies of food, water, medicines and supplies in by air via the Soviet controlled air 'corridors,' flying over Soviet East Germany and into the airports of Tempelhof and Tegel in West Berlin. That Airlift started in June of 1948 and continued for a year till May 1949 when the Russians realized they had been defeated in their plot, and finally lifted the blockade.

I returned to base in the U.S.

On November 9th, 1989 the Berlin Wall did indeed come crashing down with great fanfare and celebration and between that day and the 22nd of November 1989 – eleven million elated East Germans crossed the border at Checkpoint Charlie into West Berlin - and freedom.

CHAPTER 42 -

AN ALTERNATE OPPORTUNITY

L inda Kelly met me upon my return home from Berlin. It was early afternoon and we went to her office and she closed the door behind us.

She was very sympathetic and kind – totally understanding my disappointment. We talked about it for some time and shared a cup of tea that she had brewed upon our arrival – then she asked me, "OK Gi – now I would like to know what you feel like you want to do as a result of this situation?"

I was puzzled and looked up at her, not understanding the question – so she added, "You have been re-assigned for the Berlin job and are now 'Management' - would you like to stay in that category, or do you wish to go back to 'In-Flight'?"

I sipped my tea, not quite sure how I wanted to answer. She let me take my time and said nothing. An airplane thundered by the building on its way skyward. The clock on the wall ticked loudly.

"Linda - I'm not sure how to answer that. If I stay Management what would that mean? I now have no job - so I must return to In-Flight."

"I understand your dilemma. When we talked before you had indicated that you would be interested to upgrade to Management if the opportunity presented itself. At this time you are Management, and if you are still of the same mind I have an idea that may work. Pan Am Express has need of an In-Flight Services Manager in Philadelphia. We could offer you that if it might be of interest. It is nothing like the job in Berlin – but it would keep you in Management for the time being till something more desirable comes up.

"Your boss would be Shelly Ufner – I believe you know each other. She is Director there, and has indicated she would love to have you, should you have any interest. She also has indicated that she is 'looking' to move on from that job so her position as Director, would be yours for the asking if or when she leaves. I understand they have about two hundred flight attendants stationed there at Philadelphia North Airport, in Bensalem."

I was silent. I did not know what I wanted and finally - said so.

"Of course, Gi. That is completely understandable. Why don't you go back and fly-the-line for a month and then when you have had time to get over the Berlin disappointment, and given the other some thought – come back and we will talk some more."

"Thank you, Linda, – it's a deal." I did not feel ready to make such a decision right then and there. I also did not realize I had such an option open to me. I just assumed that I would go back to flying-the-line. I got up, thanked her very much for her help and understanding, and promised to get back with her as soon as I had had a little time to think this all through.

Life returned to normal and I regained my equilibrium. I called scheduling and volunteered to fly "in the pool" for a month – which they welcomed with delight and immediately scheduled me to fly a six day pattern to London, Paris and Rome.

I also called Shelly Ufner and talked the offer over with her at some length. She was seriously looking for something outside Pan Am because she felt that she had hit her ceiling of opportunity within the company.

****

It was 1990 and I was going to be forty-nine years old in a month. The airplanes were getting bigger and the loads were getting heavier and I was starting to feel my forty-nine years in my knees and back.

I called Linda and told her I would like to take the job in Bensalem. She was excited for me and said she would put it into place for me to start March 1st. I was to take five days off after my next trip to find somewhere to live in Bensalem. I did that, and found a nice ground floor apartment in a tree lined complex of cottage style buildings two stories high, backing onto a large park. Little Willie, Nephie cat person and I moved in, on Friday, the 1st March, 1990.

On Monday morning at seven o'clock sharp I reported to my new assignment as Manager of In-flight Services with Pan Am Express. It was an interesting learning curve and a far cry from my past life. It was structured, it was intense, it was confining and repetitive – but I learned a lot about a lot of things I had never been exposed to before. The hardest thing for me to learn was that I would be in that office every day from Monday to Friday from seven in the morning till six or seven every night, tackling anything from discipline to paychecks in a location – North Philly – that I hated.

I am NOT an office type person. It was an enormous adjustment. It was decided (not by me) that I not qualify on the small – one flight attendant - airplanes they flew as "feeders" for Pan Am's main-line flights. They did not want me to fly – which was a little strange for me – but I accepted it because I did not have a veterinarian here that I trusted with my critters. So that worked for me.

However, only for now.

In August of the following year Shelly told me she had an interview appointment with a small carrier based in Maryland. I wished her luck and wondered what this would mean for me. She left for the main Philadelphia airport bright and early one Friday morning to catch her flight to the town of Salisbury across the Chesapeake Bay in Maryland. It was not until the following Monday that I saw her again to ask her how she made out at her interview.

She laughed in total disgust and said, "Oh my Lord Gi – it was awful. It was this little rinky-dink carrier in a little hick town in the boonies of Maryland – No Thank You - it was the end of the world and I am not going there!!"

I was floored. What in the world did this mean for me and my future? I had stayed put for a year – learning a lot, but I was stifling. I needed out – or a change. I was at the point of seriously thinking about returning to the line.

Upon leaving her office in confusion, I suddenly remembered a conversation I had had at the Philly airport two weeks before. I was in Pan Am uniform; we had a mechanical delay of several hours and I was sitting in the airport near our gate – waiting for the OK to go and check that the flight attendant on our departing flight would still be good and legal to take that flight. With my ID and being in uniform helped me get to anywhere in the airport I needed to be – including any crew room located "air side" of the terminal.

While there I sat next to a sweet, elderly gentleman who asked me what I planned to do when Pan Am went 'under?'

"Of course," he pressed gently, "You do accept, that it is going 'under' - don't you?"

I introduced myself and he did the same. He too was delayed, and we talked for a goodly while.

I explained that I was one of thousands of people around the world, wearing this uniform that could not accept that fact. He was forcing me to face and acknowledge that the storm that had broken over Lockerbie in Scotland that devastating night in 1988 – had not left us. We have not been able to recover. Pan American – the world's most experienced airline, with a logo recognized around the world second only to Coca-Cola – was left very fragile and very vulnerable since that dark horrific night.

Yes – that devastating, looming storm, had been hanging over us since 1988. It had slowly and cruelly blanketed our amazing airline and threatening it, since that terrible day. The storm has progressed one day, one month, one year at a time, until this moment when we are unable to shake the final, dark, blanket of demise. We MUST accept reality – as devastating as it is - it is almost over!

He and I talked for a long time. He asked me what I had been doing with Pan American and how long I had been with them. What were my plans?

Suddenly, his flight was called and he got up to leave.

"I have a small 'feeder' carrier based on The Eastern Shore," he said quietly, before leaving. "I need someone with your experience and background. Here is my card – please call me."

I reached out my hand to take the card and said with a puzzled look on my face, "The Eastern Shore – isn't that where we are now?"

"Indeed it is not, my dear young lady – we are on the East Coast here. The Eastern Shore is across the Chesapeake." He smiled broadly, waved and was gone.

After talking with Shelly, I remembered my conversation with that sweet man at the Philly airport. I could not wait to get home and dig in my uniform pocket to retrieve the card I had completely forgotten about till this moment in time.

That night I retrieved it. Richard A. Henson. Henson Aviation, Salisbury. Maryland. Could that be where Shelly had been to interview? They were looking for a Director of In-Flight Services for ninety flight attendants.

Later that week after an evening meeting to discuss the possible dismissal of a flight attendant, I asked Shelly again about her interview. She reiterated her negativity – it was an awful place – she could never live there.

I asked her if she would mind if I connected with them for a possible interview. She looked at me as though I had three heads.

"Gi, of course not – here let me give you all the contact information. Are you sure that is what you want to do?" She looked at me in disbelief – but also with some concern. "Gi, it is w-a-y off the beaten track. In the boonies and cut off from the world, by the Bay. You and I have way too much going for us to go there. Do go check it out, but please think this through before you make any decisions." I left her office with all the information not knowing in the least what I planned to do with it.

I sat on it for a whole ten days wondering what I should do. I did not know what I wanted, but I did know that I needed something different, and I really did not want to go back to 'line flying.'

After much consideration, I finally placed a call to the office of a Mr. Steve Farrow at Henson Airlines, The Piedmont Connection, in Salisbury, Maryland.

Mr. Farrow's secretary called me back the next day and made arrangements for me to come to the Eastern Shore for an interview five days later. She sent me flight information for Friday, October 3rd 1991 arriving in Salisbury at 10:00 a.m. She said she will be there to meet me.

At 08:35 a.m. I boarded the smallest airplane I had ever considered flying in, on a scheduled flight. It was a Beech 99. I was one of eight passengers and two pilots. OK – so the First Officer made sure we were all belted and secured and then closed the aircraft door and jumped back into the cockpit. The two engines burst into life one by one, and we were on our way.

I smiled to myself on the forty-minute ride over the Chesapeake Bay wondering why Henson Airlines needed a Director of In-Flight Services if they were flying Beech 99s which had no flight attendants.

Upon landing, I walked across the tarmac to the small terminal building and was immediately greeted by a very professional young lady who introduced herself as Steve Farrow's secretary. We had an immediate connection, and she bid me follow her to the offices behind the terminal. Which I did.

We entered the double doors of the main building and climbed the stairs to the offices of Steve Farrow and the other major officers of Henson Airlines – including Richard A Henson who I had met but was not there that day. Steve Farrow was expecting me and I had a feeling that he had watched our walk from the terminal to this building - as his large office windows faced that side of the airport. He greeted me very graciously and with a firm handshake - then bid me have a seat.

We sat across from each other for many minutes without speaking. I looked up at Steve silently, waiting for an opening. Finally, he said with a big smile on his face.

"Welcome to Henson Airlines and the Eastern Shore. I am very happy that you are here and decided to call us. We are very much in need of someone to take over the In-Flight department but have no one in-house. We have been looking for a goodly while to find just the right person"

Time seemed to stand still. It was very strange. Steve and I connected – I could feel it. We talked – and talked – and talked – about everything and nothing. I had no idea that I was having an interview – we just talked.

The afternoon just flew by and he finally said, "I have made arrangements to meet my wife for dinner and would love it if you could join us – or do you have to get back?" I said that would be lovely – I could take the later flight back to Philly.

On the way to the restaurant he told me a little bit about Henson Airlines and how it got started. He chuckled full of merriment when I told him about my meeting with Mr. Henson.

"He is my uncle – and that sounds like a conversation he would have with someone like you."

We had a delightful dinner at a restaurant called Waterman's, and his wife Donna was charming and really good company. It was a very pleasant experience full of merriment and lively conversation. Finally, they dropped me off at the airport in order to get the last flight back to Philly.

Steve shook my hand and said, "This was fun - I will be in touch."

I thanked them both and made my way to the gate, and home. My flight home was on a Dash 8 airplane. An unknown entity – but it had one flight attendant - Cindy.

Two days later I got an Express envelope delivered to my desk from Henson Airlines, offering me a job as their Director of In-Flight Service, effective November 1st 1991.

I was panic stricken at the idea of leaving Pan American. It had been my life, my love and security for so many years. I had matured with Pan Am – my children had grown up living and benefitting from my association with Pan Am – and now I was looking to leave it?

I spent the next days, wrapping my mind around this mammoth and unthinkable idea. I had a lot to think about. Yes, I wanted – no needed – a change and this seemed like such a perfect opportunity. A new challenge. Henson offered all that I had hoped for in a beautiful new environment, off the beaten track across the Chesapeake Bay. It had serious drawbacks however that needed to be thought through.

When I returned to the US from Berlin I had been made Management – but I had retained my Purser pay and status because I was basically "in limbo" till I found my permanent status in the scheme of things. Transferring to Henson would mean a $20,000 pay cut. That was a lot of money....

The Eagle needed space and time out - over water to think this through. Pan American World Airways – the company that I loved, had grown up in and that had taught me so very much - was in a death spiral.

Unthinkable – but true.

The mighty bird roosted silently before sailing for hours over wide stretches of calming water - lost in deep thought and emotion.

A giant door was swinging dramatically - shut.

But... perhaps there is a crack of light in a distant window?

CHAPTER 43 -

ANOTHER NEW BEGINNING

U pon arriving on the Eastern Shore, I moved into a cute little house with a large backyard that I had found on the outskirts of Salisbury. I was delighted to find that everything I needed was less than ten minutes away in such a small town. The house was close to the airport and off the beaten track, sitting at the end of a dead-end street. My two critters examined the back yard together and at great length – Nephie-cat-person being the most picky – but to my relief, both came back inside wiggling their excited approval. I was happy. They liked my choice.

I reported to the office of Steve Farrow at seven a.m. the following day to assume my job as Director of In-Flight Services for Henson Airlines. He had his secretary - that I knew and really liked - show me around the building and introduce me to everyone I would need to know. The maintenance manager, the scheduling and operations manager and the chief pilot to name a few - after which she showed me my office. I was tickled pink. It was right next to the chief pilot at the end of a long hallway and had two large long windows overlooking the parking lot and a green area separating the building and the main entrance to the terminal at the airport road. She left me there, to settle in.

I unpacked and set up my desk, setting out a picture of my kids at The Taj Mahal in New Delhi, my dog and cat and my Mum. I had found that it 'softens' an area that could be very scary and uncomfortable to flight attendants that had been summoned for a meeting to my office. It made me a lot more 'real,' human and approachable, and would often break a difficult silence.

While I was doing that a lady knocked on my door and introduced herself as Peggy Hart. Peggy said she was the secretary to the Director of Pilot Training and was in the office next door. She seemed very nice and told me to let her know if she could be of any help in or out of the office. She had lived on the 'Shore' all her life and would be happy to help me find my way around. I thanked her gratefully and told her I just might have to take her up on her offer before too long.

Next, I had another caller. She introduced herself as my secretary, stating that the chief pilot and I would be sharing her, and her office was directly across the hall from mine. The phone in that office shrilled loudly and she ran to answer it – excusing herself, stating with a wave of her hand, that it is almost always an emergency of some kind – to somebody!

As she ran out of my door, she bumped into someone else attempting to come in. I looked up smiling at the collision and got up to welcome my new visitor with an out-stretched hand.

"Good Morning Gisela – welcome to Henson Airlines. I am Kathie Dorick, a flight attendant here almost since the airline began – and I am now in charge of training. I hope you have been given a warm welcome by everyone – because we need you a lot!"

"Well hello – Good Morning Kathie. Indeed, everyone has been amazing – come in and have a seat."

She did – we hit it off immediately and talked for an hour. She was a wonderful lady and I knew right away that I had a great person in 'my corner' and I would be calling on her for help many times in the days to come. She told me I had a Manager of In-Flight Services – Donna Shockley – but she was in Norfolk on an errand for Steve – something to do with the Union. She will be back tomorrow."

I looked at her questioningly and asked her with a pained look "Do we have Union problems at Henson?" I had become familiar with those at Pan Am and was not too delighted to hear we might be 'sideways' with the Union here also. It is usually a very time-consuming problem, and is inclined to invariably take your eye off the ball for many hours at a time.

Kathie shrugged. "Not really – we have a pretty good relationship with the union reps. here." I was relieved to hear it, so changed the subject.

"Kathie, please tell me about the two aircraft types you are flying at Henson. I am not at all familiar with either one – and while I think of it, please schedule me in on the next training class."

She looked at me as though I had three heads. "Why would I do that – I'll be happy to show you over each one of the two Dashes, but you will not need a training class." I looked at her in disbelief.

"Kathie - of course you must train me – I am only qualified on the Boeing 707,727, 747 and Airbus 300s – I have never even seen your Dash 8's before."

"I know, but you will not be operating them so you won't need a training class."

I jumped to my feet "What do you mean – of course I will be flying – I need to qualify."

"Gisela, I was told you will not be flying. They don't WANT you to fly." I sat down again and we looked at each other in strained silence. Finally I said quietly.

"Kathie - please read my lips – that will not work for me. I have been around airlines long enough to know that I will get more information about what is on everyone's mind down-line - in crew-rooms, than I ever will here in this office. If I am going to be their boss, I need to know what they do and how it is done – I NEED TO QUALIFY!"

She grinned broadly and said "I love what you say – but good luck getting there!" with that she got to her feet, said she was in an office around the corner and she will help me however she could – and vanished out of the door. I sat in silence totally confused.

A few minutes later I heard John Buchanan, the Chief Pilot laughing loudly in the hallway and say to what might have been Kathie's disappearing form, "She sounds like everything we need – BUT Good Luck with that idea," and laughed delightedly on his way back to his desk.

I sat stunned looking out of the window at three joggers running down Airline Highway. Not flying had not worked for me in Bensalem. I cannot discipline people for not doing their job – if I didn't know what their job was supposed to be. It had not occurred to me to talk about this with Steve Farrow. I assumed it was understood that I would qualify to fly - as part of the job. Apparently I had been mistaken.

When I had said good bye to all the folks I had worked with in Bensalem – some had given me good-natured teasing about the fact that I was following our tough, inflexible ex-boss to Henson Airlines. It seems that that gentleman had indeed proceeded me here – but I did not know him, so took the tease with a pinch of salt. I had not been qualified to fly on the Pan Am Express aircraft either – the idea being I was now Management and not crew and therefore I was to dress in business attire and closet my uniform in mothballs.

Was it possible that this idea was his influence at Henson also? We had not been introduced – I did not know the man although his office was right next door to Steve Farrow.

My blood ran cold. I needed to get this straight immediately or I could not continue here.

John Buchanan's smiling face appeared in my doorway and jogged me back to reality.

"Gisela, Steve just called and asked me to have you please join us in the conference room for an Ops. meeting at two o'clock. I'm on my way down now." He stood propping up my doorway. "Are you OK – you look like someone left you standing on the tarmac watching the airplane depart without you."

I jumped up pulling myself together, and grabbing a pad and pencil followed his fleeing form down the hallway.

The Ops. Meeting consisted of the same group of men I had been introduced to that morning plus the Director of Training for the pilots. This group was the brains and 'cog of the wheel' for Henson Airlines – that made it all work, flow and come together. I was introduced and then we went to work on running a safe, on-time airline, feeding the main hubs down the Eastern Seaboard from New York to Florida.

The meeting over, I jumped up and asked Steve if he had a minute to talk to me before going back to his office.

He looked at me enquiringly and said, "Sure Gi, what's on your mind?"

I waited for everyone else to leave the room which took a little while as they all stopped to wish me luck and to let them know if they could help me with anything. They were all very welcoming and I really got the feeling that they were relieved and happy to have me join the team, which was very encouraging. Then I got straight to the point.

"Steve, I got to meet Kathie Dorick this afternoon and she told me something you and I had not discussed but is really important to me."

"Oh good - Kathie is a really good flight attendant and will be a great help to you. You also have Donna Shockley – she is down-line but will be here tomorrow."

"Yes, so Kathie said – I will be glad to meet her – but now I have a question for you. Are you not expecting me to fly now and again – as needed to and from our bases down-line? Because I feel very strongly that I must do so in order to do a good job as Director. It is imperative for me to know exactly what their job is, if I am expected to oversee and criticize them for not doing it. I cannot possibly do that if I am not qualified to fly on an airplane I am not familiar with. I need to experience every-thing they do, and where and how they are supposed to do it – otherwise I will have no credibility with them."

He sat way back in his chair and there was a long silence, as he studied my obvious distress.

Finally, he said quietly, "We don't want you to fly. We have brought you in from outside the company on purpose, instead of upgrading someone from within. We think it better for you – you will have more 'clout' with the flight attendants if you stay here in the Head Office where you have all the help and support in the world. We don't want you to be 'one of them' in their eyes. You have Donna – she can fly when needed."

I was floored – deflated – blown away. I looked at him in quiet desperation, not knowing how to proceed. This was my new boss and we really liked each other – but – we did not KNOW each other. He had no idea what made me tick and now I was wondering if he really knew what my job entailed. Another thing I had learned about him in the short time I had been there was that he had never been a crew member. He was a very clever, intelligent man who ran that airline with great skill and had surrounded himself with exceptionally good, knowledgeable people, responsible for each department. He was a very valuable, able asset to Henson Airlines – a true 'chip off the old block' for Old Mr. Henson - BUT he had never actually DONE any of it – on the line, hand's on.

I got up and walked to the window. I suddenly needed space and fresh air. After a while I tuned slowly to face him – he had been silent, letting me get myself back together.

I turned a chair around to lean on and then said looking down at him, "Steve - I left flying-the-line and transferred to Management with Pan Am in order to stop flying-the-line. When I was given the job at Express, the powers that be there also had the same notion as you. I was not to fly and I was to dress in business attire every day and stay 'on site.' That was not what I had in mind – I just did not want to fly a regular scheduled line as a Purser anymore. All Management, including our Supervisors had flown the line before becoming Management – it was a necessary part of their ability to do the job effectively.

"I have to confess it cramped my style beyond belief. I had no idea how it would cut me off from the very people I was supposed to supervise. I also never met any of my flight attendants unless I was disciplining them – so, I became the 'hated hammer.' Trust me – it did not work. I beg you – don't ask me to operate like that – because I cannot – will not.

"I am not saying that I must fly a regular schedule – I'm just saying that I should fly a 'leg' every now and then – maybe help scheduling out instead of calling out a reserve. Just so the crews get to see me out there, doing what they do and getting to know them and what they face and do every day. It just makes me more 'real' – it does not take away from my title, but it will enable me to be a better Director of In-Flight Services."

After this long tirade was over the silence between us was deafening. I looked down at him in despair. I NEEDED to WEAR the airplane – get to know it inside and out before I could do a good job for the Company and do my flight attendants justice. Did Steve understand that – had my tirade made any sense to him?

He sat examining his nails in great detail. Finally, he sat up and said, "Sit down – let's talk this through."

An hour later I walked into Kathie's office to schedule my training.

CHAPTER 44 -

A NEW BEGINNING AND A SAD END

S teve was an amazing boss. He was always there when I needed him 24/7. He mentored me, taught me, stabilized me when needed and always 'had my back' - even when it was politically risky within the company to do so. I worked hard, was totally dependable and stood up to admit if I screwed up. Over the ten years that I worked for him we would have a love, hate relationship on a very business level – disagreeing many times on things – but he knew I had the Company's back too, and would never let him down.

He shone - when we shone, and he respected and accepted my advice many times against his better judgement or ruling from above. He operated many times with his hands tied, which, sadly - I believe the crews were not aware of. The guys at Pan Am

Express had warned me – but then I had no form of reference. Now I understood how much Steve had my back against decisions made from the Director's office - one notch above his.

I found that I had inherited the most amazing group of young people. My flight attendants as a whole, were hard working, flexible, dependable – but they were human beings not robots. It was the latter that I had the hardest time on defending to the Company. Steve and the powers that be above his pay grade, did not like me to get too close to them – or to learn too much about them. They felt that was not my job – none of my business.

Just get them to do the job they were hired to do – was the order.

I however, had a conflict with the Company regarding this perimeter. I felt very strongly, that you cannot get them to do their job if you have no idea who they are or anything about their lives. Their lives HAVE to work – if they do not, the job will suffer. As a result, against all odds, I made it my business to learn everything I could about all ninety of them, and as the months and years progressed the numbers kept getting higher as our needs grew for more airplanes and more flight attendants. The two aircraft flown by Henson Airlines at that time were the De Havilland Dash 7 and Dash 8 both wonderful, dependable Turbo props, and required only one flight attendant. Although we always had reserves scheduled, it was sometimes hard or even impossible to get a reserve to the airplane down-line on time after an overnight sick call, and we would have to cancel.

I tried to be available at every 'recurrent training' session wherever it might be so that we could communicate and interact one on one. It worked. I also would help scheduling out when they had no one to fly the trip which worked for me because I could then connect with my flight attendants in crew rooms down-line. They would call the office or would track me down in the system if they needed something and I had an 'open door' policy 24/7 wherever we were.

Not all liked me – not all trusted me because I was an outsider – and that was OK. However, when any one of them was in trouble, or needed a favor, they would call the one person they knew would understand – be fair - and would try and help. Me.

This was the fourth airline of my career and what I loved and found to be universal with airlines is that when you join them - you join a "family." As crew members you were connected and joined to each other by friendship and loyalty - to a fault. It is very special and you have to have 'lived it' to understand it - and so it was even with this tiny off the beaten track feeder airline. They were a family and I was not yet a member.

One day a flight attendant had a Mother who needed a heart transplant. OK, so we needed to adjust her schedule so that she could spend the most time possible with her Mother and still keep a working schedule. The Company had a fit. It is none of my business what is happening with our flight attendants in their personal lives. They have a scheduled line for the month and need to fly it. Make sure they do. If they cannot or are unable to - then they need to resign.

EXCUSE ME – NO - that is no way to go.

I'm sorry, but it is my business – and I did the best to maintain the schedule and still make it work for that family over a two-year period - wheeling and dealing with scheduling. Years later I got the most amazing 'thank you' note from that family that I treasure to this day.

Another time, scheduling would call me in frustration to say that a flight attendant was sick in a hotel down-line with blown ear drums. They have no idea how long she would have to stay there. A doctor said she may never be able to fly again – she had been there for three days – what did I want to do about it.

"Limo her home" I said without hesitation – EERRRRR NO – the Company says they cannot do that - yet. What does that mean – 'yet?' Of course, that flight attendant needs to go and be at home – NOW – we cannot wait for 'yet.'

I drove to Philly in my car, got her and drove her home to her base in New Bern. She was in tears when she saw me, a young person scared, in pain, having spent three days in a bland hotel room with no way to get home to her family or her doctor.

Battles like this were a daily occurrence. However, when I would help the Company out on an originating flight out of Salisbury at 05:00 on a Sunday morning, or on a Christmas Holiday when they had a sick call and no one to cover – Steve always made sure he had my back. One day Ops called me in my office around lunch time on a Friday afternoon to see if I could help them out of a really bad situation. We had to cancel a series of flights due to a sick call with no reserves and were parking nearly one hundred people where they did not want to be, on three legs of a flight pattern. I said I would take the flight on one condition - if Steve could guarantee to get me home before midnight – I had no one to watch my critters and I had been gone since seven that morning.

He gave me his word and I flew the trip. Saved stranding almost one hundred passengers and three delayed flights from being canceled. This translated into much revenue, prestige and credibility for the Company. Steve was as good as his word and sent a King Air to pick me up after the last leg into New Bern to fly me home before the bewitching hour.

We were a team. Not just him and I - but all of the necessary department heads that make an airline fly reliably, dependably and on-time. We had daily, early morning briefings, so that we were all on the same page for the day. This was critical and so very helpful and I found myself working very closely with the Director of Operations and Scheduling. His name was Tom Hubric and he was a piece of work and a real character. He had grown up in the airline business from the time he was a boy in Buffalo New York and had more funny airline stories and jokes that he had lived through, than anyone I had ever met. He ran a tight ship down in Ops – but we hit it off and we made that relationship work for both of us. He would help me and I would help him any time I could. Besides he had been married to a flight attendant for many years so we were very much "in sync."

Tom helped me with a problem shortly after my arrival that made me very unpopular with the senior pilots in the company. I noticed that the lines of flying were constructed mainly with "out and backs." These were one day trips very much prized by the senior pilots because it meant they returned home every night to wife and family.

This however, was problematic for my young flight attendants on their pay scale. It kept their hours low and they received no per diem - so Tom and I worked on it so that the flying was much more mixed with some three and four day trips.

One day I was down in Ops trying to figure out a scheduling problem with Tom Hubric, when he said something in passing – that blew my mind.

"This is an easy 'fix' Gi - too bad we don't have a fix for the Concord offer."

"Really," I said somewhat distracted, still reading my notes.

"What offer is that?"

"Well, we were offered an amazing opportunity to become The Concord Connection with British Airways this morning – to fly a connection from Washington to New York. The Concord has cancelled the Washington flights and that has frustrated many regular passengers that have learned to rely on that European connection. So, they were wondering if one of the "feeder airlines" could fly a connection to New York to connect with Concord three times a week. They offered it to us - but sadly, we turned it down because we don't have the aircraft or the flight attendants capable to do the kind of upgraded cabin service they require."

My head jerked up and I forced Tom to face me. "Are you kidding, we turned it down, WHO turned it down, OF COURSE we can do this. I used to do service like this for a living. Why was I not consulted – who made the decision – this is CRAZY." I turned and started to run to the door.

"Hey - wait a minute – where are you headed?" Tom asked completely dumbfounded at my reaction.

"To talk to Steve of course – what idiot turned us down – of course we can do this – I have got 'a go see Steve." and I ran out of Ops and took the stairs to Steve's office two at a time. When I arrived there, I was very undignifiedly out of breath and he looked up in amazement from the papers on his desk, when he saw my disheveled form presenting itself in front of it – with the giant form of Tom Hubric close behind.

"Where is the fire?" he asked with a grin on his face pushing back from his desk with his arms behind his head – thoroughly bemused and relaxed at this intrusion.

"Steve - Thomas just told me we were offered a Concord

connection and we turned it down – could that be true?" I blurted out accusingly. "Why would we do that?" Steve's eyes got as big as saucers and with eyebrows raised in confusion looked from Tom to me and back again. This was not at all what he expected when two of his most critical officers presented themselves in such stormy fashion in front of his desk.

After a long silent pause, Steve got slowly to his feet, and walked over to the far corner of his office pulled another chair from in front of the giant window and placed it carefully next to the one in front of his desk.

"Sit both of you – let's talk this through."

We did. For the next two hours.

"The Company" he said quietly after settling back behind his desk, "Has two mammoth problems we felt made such a thing as the Concord Connection impossible – while being very honored at being asked. British Airways has not offered this to any other "feeder carrier"- feeling that we were the only one that they could trust to pull it off – but guys we don't have the ability to do it."

"Why not?" I blurted out in frustration. "My flight attendants can be taught to do this in a heartbeat – Steve this is not a problem."

He looked at me for a while in silence, realizing I think, for the first time, that with my background I might be right.

"Gi, our Dash 8 is not equipped to handle the required commissary items. We have no galley to house the food, trays, china, linen, glass and Champagne they expect to serve on this flight." he said looking Tom straight in the eye, expecting verification from him about the problem. But, now that I thought I had convinced Steve that my flight attendants would be able to do this I turned to Tom in desperation.

"Well" I said, in helpless frustration. "Thomas, is that true – you cannot make this work?"

Tom Hubric was a giant of a man and built like a Mack truck. He now heaved his mighty frame out of the chair that had held him captive for some time and started pacing the office boundaries, not prepared for this turn of events.

HOW had this suddenly become 'HIS' problem?!?

"Thomas, this is not brain surgery." I finally said. "They don't want a six-course dinner service – all they want is continental breakfast and a little Champagne or Mimosas at 06:00 in the morning."

"OK, OK let me think about it. Let me talk to maintenance and see what we can come up with." he finally said sinking back down in his chair.

We talked on for a while more – Tom promising to see if maintenance could come up with may be one or two airplanes in the fleet that could be modified to the specifications to fly this service. It would be such a feather in our cap, and the two men became excited at the idea that we could possibly make it happen.

Three days later I was summoned to Steve's office at 07:00 in the morning. Tom Hubric was waiting for me when I got there and Steve bade us both sit.

"Gi, we think we have been able to work out flying the Concord connection if you think you can make it work with training for your flight attendants. We have decided to modify two of our Dash 8 aircraft with the necessary equipment and Tom will make sure that one of those two aircraft is always in place to fly the connection. How do you plan to make it work with your people?"

I was ecstatic at this news, and had given the problem some thought. Since the flying would be very local, I decided it would make sense to just train the Salisbury based flight attendants, if Tom, who controlled the scheduling department as well as Operations, could ensure that they along with the airplane, would be the only ones required to fly it. It would take a lot of very skilled maneuvering of aircraft and personnel to pull this off. BUT –OH dear Lord - it could be done.

As expected, my flight attendants took to it like fish to water, placing a crisp white linen napkin on the tray table and serving continental breakfast on beautiful china and Champagne and Mimosas in crystal stemware. We only booked one passenger to each row of two seats which gave everyone lots of room and limited the passenger load to twelve which the new galley configuration could handle.

My Salisbury based flight attendants were STARS - as I knew they would be – and I was so very proud of their achievement. British Airways was ecstatic and could not thank us enough for a job well done.

I loved my job and found my prior experience regarding so many different types of passengers of all nations and cultures to be very helpful in the training of my flight attendants as we continued to grow in size and scope. We very often now had people of many nations getting off the main-line carriers onto our airplanes, and I was able to give them a 'head's up' on certain idiosyncrasies, mannerisms, beliefs or religious needs for different cultures which was very helpful to my flight attendants that had never experienced such things before. Suddenly the world was open and alive for them and they were now a part of it.

For this necessary information I almost lost my job one dark day when our CEO became irate and extremely insulted when he joined us impromptu at an Ops meeting and learned that I had warned and coached a group of flight attendants on how to handle a certain young man that had been extremely problematic, drunk and disruptive for many months on several of our flights. This young man flew the same route every month on his way home from a job on the rigs in the Gulf of Mexico and he happened to have the same ethnic background as our CEO. It was a very serious situation down-line, and my young female flight attendants threatened to refuse to work the flight if he was on board. For me - It was an easy fix - and I instructed my people on how to handle such a passenger situation without incident.

Our CEO however did not appreciate my "fix" or how I handled the situation for In-Flight Services. I withstood his wrath in the meeting for some time, as he dressed me down royally, accusing me of prejudice and bias due to my British upbringing in front of all present. I however, could not – and would not – agree to do anything different to protect my flight attendants from abuse or aggression on board that airplane and stood quietly by all I had done. He knew that and it made him even more angry.

I know Steve stood up for me that day too, but it was touch and go. By now we had about three hundred flight attendants and we had received the enormous honor of changing our name to Piedmont Airlines after that wonderful airline of old, that had long ago hung up is wings. As a result, it would have been extremely problematic for Steve to lose his Director of In-Flight services now. So before going home that evening I went over to his office to asked him if I still had a job.

I found him sitting all alone in his office with his feet up on the desk staring out of the enormous window overlooking the runway.

He looked up when he saw me, his eyes troubled and a little helpless and said, "I don't know Gi – I don't know. Could you maybe bring yourself to apologize for the implication?"

I pulled up a chair across from where he was seated and looked him straight in the eye. Neither one of us blinked.

"No sir," I stated flatly - feeling his worried concern. "This is not a matter of 'implication' - sadly, this is reality and I need my flight attendants not to be intimidated but to understand and know how to handle it."

This is why I felt so strongly that you HAVE to have been a crew member and lived through some of these traumas in order to understand them on board an airplane. Especially if you are the ONLY flight attendant on board to handle the situation.

I understood - our CEO did not.

Somehow it all blew over – time passed as though this incident had never happened and I never heard of the problem again. Neither was my judgement or policy ever questioned again either.

****

It was almost exactly one month to the day that I had started my new job, when the curtain finally closed on the old one, and an Icon of American aviation died. At exactly 2:00 p.m. on December 4th, 1991 a Pan American Clipper took off from a tiny island - a multicolored jewel set in a wide expanse of turquoise ocean, and slowly turned North East as the soft Trade Winds directed. The Clipper, a Boeing 727 - Flight 436, took off from Bridgetown Barbados, heading to Miami the city of that iconic Company's birth.

This was to be the last flight for this amazing airline. Pan American World Airways was lost. It had finally succumbed to corporate inaptitude, governmental indifference and an inability to change with the world it had helped to bring together. The company that started 64 years ago and could boast that in 1943 Franklin D. Roosevelt left from Dinner Key aboard a Pan Am Dixie Clipper bound for Casablanca – the first American President to fly while in office – had just tragically, flown into the history books.

Today Pan American World Airways became a memory.

The Eagle roosted high above the calming waterways of the Chesapeake Bay in sadness and shock. It was the end of an Icon - but it was also the end of a lifestyle – a life of years of memories, of growth and learning for the Eagle and her offspring. So very many years of a life lived, loved and enjoyed that will never be forgotten and cannot be replaced.

CHAPTER 45 -

THE END OF AN ERA

Years passed. I loved my job. I loved the Eastern Shore of Maryland with the Chesapeake Bay and all its surrounding water. I loved my flight attendants who kept growing in numbers – but I was getting old. It was time to consider hanging up my wings.

I had moved several times. Once out to Nanticoke – onto the wide expanse of river estuary spilling gleefully into the Chesapeake Bay. I loved waking up to that open, moody stretch of water every day, blanketed in bright or angry sky. On my days off I would sit all day surrounded by this ambiance on the bulkhead, fishing or waiting for the crabs to bite on my traps. Or, sometimes I'd watch the drama of a thunderstorm in thrilled wonder from my giant living room window, as the estuary became a frenzy of churning water and the sky turned into a spectacle of whirling angry thunderheads. Then the sky would be suddenly punctuated by amazing zigzags of wild lightning bursts and I would hold my breath - waiting in awe for what would surely follow - the shattering blasts of thunder. The wild churning water seemed to also await this mighty surge of energy as it swept with great drama and raging abandon into the mighty Sound of the Bay.

This was my heaven – but it could not last. I really loved it there but it was too far out – it would take me forty five minutes to drive the distance between the house in Nanticoke and the airport, and that was not convenient if we had scheduling problems. That was proven to me one day in living color after an unusually heavy snowstorm hit the Eastern Shore.

I had to leave my car on the street because I was unable to clear the long 100 foot expanse of driveway from the street to my house, of snow. I had just shoveled a small path, the width of the snow shovel, so that little Willie could go out and do his business because the snow was up to his chin.

The next morning at O Dark Thirty, scheduling called me in panic. Could I please help them out, they had no flight attendant to fly the originator out of Salisbury at six o'clock that morning and it was booked full with connections to everywhere including international flights. OK – I'll be right there I told them - and started climbing into my uniform. Ten minutes later I locked the house, and made my way gingerly down the long snowy driveway to my car, in the freezing dark morning air. Only problem was – I could not find it. It had been beautifully and completely plowed under, by the City plow truck the night before.

As a result, I finally and very reluctantly, bought a little house in town – in an area with many trees and a big yard. It was a very nice house in a beautiful area, ten minutes from the airport – but OH how I missed my life on that wide expanse of water leading into the Bay.

When I first arrived on the Eastern Shore I had joined the local Rotary Club. I felt it was necessary to do so – it gave me a good overview of what was happening on the Shore businesswise and it would also alert people to Piedmont Airlines and the service we had to offer. This also proved to be my only social connection. I felt very strongly that I could not ever mix business with pleasure and as a result did not socialize with anyone at Piedmont Airlines. In my capacity as Director of In-Flight Services I could not party with them one night and the next day discipline them for some infraction.

It was lonely in the beginning, but I was so completely involved in my job at the time that I did not miss it. Much later, I would slowly start to make friends through my Rotary connections. It was here that I was introduced and started dating a widower who had built a house on the water in the little picturesque town of St Michaels. Bob Johnson had been widowed five years before and had a daughter living in Salisbury with her husband and two children. This man was very different from any man I had previously dated. He was quiet, calm and unassuming and was a retired engineer with General Electric. He was totally unlike all the loud, boisterous "Jock types" I had been involved with before. I was blown away – this man with his quiet strong sense of humor and I, really hit it off. We dated and shared much over a two year period.

I loved his house on the water in St Michaels and his large old goofy Chesapeake Retriever Babes, and my little rescued dachshund/beagle mix, Sammi, hit it off too – much to our delight. Babes would take little Sammi off and into the woods of the five acre property in St Michaels and introduce her to all her favorite spots. This would include the neighbor on the edge of the property down by the water who always had cookies on hand when visited by these two buddies. Babes also tolerated and totally ignored

417

Lexie cat person, an ornery, very vocal Siamese cat my old Pan Am friend Lizzie, had given me after the cat we had shared years ago, Nephie, died.

Life was good - full and a lot of fun. However, I was about to turn sixty and it was time to hang up my wings. My children were all on their own in different parts of the country - two married with children of their own. Bob had four wonderful kids also with families, one of which was a daughter that lived on the Shore in Salisbury. It would be wonderful to have the time to make the rounds and visit them now and again.

Bob and I decided that under the circumstances we really should get married. Both of us agreed that we had found something very special in each other that we had never experienced before in a relationship and we must hold onto and treasure it for the rest of whatever life we had left. We planned to buy a camper and load our critters in the back, and explore the country. Bob had grown up on a farm in New York and had really loved the state of Maine – he wanted to show it to me. He was a hunter and loved the wild out-doors. We had visited the farm he grew up on in New York many times so that he could hunt and introduce me to his past-time and passion next to sailing and the water.

When I had joined Pan Am it was an international airline that flew only into the gateway cities of the US. We had no domestic routes, so although I had lived most of my adult life in the US I had not seen very much of the country at all. I had lived in San Francisco, New York, New Jersey, New Orleans, Miami, Herndon, Virginia and now the Eastern Shore, but that was it. Bob decided he would show me the rest of all his favorite spots over the next thirty years. There was even a wonderful country song by Tim McGraw called that, "The Next Thirty Years." We adopted it – that became "our song."

That was the plan, and in February 2001 I hung up my wings. The last year at Piedmont had been difficult, stressful and downright problematic. Steve Farrow and the Company elected to make changes to personnel that I was not comfortable with and could not condone. The Company was continuing to grow and I no longer felt comfortable growing with it. It was time to 'let go,' start the rest of my life - and marry Bob.

Piedmont Airlines and Steve Farrow gave me a really wonderful 'send off' retirement party to celebrate my ten years with the airline. A month later Bob and I quietly got married in a tiny chapel in St Michaels with just our neighbors as witnesses. I sold my house in Salisbury and moved into Bob's house on the water.

Life was perfect – I could not recall every being this content, having no one else to worry about in this most perfect of settings - except the two of us.

We spent a lot of time fishing in the Chesapeake or working on the beautiful five acres we called home along that expanse of open water. Our house was called "Osprey Landing" and we had a large nest of these awesome birds on a piling right at the end of our pier. The same pair of birds, who mate for life, would come back every year in March, restore their nest and raise two babies. We had the pleasure of observing this for the next four months till those babies learned to fly, were grown and gone.

In August of that year we decided to invite our friends and families to celebrate our marriage since we had done the 'deed' so quietly and without inviting anyone. That was the way we wanted it - but now we needed to celebrate and did so with food, booze, music and gay abandon on a little paddlewheeler party boat called the Dorothy May. We found her in the little town of Cambridge and fifty of the most important people in our lives came from far and wide to cruise and party with us on the beautiful Chesapeake Bay.

We bought a camper and since neither one of us had ever owned such a contraption before, we had to practice using it before we dare take it on the road to far off places with our critters in the back. Twice we took it to a little camp site down the peninsula on the Chesapeake side, towards Norfolk. There we were joined by Bob's daughter and her family to show us the ropes. They had owned a camper for years and were old hats at this camping stuff. It was new to both of us and we had so much fun getting acquainted with our new toy, and excited at all the possibilities it offered.

Around this time we lost Babes. She was very old and could no longer get to her feet. We were heartbroken but her time had come to cross 'the Rainbow bridge.' We had our favorite Veterinarian come to the house and then Bob took the Kaboda tractor and dug a big hole on a slight incline under a giant fir tree at the edge of the property. This is where she would love to lay for hours on end and gaze out over the water. This was 'her place' and we could always find her there when she was not on a trail somewhere with Sammi in tow on a mission to find cookies. It was a perfect resting place for a sweet dog that had lived a full life, loved by all she met. I planted a rose bush there in her memory and it was always a mass of red blossoms.

In August 2003 we headed down to Bald Head Island, North Carolina in the Cape Fear estuary. My son Mark had a beautiful summer home there and encouraged us to use it whenever we felt like driving down. We were very excited and decided to invite Bob's eldest daughter and her husband to come down from their home in Pennsylvania and join us, as well as a friend of Bob's and his wife, from his days at General Electric.

There were no cars on the island, only golf carts and bicycles, so we found a good place in the giant parking lot on the main land to leave the truck, and rode the ferry to the island. Little Sammi was the only one not happy with our plans – she hated the cramped conditions on the ferry – so Bob picked her up and held her on his lap for the 30 minute ride.

They had become inseparable – she followed him everywhere – even on his daily three mile walk. He would walk the long three hundred foot driveway to the road from the house with her by his side in all weather. Then he would tell her to "stay and wait" and she would sit there under a tree until his return. The companionship was appreciated and sought after, because when Bob went anywhere around the property or to the store in Easton in the truck, he would call or look for her to join him. Sammi however, did not 'dig' boats and all the push and crush of people on the ferry was not a happy place for a little twenty pound dog with short legs.

We were delivered to the house by the island shuttle, and it took a while to haul all our stuff into the house. Besides our bag of clothes we also had two coolers full of meat and perishables for the week. Enough for three couples. We would take the golf cart to the little island grocery store tomorrow and pick up some fruit and vegetables and salad fixings to go with it and anything else we might need.

This we did after we got up the next morning and Bob had taken his three mile walk around the island. Here he did that without Sammi. It was a beautiful day – not too hot yet, with a slight breeze off the ocean. We had enjoyed a leisurely breakfast sitting on the top balcony of the house overlooking the Atlantic that rolled into shore gently this morning, with just the occasional white cap.

The store was quite busy with vacationers from all over the US and I poked around looking for some post cards to send to my adopted London family. They did not have much choice and I ended up picking up a couple of cards that were the same. I liked them because they were of a fisherman throwing his line into a shimmering surf. I was tickled because the man was the splitting image of Bob and we laughed about it on our way home in the cart.

We unloaded and put everything away and found that it was

getting close to noon when Bob needed to go meet our visitors off the mid-day ferry with the golf cart. Only Bob's friends from Atlanta were on this ferry – his daughter and her husband would not be arriving till later this evening because they had a long drive down from Pennsylvania. I told him to go alone because there would not be room for all of us plus their bags on the little cart.

When they arrived and stowed their bags in their allotted room, we had the best time. This was the first time I had met them and it was fun getting to know them sitting on the balcony in this awesome sunshine looking out onto a sparkling ocean. We laughed and Bob and they reminisced and told funny stories about their time together at GE - while the Bloody Mary's flowed with gay abandon. It was such fun and we could not wait for the other two to join us.

Suddenly Bob said, "OK guys – enough of this revelry – we are at the beach on a beautiful day – we need to go swim."

Of course we did, and without further ado we all went down to our bedrooms and changed into bathing suits. Thus suitably attired we set off across the yard to the beach laughing all the way. It was so much fun and Bob was so happy to be able to share all this with his old friend.

When we got to the water however, I decided that the surf was a tad too much for me to handle. It rolled in and as I stood with the water swirling around my knees I had trouble staying on my feet. So I waved at them and said "You guys go – have fun I'm going to make myself a little nest here on the beach." I did that and Bob waved at me cheerfully and dove in and started swimming out with strong strokes. He was a good swimmer and loved the water – especially the ocean. I was sad that I dare not go out and join them but the wind had picked up and the surf was too strong for me to be comfortable.

I sat there watching them having fun. We were the only people out there – a few people were out walking the beach with their dogs – but it was wonderful – they were alone in the bright azure, sparkling water. My cup runneth over.

My world had become very special. It was safe. Peaceful. It was fun and my retirement years were stretching before me so full of potential and new experiences. I was relaxed and happy to let the sun and the wind seep deep into my soul as I stretched out lazily into the warm sand.

Suddenly I heard a shout, carried on the wind out of the depth of the ocean. I shot upright coming sluggishly out of my revelry and saw Ted stand up and start waving at me wildly - yelling something I could not hear because of the wind. I stood and looked in alarm to where the three of them were swimming. Then I saw Ted bend over and start pulling Bob through the water towards me.

In panic I rushed into the surf - all caution forgotten - and helped pull my unconscious husband onto dry land. We started rubbing him down with the towel all the while patting his face begging him to open his eyes and respond to our frantic efforts.

His eyes rolled and I could not find a pulse – I jumped into action and started doing compressions on his chest. I yelled at Ted to watch me and then take over while I swished out his mouth and tried to breathe life saving air into his lungs. I yelled at Angela to run in to a neighbor's house and beg them to dial 911.

At that moment I suddenly felt strong arms come around from behind me and a quiet voice said, "I'm a doctor let me take over – let me help you – the medics are on their way."

I don't remember very much after that – except that suddenly an ambulance was racing across the hard sand towards us and the medics worked tirelessly with that doctor, who was our next door neighbor and happened to be watching us when Ted yelled his alarm. They worked for about an hour with everything known to man to try and bring life back into Bob's listless body.

They were unsuccessful. I was a widow.

They loaded my dead husband into the ambulance and begged the crowd that had gathered to watch the unexpected drama, disburse. Then they turned to me and asked me if I would like a few quiet minutes alone with him in the ambulance, before they drove to the barge to transport him to the hospital morgue on the mainland. I nodded dumbly – my body reacting as if in a nightmare. I was numb with shock and disbelief. We had only been married two and a half years.

IT WAS A NIGHTMARE.

The Eagle had somehow managed to fly into a parallel universe. In one split second that mighty bird's whole world had splintered into a gazillion pieces.

CHAPTER 46 -

MOVING ON

Moving on in this new world that I found myself in was problematic and traumatic. Nothing that I had lived through in my sixty-two years had prepared me for this – and I had lived through some very sad and troubling times. Not only did I have to shake my numb body and brain back into this reality, but I found I had to care for an animal that seemed as traumatized as I was.

Little Sammi spent her time running between the barn and the truck looking for Bob. She would sit there for hours waiting. Just patiently waiting. Nothing I said or did could console her and she did not want to eat. One morning I could not find her. I combed our five acres of woods and waterfront, calling her. She was nowhere. When she had not returned by the afternoon, I started calling around to my neighbors to see if they had seen her.

NO.

At four o'clock that afternoon my neighbor's car pulled into my driveway. She lived about a mile further up Bozman Nevitt Road and was very fond of Sammi. The little dog would stay with her and her husband if Bob and I had somewhere to go overnight or on a weekend – she also was the provider of Babes and Sammi's cookie 'trecks' which Sammi had continued now that she was alone.

I ran out to see if she had any news because she had indicated that she would go out and help in my search. She beckoned me to approach the car because she did not attempt to get out. I walked around to her side where she had rolled down the window and there was Sammi asleep on her lap. She had found her up by the road in her 'spot' under the tree where she would wait for Bob to return from his walk.

The property sold in two weeks after it was put on the market. The house and grounds were both too big for me to care for. It was a heartbreaking decision but had to be made quickly while both were still in pristine condition. It was bought by a heart surgeon from Baltimore, and I moved into a charming little house on a lake back down in Salisbury.

My old friends there, all circled the wagons around me, and helped me gradually pull out of my depression. The little house also helped. The lake was twenty-six acres of pure clear water fed by three natural springs and I had one acre of yard with NOTHING growing on it except grass. I set to – digging holes and planting trees and flowers. Gardening, I discovered, was an excellent emotional pain and stress reliever, and after three years I had created a mini paradise with six giant Weeping Willow trees cutting me off from the road for privacy. My long driveway had white Crape Myrtle trees on either side forming an arch all the way to the house. I ran a split-log fence around the entire property and built a dock out into the lake - which had fish and turtles and wild life in abundance.

My kids loved to come and visit me here with their families, to fish, boat and play in and on the lake. Jumping off the small dock into a pool of eighteen feet of crystal clear water was the biggest thrill and never got old.

The lake was also on the 'fly zone' for migrating swans and geese and some evenings I would sit on my dock with a glass of wine and enjoy watching them arrive in droves and cover the lake in noisy excitement. Then early the next morning I would sit on my deck with my coffee, and watch them take off to find food in the plowed fields all over the Eastern Shore. The geese would come first and when they had moved on later in the Fall, the swans would come and fill the lake like falling snow.

I opened a little antique business in Salisbury, when I was not digging in my garden. I sold antique furniture and clocks which was fun and also kept me busy, while making wonderful new friends with similar interests. It did well.

My dear friend Elizabeth - from my Pan American days had moved to Florida and begged me to come down and visit her. She had settled with her husband in a magical little town in Lake County, Florida, which was thirty miles directly west of Daytona - called Mount Dora. It sat high up – overlooking Lake Dora – hence its name MOUNT Dora which was very picturesque and had a grand elevation of 184 feet above sea level. This whole area of Florida was one mass of lakes and water ways with the St Johns river on one side flowing through it also.

I took Lizzie up on her offer and went down to stay with her and promptly fell in love with Mount Dora. It was a sleepy little town that reminded me very much of St Michaels – very un-Florida like with many old historical homes and little boutiques, shops, restaurants and antiques – all surrounded by miles of water. This also was 'Pan Am country' and many Pan Am crew members had made this area home.

I bought a cute little house in Mount Dora on a quiet cul de sac and became a 'Snowbird." Three years later I decided to make the move permanent. I closed the little Antique Shop that I had started after Bob died – sold my precious little house on the lake – piled Lexie cat person and two new rescued dogs, Sandi and Bindi in the car, and with my little utility trailer that was bursting at the seams, in tow - we moved to Florida.

I loved Mount Dora. Made many wonderful friends. Opened up a new Antique shop at Renninger's - a large Antique Emporium there, and I settled down happily to a new and busy life with Sandi and Bindi and a bad, vocal old Siamese cat that loved to sit in her chair on the lenai and watch the lizards play. Little Sammi had crossed the Rainbow bridge a year before and I had done what I promised Bob I would do while with him in the ambulance the day he died. I held his hand and promised him I would bury Sammi with him when her time came – which I did - I buried her ashes on his grave in St Michaels. They were together again and it made me smile.

It was thanks to these last wonderful years of healing on the beautiful Eastern Shore of the Chesapeake Bay and to the many amazing, caring friends I had found there as well as in my new home in Mount Dora that enabled an amazing transformation to take place. Their help, support and encouragement meant the mighty Eagle once again could hold its head up high - now able to soar once again over mighty waters, and go on - alone.

Epilogue - *Some thoughts upon review...*

These, my memories, are spread over almost eighty years of time, starting in a bygone era of naivety, glamor, hard work, courtesy, consideration and – yes – even sexism. Expectations and behaviors in those early years would now be considered downright sexual harassment or cultural insensitivity to the point of racism.

Our actions and behaviors at that time however, were nothing of the sort. Indeed, we lived in a time of courtesy, chivalry and personal attention to detail and kindness for everyone we came in contact with. All of these things seem sadly lacking in today's impersonal – high tech world. Today a flight attendant has to worry if he/she may even dare touch to aid a passenger in certain situations for fear of legal action.

All the intense attention to detail that we were taught by Pan American in our classes of yester-year, seem to have flown by the wayside. Be it the attention paid to a perfectly cooked roast of beef or to the trick of a perfect three-minute egg cooked at 30,000 feet. Or even the representation we upheld on, or off the airplane of Pan Am – an amazing airline - that taught the world to fly – its round blue logo known around the world as America's flag carrier.

All this has now faded and been replaced by rudeness, microwaved meals in tinfoil, non-existing dress codes and oversold flights. Sad indeed.

I am however delighted, and it was my pleasure to live in those golden days of old – loved them, lived them and rejoiced in re-living them over again while writing these pages. I met some wonderful people and enjoyed visiting truly amazing places – none of this could have happened had the Eagle not had the courage and vision at a very young age - to want to fly and to move heaven and earth to accomplish it.

I'd like to close this book with the farewell Recruiting and Training song we created at the end of our five year training assignment - for Amie Peroz Manager In-Flight Service Standards and our boss in the Training Academy in Miami. Hector Adler was the VP In-Flight and Dining Services. I had mentioned it in Chapter 40 and thought it would be fun to add it here in its entirety.

Sung to the tune of "*Leaving on a Jet Plane*."

> Our bags are packed, we're ready to go,
> We're standing here outside our doors,
> We hate to call you up and get phone mail.
>
> We're flexible, we're never late,
> We're always willing to relocate,
> We also love to travel even more.
>
> Kiss them and say goodbye
> Tell them that you have to fly
> Maybe you'll be home by next July.
>
> WE'RE LEAVING ON A JET PLANE
> DON'T KNOW WHEN WE'LL BE BACK AGAIN
> OH AMIE, JUST TELL US WHERE TO GO.
>
> Break your lease, leave your job,
> Sell your car, shoot the dog,
> Just tell me if a SPA fits in your life -
>
> We'll recruit and we will train
> Anywhere through snow or rain,
> A T.E.R is all we want from you.
>
> Kiss them and say goodbye,
> Tell them you have to fly
> Maybe you'll be home by next July.

WE'RE LEAVING ON A JET PLANE
DON'T KNOW WHEN WE'LL BE BACK AGAIN.
OH AMIE, JUST TELL US WHO TO HIRE.

We gave you diamonds in the rough,
We turned them into super stuff,
We made them starve and jog from dawn to dusk,
OH AMIE, JUST TELL US WHO TO TRAIN.

We'll drive the hearse, we'll work the drones,
We'll never ask to see our homes,
We'll do wizz watch from dusk to early morn.

Kiss them and say goodbye,
Tell them you have to fly
Maybe you'll be home by next July.

WE'RE LEAVING ON A JET PLANE
DON'T KNOW WHEN WE'LL BE BACK AGAIN
OH AMIE, JUST TELL US WHO TO TRAIN.

You recruited us and trained a team,
When even eight hundred was but a dream -
Then Hector said we need four hundred more.

So now they're all dressed in Pan Am blue,
We did it all because of you -
So remember - when you start it up again,

Kiss us and say goodbye
You told us that we had to fly
Do not call us until late next July

WE'RE LEAVING ON A JET PLANE
DON'T KNOW WHEN WE'LL BE BACK AGAIN
OH AMIE, YOU KNOW WHERE YOU CAN GO!!!!!!!

Once the wings go on, they never come off whether they can be seen or not. It fuses to the soul through adversity, fear and adrenaline, and no one who has ever worn them with pride, integrity and guts can ever sleep through the 'call of the wild' that wafts through bedroom windows in the deep of the night. When a good flyer leaves the 'job' and retires, many are jealous, some are pleased and yet others, who may have already retired, wonder. We wonder if he knows what he is leaving behind, because we already know. We know, for example, that after a lifetime of camaraderie that few experience, it will remain as a longing for those past times. We know in the world of flying there is a fellowship that lasts long after the flight suits are hung up in the back of the closet. We know even if he throws them away, they will be on him with every step and breath that remains in his life. We also know how the very bearing of the man speaks of what he was and in his heart still is.

Because we flew, we envy no man on earth.
-Author Unknown

Printed in Great Britain
by Amazon